Adolescent Psychology

John J. Mitchell

Holt, Rinehart and Winston of Canada, Limited

Toronto

Canadian Cataloguing in Publication Data

Mitchell, John J., 1941-
  Adolescent Psychology

Bibliography: p.
Includes index.

ISBN 0-03-920018-3

1. Adolescent psychology.   I. Title

BF724.M58   155.5   C78-001485-5

Library of Congress

Catalog Card No.:   78-62010

Mitchell, John J.
  Adolescent Psychology.

Toronto, Canada/New York, N.Y.: Holt, Rinehart and Winston

256 p.

7812   780807

Printed in Canada

1   2   3   4   5   82   81   80   79

ACKNOWLEDGEMENTS

I would like to acknowledge the people who helped in the researching, editing, and writing of this book. Genevieve Thomas, Collette Schaeffer, and Diane Tomm all worked diligently in typing the manuscript. Steve Lewis and Robert Haymond were valued research assistants. Most especially, my father, Robert Vincent Mitchell, served as a constructive editor and consultant.

J.J. Mitchell
Edmonton, Alberta
December, 1978

DEDICATION

This book is dedicated to my son, John Joseph, from whom I learn daily about youth and life.

Table of Contents

Part II: The Psychology of the Adolescent

Part One:
The Three Ages
of Adolescence

Chapter One

A Personal Introduction

This book is about adolescents. For all intents and purposes, that means teenagers; however, stretching a year or two in either direction will not markedly affect the contents of the book nor the forms of youth.

This book is written in a rather informal style partly because it reads easier this way, partly because I am among the many professors who have grown weary of unnecessary jargon, and partly because adolescents themselves are best portrayed when literary style is somewhat loose and freewheeling. My focus is primarily upon normal growth, and although a special chapter is devoted to psychological problems related to adolescence, this book does not portray youth as a diseased lot.

Adolescent Psychology breaks the adolescent experience into three distinct ages and systematically documents the unique features of each age. Many important facts of adolescent life, to be *properly* understood, must be placed in an age-span perspective. Therefore, in this book, the treatment of adolescent sexuality, adolescent storm and stress, and adolescent physical growth is delineated in a more definitive manner than is customary in textbooks where adolescents are unfairly clustered into one single growth category.

The book is divided into three unique sections. The first section analyzes the physical, social, mental and emotional aspects of early adolescence, middle adolescence, and late adolescence. The second section describes the basic psychological needs of adolescence; the unique types of stress and strain encountered during these years; and, the nature of adolescent sexuality. The third section (which is completely different in style and approach from the first two sections) deals with some myths about adolescents and how these myths cloud our understanding of the adolescent experience.

1

Some General Assumptions

This introductory chapter is intentionally brief. However, before getting into the "body" of the book, I would like to advise the reader of some of the assumptions which I hold concerning adolescents in our culture. My reason for doing this is simply because it enhances fairness to the reader. Authors who do not freely admit their biases usually camouflage them with the bravado of pseudo-objectivity, or hide them under the pretense of "what experts in the field have to say". The end result is that the reader is partly deceived and the author is partly deceptive. Therefore, I would like to take a few pages to inform the reader of some of my personal viewpoints and assumptions about youth which I take to my investigation of adolescent psychology.

1) Adolescents must cope with day-to-day problems of living just like everyone else. They must learn how to live off their wits; how to get along with others; how to make do within bulky institutions; how to get what they can without offending too many significant others; how to meet their basic physical, psychological, and social needs; how to make themselves feel worthwhile and human; how to get feelings of support and sympathy from others; how to develop intimate relationships and a sense of general worthwhileness. In essence, they confront the same general interaction problems which we all experience and they do so with existential urgency.

2) Adolescents *tend* to be physical, sensual, and hyperactive. They often have strong passions and crave intensity. They infrequently have surplus energy and a certain amount of nervous energy which must be siphoned off into one channel or another.

Their surplus energy gives outside viewers an impression of a chaotic, nonordered life-style, which in its most disciplined moments is still helter-skelter. This however, is not the case. Adolescent activity is virtually always functional with each behaviour doing its bit to facilitate the gratification of this or prevent the onset of that. And, just as adults let off steam when they get too pent up with frustration or nervous energy, many adolescents are continually in the process of releasing the surplus energy which characterizes their normal condition.

3. In many respects, middle and late adolescents are young adults capable of engaging in a variety of roles basically reserved for adults. They are capable of assuming a wide variety of occupational, sexual, and interpersonal roles which our society alternately condones and

disapproves with regard to them. Some adolescents are smooth enough (as well as shrewd enough) to make it as entrepreneurs, although the kinds of business they can get into are quite limited. Some are keen enough to be con-men; others have the brain power to handle physics and calculus at the university level. Untold thousands have married while in their teen years and have proved to be good marriage partners and parents (although youth who wait until their twenties to marry have a much better chance of a successful marriage). And adolescents are considered mature enough by many societies to serve in the military, to vote, and to be sent to prison if they break the law, to teach and to preach, and to intern for the most essential professional jobs.

At the same time, however, the adolescents have within them much of the child. They have strong feelings of dependency upon parents and authority figures. Adolescents will, on occasion, display immature and regressive behaviour. They seem to straddle the fence between young adulthood and late childhood, somehow assuming that whenever their balance takes them in one direction others will (and should) adjust to their changing posture. In one breath, they consider leaving home for good and in the next are resentful because parents will not watch the TV shows they prefer. They are capable of ruthless social cruelty yet may experience shattering anxiety when spoken to harshly or reprimanded for an impulsive act. Adolescents challenge parents or teachers to account for adult hypocrisy while being blind to their own. There is much of the child in the adolescent (especially the early adolescent). The fact that the child is so delicately woven with the adult makes the adolescent an incredible challenge to those who strive to ''psychologize'' these years.

4) Adolescents want to know with a certain amount of assuredness that a promising future is in store for them. Like all humans, they are egocentric, self-centred and concerned with looking out for their own best interests. They become bored and impatient with things which on the surface do not appear fruitful or meaningful. They dislike preparing for something which they neither understand nor appreciate. When the future appears to stack up properly, when it seems promising and hopeful, adolescents run headlong into it with openness and fervour.

Today many adolescents have a gut level fear of the future. Why this is so is hard to say, but the fear is obvious to professionals who deal with adolescents, especially those who have legal or psychological troubles. Part of the fear stems from cognitive disapproval of many trends, values, and priorities of the larger society, and part of it stems from the immaturity inherent to this developmental stage.

5. Adolescents have their own ethical and moral concepts acquired from parents, conditioned into them by societal institutions, and generated on their own through trial and error, insight and chance.

Their ethical network to a great extent determines their sexual behaviour. Many adults fail to understand this, believing instead that adolescents are burgeoning carriers of sexual energy and ambition, who are capable of being triggered by every suggestive gesture, thought, or picture. Much to their surprise (and I think, disappointment) adults find on close inspection that their adolescent children are highly ethic-bound in their sexual behaviour. The ethics which govern adolescent sexuality are not the same as for the adult, but nevertheless, ethics are there.

6. Adolescents are much more than mere receptors of social roles. Adolescents today, probably more than in previous generations, critically analyze cultural customs and folkways. They are quite capable of liking or disliking something on its own merit. Some psychologists view the adolescent as a cloud drifting in accord with the pressures and currents surrounding it, or like a billiard ball which careens and ricochets in predictable sequence. This, however, is a limited deterministic viewpoint. Teenagers initiate action. They act and *re*act. But when they do act it may be a reflection of their own choices rather than merely because someone else does it, or because it is socially prescribed. In other words, adolescents are self-directing human beings and the way they behave cannot be reduced to any set of deterministic principles.

7. Adolescents know how to cheat, exploit, and take advantage of other people just like their more sophisticated elders. Most of them have enough common sense to recognize that when forced to adjust to a large, impersonal institution (such as a high school with 2,000 students) one must do a certain amount of jockeying and manipulating in order to preserve a sense of individuality. Most textbooks of adolescent psychology do not mention that this type of behaviour *is intrinsic to the condition of adolescence*. Somehow it is felt that adolescents should endlessly adjust to parents who do not completely understand their needs; and to rules which pretend their needs do not exist.

8. Many psychological characteristics that accompany adolescence are developmental in nature and modify with time. Many adolescents at age 17 have startling memories of their "childishness" at age 15. The job of the psychologist is to determine which characteristics of the adolescent are due to developmental traits and which are the building

4

blocks upon which adult behaviour is founded; which is fad and which is fact.

9. The basic virtues of truth, beauty, and goodness are found in ample abundance among today's youth. The degree to which these virtues exist because youth were properly trained and socialized is a credit to parents and to the adult society in general. The degree to which adolescents have had to teach themselves virtues because of an absence of adequate models is a tribute to their internal fortitude and self-direction.

10. Sexual problems are central to the adolescent experience and are related to a wide range of personal realities: body image, self-concept, feelings of masculinity or feminity, feelings of adequacy, acceptance, popularity, intimacy, belongingness, and general worthwhileness are all related to sexuality during the adolescent years.

Adolescent textbooks don't mention it, as a rule, but sexual behaviour is (or can be) fun, pleasurable, and exciting. There is virtually no way that sexual behaviour could be eliminated from the repertoire of adolescent activities in our culture. *In a sense of christian principles* ○ ○ ○

Some Further Observations and Assumptions

1. The adolescent subculture is increasing in its social, political, financial, and moral impact on the total society. It has the attributes of assuming cultural identity into itself and can be expected to influence, in certain circumstances dominate, other societal institutions in the near future.

2. Young men and women in their teenage years do not necessarily follow the footsteps of their parents: they are capable of generating new ideas, customs, and ways of living. This is more prevalent today than in previous generations and has tremendous social implications for the global society.

3. There are many aspects to our society (some institutional and some ideological) which conspire against normal needs of the adolescent, resulting in conflict and hostility between youth and society.

4. Many adolescents camouflage their true psychological motives under the guise of protesting societal weaknesses and limitations. It is difficult for the neutral bystander to determine when adolescents *are acting out their own internal confusion and when they are legitimately protesting a social condition which deserves protest.*

5. Adolescents tend to be egocentric. As a rule they understand first-person experiences better than abstract experiences and prefer to be around people whose life-style accentuates first-person subjective experiences. Because of this they are susceptible to idols, heroes, and pied pipers of a seemingly endless variety.

6. Adolescents accumulate hostility towards adults who refuse to acknowledge their integrity and personal identity. Sometimes the hostility is repressed, sometimes not. Our culture has probably seen the last of the days when an adult could categorically intimidate an adolescent merely by merit of being older.

7. Adolescents are predisposed toward liking, even admiring authority which acknowledges their integrity and identity. This, however, is not categorical because adolescents also require that adults preserve their own identity in addition to that aura of superiority they are *somewhat* entitled to by merit of age.

Chapter Two

The Early-Adolescent Period: Child-Adolescence

Adolescence covers too many years and too much growth to be properly understood as only one developmental period. The differences between the early and later years of adolescence are profound and we do not treat these differences with enough respect. The most consistent error is to treat early adolescents as if they were more mature and self-directing than they are, and to treat late adolescents as if they were more juvenile than they are. We prematurely impose adolescence on youngsters who are child-like in the essence of their personality, especially the 11-, 12- and 13-year-olds; and then during late adolescence when they are ready to grow into adult maturity we prevent them from doing so. Both of these errors derive from our inability to create viable involvements which suit the talent and aptitude of adolescents.

In terms of chronological ages, the years which fit the early-adolescent period are 12, 13, and 14 for boys and 11, 12 and 13 for girls. The sexes are treated differently because they are different. Girls reach puberty at an earlier age, they reach the peak of their height and weight sooner, and they achieve their adult body at an earlier age than boys. Of the three adolescent ages, early adolescence is where the greatest maturity difference between the sexes manifests itself. Fourteen-year-old boys, for example, have reached a level of sexual maturity for their sex which is comparable to that reached by girls at about age 13.

If you skip ahead to the next chapter you will note that I include in the *middle*-adolescent period the years 14, 15 and 16 for boys and 13, 14, 15 and 16 for girls. The overlap between the upper limits of the early group and the lower limits of the middle group is intentional, and designed to indicate that we are most concerned with general age clusters rather than rigid chronological years. I believe, however, that the consistency of growth trends throughout the second decade of life is sufficiently strong to categorize by age and that valuable insight into the adolescent world is gained by doing so.

9

When youth begin adolescence, they have been out of childhood less than a year. Their lives have been lived as children, and childhood is what they know best. Nevertheless, the body grows steadily toward puberty, and the world over, the attainment of puberty is the objective sign that childhood has seen its day. Early adolescents straddle the world of child and adolescent, sometimes thinking as one then as the other, sometimes feeling like one then like the other, sometimes looking like one then like the other. To think of them as children is wrong. They are not children. To think of them as full-fledged adolescents is also wrong because they are not. To think of them as late adolescents (what I call the adolescent-adults) is completely fictitious.

These are years of transition, of learning new roles and rules, and of accepting a body which changes significantly every six months or so. The pull unquestionably comes from adolescence, and in this regard our youngster can be understood as one. The push, however, comes from childhood and it flavours all experience and taste. Just as late adolescents take into the adult world the remnants of their adolescent perceptions and attitudes, so do early adolescents bring their childhood to adolescence. For all of these reasons I call the earliest years of adolescence the stage of ''child-adolescence''. The term suggests a mixture of the two worlds, and makes clear the fundamental differences between this age and the final period of adolescence known as *adult*-adolescence. The period sandwiched between these two vital times of life I call *adolescence* because it is here that youth most honestly resemble the images and stereotypes our culture holds of ''adolescence''.

In this chapter, I shall present what I consider the most important facts of the early-adolescent experience in North America. I shall not burden the reader with excessive ''caution'' comments about individual differences or how each young person is an individual who must be understood in his or her own right. This I assume everyone knows. My prime task will be to isolate the common themes of youth and to try to determine the extent to which they are a product of our unique cultural configuration, the degree to which they are the result of the realities inherent to youth, and when necessary, I will try to deal with other possibilities and interpretations.

The early years of adolescence are dominated by body growth and social outreaching: considerable emphasis will be placed on them in this chapter. A special attempt will be made to point out how the three ages of adolescence relate to each other, how they overlap and contribute to mutual development, and how they create tension vital to growth.

The Body

The relentless growth of the body is the dominant theme during the early-adolescent period. The child-body gives way to the adolescent-body as predesigned in the human genetic blueprint. No other period during the second decade of life rivals these growth advances and none incubates such potential for social and emotional change.

Two separate growth periods are experienced during early adolescence. Developmental psychologists usually refer to them as *latency* and *puberty* and the differences between them are remarkable. The latency period is a time of stable, consistent growth; by adolescent standards it is comparatively trouble-free and uneventful. The puberty period, and the time immediately before it, is a zesty, fast-paced era with body parts undergoing remarkable growth, and to establish a "feel" for its impact on the total person, we shall overview the growth highlights of puberty because they constitute the nuclear ingredients which govern body experience, and, of course, they are the physical facts of "my" personal body.

About two years before puberty the body begins readying itself for the forthcoming upheaval. In this period, known as *pubescence,* the body undergoes an increased rate of physical growth and awakens from the slumber of latency.

Sexual maturity begins at puberty. In girls, it is signalled by the first menstrual flow, one of the most vital events in their lives. One of the most famous adolescents of our century, Anne Frank, says of it, "Oh, I'm so longing to have it too; it seems so important." For boys, the signs are less definite, with the most reliable indicator being the presence of spermatozoa in the urine. (The reliability of this signal is offset by that the fact that it requires a microscope, a scientist who knows what to look for, and a urine specimen.) To state that puberty for male *or* female is announced by *one* particular event is unfair because puberty is a process that affects all body subsystems and includes much more than *only* sexual maturity.

The hormones responsible for masculine traits (androgens) and those responsible for feminine traits (estrogens) are both produced in *every* person. However, with puberty in girls occurs a sharp increase in the production of estrogens, and in boys a corresponding increase in the production of androgens. These hormones catalyze the growth of all primary and secondary sexual characteristics. *Primary* sexual characteristics concern those parts of the anatomy directly involved in repro-

11

duction, particularly the genitalia. *Secondary* sexual characteristics are species traits common to either male or female, but not directly involved in reproduction. Secondary traits for males include deepening of voice, growth of body hair, expansion of chest cavity; for females: rounding of the pelvis, growth of breasts, increase of fatty tissue. The first menstrual flow begins for about 75 percent of all girls during the twelfth, thirteenth, or fourteenth year. The *average* age is about 12 years, ten months. However, the "normal" range can be extended two years in each direction. The menstrual cycle tends to be inconsistent and somewhat unpredictable the first year or so after it begins, and the fact that a girl menstruates does not confirm that she is able to conceive or to bear a child. The ovaries may not be able as yet to produce eggs capable of being fertilized, and the uterus may not be sufficiently mature to house a fetus. Quite commonly, the female is not capable of becoming pregnant during the year after the first menstrual flow; however, as the birth records throughout North America prove, many are capable. During the past 100 years, puberty for girls has begun earlier. The average age for menarche has dropped from 17 to 13 in the last 100 years or so, and is still falling. The onset of menarche (the first menstrual flow) varies considerably from culture to culture because of differing nutritional standards. Girls in Western European countries have median menarcheal ages of about 12.8 to 13.2 years; in contrast with this, girls in the Highlands of New Guinea begin their menstrual cycle at about age 18, and those from Central Africa at about age 17. Well-nourished African girls have a median age of about 13.4, whereas Asian girls at the same nutritional level as Europeans begin menarche at an almost identical age, though slightly lower. These data demonstrate how nutritional factors influence natural growth processes and further confirm that environment can influence, either positively or negatively, intrinsic growth tendencies. (Data taken from Tanner, 1972, p. 22.)

Other changes are taking place simultaneously. The breasts enlarge, the nipples (areolas) expand and usually become darker in colour. Breast development through the bud stage usually takes place *before* the menarche, and to mature size between the ages of 12 and 14, a biological fact which holds considerable social importance in the early-adolescent peer world. The external genitalia enlarge but retain their basic shape and appearance; straight, pigmented pubic hair appears which eventually becomes kinky and more coarse. Underarm hair appears as does a certain amount of facial hair, especially on the upper lip and upper jaw. The pelvic girdle expands, and this is the final indicator that the young girl is not far away from womanhood — at least in the biological sense.

Puberty occurs later for boys than for girls in accord with the fact that girls are, as a rule, developmentally more advanced during the first 15 years of life. Most girls complete the puberty growth spurt between their thirteenth and fourteenth birthdays, while boys continue until the fifteenth birthday and beyond. This age difference in reaching maturity carries considerable social implication.

The primary sex organs of the male grow rapidly during puberty. The testes increase in size and volume, and the penis grows to almost complete adult size. The shaft of the penis becomes longer, wider, and thicker, and the glans grow considerably. Facial hair begins to appear, first as down and later as coarse whiskery hair, and the pubic hair follows the same general pattern. The voice deepens noticeably due to enlargement of the larynx. The body musculature hastens its growth causing arms and legs to become stronger.

For boys and girls alike, a number of similar events take place during puberty. The skin tends to become coarser and more porous; the sebaceous glands become more active and produce an oily secretion which contributes to the adolescent's vulnerability to complexion problems. The composition of sweat changes, becoming much stronger in odour. All these tend to make one more self-conscious and to tax the self-image.

The practice of masturbation becomes firmly established during adolescence for boys and girls. Most recent research indicates that virtually all boys masturbate, with greatest frequency during middle and late adolescence. Girls masturbate less often, with less likelihood of reaching orgasm.

Many of the apparent changes which take place during puberty are in direct response to the incredible pace of skeletal growth. During early adolescence, bones increase in length and size as well as in density and hardness. The long bones in the arms and legs are most obvious in their extension, but dramatic changes are simultaneously taking place in less conspicuous locations such as the wrists, ankles, ribs, shoulders, and pelvis. The rate at which the skeleton grows toward maturity is called *skeletal age;* knowledge of this tells us a good deal about future growth patterns. For girls, skeletal age is highly correlated with the age at which puberty begins. A *seven*-year-old girl with a skeletal age of *eight* years is one whose overall skeletal growth is proceeding at a pace in advance of her chronological age. Girls with such skeletal precocity tend to begin puberty slightly sooner than girls with normal skeletal age and considerably sooner than girls whose skeletal age is behind their chronological age. The rule is this: girls with advanced skeletal age begin puberty at an early age, girls with normal skeletal age begin puberty at the average age, and girls with below average skeletal age begin puberty late. This serves to remind us of the organismic unity of the growing body and the interdependence of body systems. We shall note time and again that this interdependency is not only biological; frequently a biological change radically influences a social or a psychological world as well.

The head and face demonstrate noticeable growth during the early-adolescent years for both sexes. The nose tends to become longer and more conspicuous; the jaw, especially in boys, assumes a more angular and impressive prominence. Sometimes the upper part of the face grows more rapidly than the lower, providing an incongruous, but developmentally natural, appearance. The extremities of the body are the first to reach full adult size; consequently, they are out of proportion to the rest of the body.

Even the naive or disinterested observer will notice the dramatic changes in height and weight which typify the early adolescent. Boys commonly begin the ninth grade a full three inches taller and 20 or more pounds heavier than they were four or five months earlier. Neither is it uncommon for a 12 or 13-year-old girl to sprout upward three inches, develop a noticeable bustline, gain 10 to 15 pounds, round out in the pelvis, and lose facial baby fat within a four-or-five-month period.

Sex differences, as one would expect, pertain in the matter of weight and height. The rate of growth for girls is most accelerated slightly before the onset of sexual maturity, whereas for boys the rate of growth continues for some time afterwards. This results in adult males being larger than adult females, even though females, for the most part, are slightly larger during early adolescence. During the peak of the adolescent growth spurt girls grow about three and one-half inches in a year and gain about 11 pounds. Boys during the peak growth, shoot four or five inches upward and add 12 to 15 pounds. Most growth in height during adolescence results from an increase in trunk length rather than from increased leg length.

As youth stretch upward, basal oxygen consumption increases; they are obliged to eat more because they need more to sustain normal body operations. As the skeleton lengthens, the need for calcium and phosphorus increases; muscles must expand to handle the burgeoning body and, consequently, the need for protein and exercise increases. Not uncommonly, rapid growth in height results in awkwardness. Muscles

14

are not efficient in controlling the body and, of course, the person must adjust to the fact that the body does not fit into the same space it once did.

The human body does not grow uniformly; some parts grow fast while other parts are static. This uneven pattern, referred to as *asynchronous growth,* provides us with ample evidence of its influence. During this period, extemities grow faster than the rest of the body, giving adults the impression that if adolescent growth trends continue, the hands will be dragging on the floor, the waist will move up to the shoulders, and thigh bones will grow out of the bottom of the rib cage.

Considerable difference in muscle tissue exists between the sexes. From the earliest years, boys possess greater volume of muscle, whereas girls have greater quantity of fatty tissue. By adulthood the male leg contains only about eight percent fat, while a woman's contains about 18 percent. The lesser amount of fat in the male body is made evident by the fact that his bones and muscles are heavier and bigger than those of the female. It is instructive to note that even with differences in fatty tissue, boys and girls have the same relative strength to body weight *before* puberty; after the onset of puberty, however, boys show an increase in relative strength which when linked with other sex differences such as the larger heart and lung of the male and the greater stamina of his muscles, usually results in the male being more suited for physical activities requiring strength and endurance. To impress this point upon the memory we should remember that when 11-year-olds arm wrestle, a girl is as likely to win as a boy; when 15-year-olds arm wrestle a girl is almost never able to defeat a boy.

The 12-year-olds of today are approximately three inches taller and 15 pounds heavier than their counterparts of 30 years ago; the average 14-year old is about five inches taller and almost 25 pounds heavier than the adolescent of this age in 1880. Without question, the youth of today are bigger than those of previous generations and are reaching sexual maturity earlier.

The Psychological Response to Physical Growth

Puberty takes a personal toll. It is difficult to imagine otherwise. The most notable psychological consequence is a general preoccupation with the body, with the way it looks and how it feels. This is a period of body shyness and sensitivity, though for the most part, these feelings are outgrown and in time replaced by what adults know as "body-consciousness". For boys this "shyness" is not always apparent because of their tendency to employ braggadoccio about things of which they are inwardly frightened.

Few youngsters of this age take their body for granted. They worry about how it looks to others, even though they possess some objective idea as to whether it is attractive by general standards. They are more likely to believe a negative comment about their appearance than a positive one, therefore, they experience considerable anguish in the presence of ridiculing peers or highly critical adults. The diaries of adolescents are filled with statements about dislike of their bodies, as typified by this entry from a nervous boy:

> I feel self-conscious. I don't want to be handsome, but I hate my present appearance. Weak, pale, small ears, big nose, 'peach fuzz', weak chin. Now my mouth is out of shape and I cannot smile, for Dr. Singer put my brace back yesterday. (Kiell, 1964, p. 54)

All youth harbor feelings of inferiority and in few areas are they more easily wounded. To alleviate tension, peers make fun of one another in a playful way, thereby venting some of their unspoken anxiety. On a given day the playfulness may or may not be taken seriously, so the game is not without psychic peril.

Because they lack confidence in their assessment of themselves, youth look to others for cues about their appearance, their attractiveness, and especially their femininity or masculinity. They need good news from outsiders and when they don't get it they are likely to think poorly of themselves. On the other hand, their understanding of outsiders is wobbly, and praise may bring a mere shrug of the shoulders or a what-do-you-know snarl. Adults, as a rule, resent this kind of retort and stop providing the ego-bolstering so essential to the self-doubting youth.

It surprises many adults to discover that even in our age of "sexual enlightenment" many young girls experience significant personal problems in accepting menstruation. Whisnant and Zegans (1975) in their investigation of how adolescent girls feel about menstruation contend that the following findings typify their sample:

1. Regardless of how early-adolescent girls get along with their mothers, they are more likely to turn to them for information about their menstrual flow than to any one else.
2. Girls frequently stop talking about their body to peers near menarche.
3. Many girls experience menarche as a disturbing and frightening event and many of them were ashamed of it even though they

believed they should not be.

4. At the time of menarche many girls avoided their fathers.
5. Many girls associated menstruation with defecation or soiling themselves, or at least, with uncleanliness.

The researchers conclude that too much emphasis is placed on teaching girls about the physical or biological aspects of menstruation and not enough on the social and psychological implications of this growth reality.

In our society the moodiness associated with adolescence begins during puberty. Emotions, though they are not as rich as they will be in a few years, add their weight to body anxiety, making the overall experience more burdensome than during pre-adolescence. Psychologists for the past 50 years have stated that this is the age when moodiness begins to take on a distinctly adolescent tinge. The crankiness of childhood deepens and dignifies and continues to do so throughout the adolescent period.

Pain, of course, is not only of the *psychological* variety although psychologists are fond of thinking so. Growing muscles ache and irritate; girls often experience discomfort in the developing breasts and in the abdomen area during menstruation. Skeletal joints, especially in the feet and shoulders, sometimes smart. The growing body creates its own discomfort and when it is aggravated by psychological pressures, by inferiority feelings and self-doubt, or by peer ridicule or adult avoidance, the growth process is that much more difficult.

The child-adolescent phase is governed by the demands of physical growth more than any other time in the adolescent period. As growth tapers it becomes less demanding and progressively more amenable. For now, however, it influences every phase of life and gives this period its dominant trait. But the world goes on, and growing body or not, youth must live within it and face up to its demands. Therefore, I shall now discuss some of the more important aspects of the phenomenology and social mechanics of early-adolescent existence.

The Social and Private World

The greatest social demands of the first stage of adolescence centre around living with peers, coping with the pressures of competing within a limited circle of comrades, and mastering the rules of social survival. Since these requirements are not simple, their mastery requires intense concentration and an exceptional amount of trial and error. Coping with bullies, rule freaks, and friends who own desired play things or possess money are all facts of social life. Most importantly, one must learn to do well whatever is prized, or to compensate in ways that make oneself the prize. The peer group acquires such power that frequently it voids parental demands as well as personal beliefs. Many an early adolescent has sold out personal convictions because of peer pressure. The peer group holds power for at least two reasons. First, peers establish the criteria for *social acceptance* and, they also determine what will lead to *social rejection*. To go against them one risks being ostracized or ridiculed — the two gravest fears of comrade-conscious youth. Second, most youth of this age do not have a genuinely developed sense of selfhood nor a thoroughly developed sense of morality. As a result the constraints which hold back a more mature personality do not actively press on the child-adolescent. As identity becomes more crystallized, and moral outlook more principled, the tendency to stand up to peer pressure increases. Until then, however, peers and self live an uncomfortable alliance, each incomplete without the other, but often miserable when together. This "uncomfortable alliance" is virtually universal among early adolescents in our culture although in less complex societies it is not as prevalent.

Sex role learning is important more for knowing what is *un*feminine or *un*masculine than for what is "proper". This is because youngsters at this age are experimenting with sexual identities and by no means have a clear outlook as to what is appropriate behaviour for their sex. They are impressed, however, with behaviour that they believe is *in*appropriate, because it is easily spotted by their peers and easily ridiculed. It makes them stand out and feel isolated. The fear of such isolation and ridicule is a basic fact of early-adolescent social adjustment and contributes greatly to their tendency toward conformity and their desire for social acceptance. As with most social realities of this age, errors are more important than successes because they carry with them the onus of ridicule or rejection.

The emotional climate is still rather juvenile and to a considerable degree accounts for the simplicity of the social arena. The *range* of emotion is wide but the emotions themselves are essentially childish. Anger, joy, affection, and sadness are experienced but not with the forcefulness which jolts the late-adolescent personality. Personal attachments lack the commitment of adult intimacy, thus their bonds are more easily severed and their existential connections more frail. Emo-

18

tion is a life force, but not a dominant one. And here we see the importance of assessing youth not only in terms of where they have been, but also in terms of where they are going. When contrasted with the phenomenology of the child, the early adolescent experiences a greater breadth *and* depth of emotion. When contrasted with the emotional makeup they will have in a few years however, they align more closely with childhood than with adulthood. One of the most exciting features of the next age of adolescence (middle adolescence) is the crossover in this alignment, that is, the transition from childlike to adultlike emotional fabric.

This is not to say that emotions are not volatile. Anger can border on the savage, and without question, many youngsters of this age would severely injure one another if they were more adept at fighting. Sorrow induced by rejection can rip the seams of an otherwise domestic personality. Jealousy, envy, and spite reach remarkable depths. The major differences between the emotions now and during the older years are in time and expense. Child-adolescents (who forget more quickly than they will in a few years) remember painful emotions dimly; they make amends with greater exactitude and promptness than will their future self. In all, emotions are not as soul-shattering nor as personally expensive as they will be.

Because of their limited emotional range, few youngsters of this age experience sexual passion as adults know it. Intimacy is not a major experience because the self is insufficiently developed to permit genuine symbiosis; religion lacks emotional fervour because it remains abstract. Each of these developmental consistencies yield to time and growth, but for now they take the form we associate more with the child than with the adult.

Egocentrism

Of the three ages of adolescence this is the most egocentric because it is closest to childhood, and also because it benefits least from expanded mental maturity. *Egocentrism* is the tendency to see the world in terms of one's immediate frame of reference, and to understand what we see in terms of what we already know. It is a perceptual, emotional, and intellectual filtering without the realization that *the filtering process dictates the experience*. All humans are egocentric because no way exists to perceive the world except through oneself. However, it is possible to backtrack in order to assess the relative role of self-ish-ness in our perception of things.

Egocentrism tends to abate when adolescents acquire the ability to view more systematically the viewpoints of others, and even more importantly, to assess the *bases* of foreign ideas. Here is how Kagan, one of the leading psychologists of our day, assesses the nature of early-adolescent thought:

> The essence of the argument is that the twelve-year-old has acquired a new cognitive competence — the disposition to examine the logic and consistency of his existing beliefs. The emergence of this competence, . . . is catalyzed by experiences that confront the adolescent with phenomena and attitudes that are not easily interpreted with his existing ideology. These intrusions nudge the preadolescent to begin an analytic reexamination of his knowledge. (1972, p. 92)

The major point is that the early adolescent begins to think with greater logic and consistency, and this influences all areas of life. Though some youngsters of this age have begun formal thought, they are novices and benefit less than they will in a few years. In consequence, when compared with older adolescents they are considerably more preoccupied with their own microcosm. For the most part, early adolescents are exempt from thinking extensively about larger issues such as government, race or religion, and when they do think about these issues their reflections are essentially personal and immediate rather than abstract and general.

Egocentrism is among the most distinguishing marks of this age because it precludes many of the existential or interpersonal traits, (such as intimacy, commitment and altruism) found in the late adolescent and at the same time makes possible the carefree exuberance and primal spontaneity characteristic of childhood.

Egocentrism results in the tendency to personalize almost everything and to view abstract matters from private biases and assumptions. It is a primary reason that I refer to this age as the period of ''child-adolescence''.

Social Outlooks

The view of society held by most youngsters is not overly encouraging because *egocentrism tends to expand into ethnocentrism.* Youth of this age tend toward high nationalism. They reflexly think that a country should always do whatever is in its own best interests. They do not know a great deal about the social forces of history nor do they understand much about their society's role in international power struggles. Their understanding of society is based more upon platitudes and pledges than on genuine insight. They frown upon anyone who opposes their country and usually believe that those who do so are perverted or malicious.

Few youngsters view their society with detachment, isolating its inferior institutions from the superior. Although they know that defects exist, they accept them as legitimate blemishes on an otherwise attractive face. Their sense of social identity rests more with authority figures than with a concept of justice. (In this regard, they are similar to most adults, though an important difference exists. For adults, the *capacity* to make such distinctions goes unused, for the child-adolescent, the capacity is not as yet crystallized.)

In some regards youth of this age are social *pre*moral. Junior high school teachers and principals, for example, have learned from experience that it is not a wise policy to have youngsters involved in judging their peers who have broken a school rule. First, their punishment is often intense and vindictive and far more punitive than the violation warrants; secondly, they often allow a guilty offender to escape punishment altogether if he or she carries social weight with the judges. Of the three ages of adolescence this is easily the most corruptible as far as social justice is concerned.

Antisocial behaviour such as fighting and bullying are important matters during this age — especially in the school setting. A research study conducted by Oliveus (1977) concluded that it is extremely difficult to reduce aggressiveness and rowdiness among preadolescent and adolescent males. Following a three year longitudinal study, Oliveus made these conclusions with regard to adolescent "bullies":

1. highly aggressive boys tend to remain aggressive throughout the three year period of ages 13-16;
2. highly aggressive boys enjoyed about average popularity among their peers; therefore, male aggressiveness does not seem to be caused by peer rejection;
3. "bullies" were average in academic achievement, therefore, their behaviour is not understood as a consequence of failure in school;
4. "bullies" were not overly anxious or insecure people; on the contrary, they appeared to have rather high self-concepts and demonstrated considerable confidence in their day-to-day activities.

In general, it was concluded that youth of this age are "naturally" prone toward aggression, that those who are most aggressive tend to stay that way over the three year period of 13-16, and that aggressiveness or being a bully is not reserved only for youth who are failures in school or rejected by their friends.

At this age youth are rather authoritarian and inclined to view the world as a place to be run and organized. Why they are inclined this way when they are simultaneously egocentric and self-centred is not clear. Adelson, in an extremely thought-provoking essay on the political imagination of youth, offers the following observation:

> What accounts for the authoritarian animus among the young? They are, to begin with, preoccupied by human wickedness. They see man as tending naturally toward the impulsive and the anarchic. They are Hobbesian — it is the war of all against all. They do not seem to have much faith in — or perhaps they do not cognize adequately — the human capacity for self-control, or the demands of conscience. (1972, p. 117)

Not all experts would phrase it this way, but I find it quite commensurate with the nature of early adolescence.

It is a good time for "isms". Nationalism, Catholicism, Nazism or most any other "ism" finds a good audience here. Those learned in the home are the easiest to assimilate and are acquired with least questioning. The great age of doubting is not far away, however, and many acquired "isms" are abandoned during the introspective intellectualism of middle adolescence. Almost all issues are viewed in terms of how they are *now*. Neither history nor the future have the importance they will acquire in later adolescent ages. Again Adelson makes a relevant observation:

> In the *early years of adolescence the child's mind is locked into the present*. In pondering political and social issues he shows little sense of history of a precise and differentiated sense of the future. The past is not seen to weight upon the present, via precedent and tradition, nor can the child perceive the manifold and varying potentialities within the present. The young adolescent will rarely look back to the antecedent sources of the present, and when he thinks of the future, or is forced to by the question we ask him, he can imagine only the immediate and direct outcome of a current event.
>
> During the middle years of adolescence, we begin to see a distinct — though modest — extension of temporal range. A sense

of the past begins to appear. (1972, p. 110)

Gangs and cliques are fairly common during this age. They represent an ideal way to escape the world of adults, to establish a more diverse identity which includes things forbidden at home, and to achieve greater social competence within the peer world. (At this time we shall not discuss the role of age segregation in our society. It is, however, an important matter which will draw our attention later in the book. The basic issue is whether youth cluster together because of natural psycho-social impulses, or whether they do so because they are herded together via the school system and learn to become so impressed with one another.)

Almost everything in the social world is interpreted through an underdeveloped sense of morality. In school, for example, rules are thought good if they favour "me", and bad if they do not. At home rules are obeyed more from habit (or fear) than from any firm conviction of their intrinsic merit.

Sexual Interests

The opposite sex is not well-regarded. Males have little interest in females although they recognize that to get along with them is a cultural requisite. Girls, because they are closer to puberty and because the menstrual flow hastens their awareness of their body and of reproduction, have slightly more interest in boys. However, the attraction between the sexes is based more upon the future and its demands than on the present and its impulses. This represents a crucial difference between the nature of sexual attraction during this period and during *late* adolescence when the sexual impulse is immediate and forceful.

In a rather matter-of-fact essay on the behaviour of early adolescents in the schools, Martin (1972) includes the following observation:

> Twelve-year-olds hang around in groups by sex. It is a rare exception when a member of one sex risks associating with members of the opposite sex. The students make this issue an important one, for example, when they work in groups and strongly prefer one-sex grouping. The attitude displayed toward the opposite sex is often humorous — "Ugh, she's a girl" — when you realize what he will be saying in three years.

Sexual desire exists and it does lead to sexual activity — though sexual intercourse is comparatively rare. Almost all researchers in the

23

area of adolescent sexuality conclude that fewer than five percent of boys and girls have experienced sexual intercourse before age 14. Schofield claims that less than one percent of the girls in his research sample admitted to sexual intercourse before the age of 14. (See Mitchell, 1974, p. 79 for further information on this topic.) The sexual impulse is not as keenly genital as during late adolescence, and does not have an independent force as it does during adulthood. Sexual interests are greatly influenced by novelty, experimentation and curiosity, and they are qualitatively different than during late adolescence. Sexuality is less intense and less erotic. Thwarting the sexual impulse rarely leads to feelings of emptiness or frustration as is common during late adolescence and early post-adolescence.

The nature of sexual *feelings* during adolescence is not agreed upon by theoreticians. The Freudian-oriented psychologists are inclined to believe that puberty brings a range of passion which the adolescent learns to sublimate or to force out of awareness. Many developmental psychologists do not agree; they claim that sexual passion is not very important in the life of the early adolescent. I agree with Kagan's assessment:

> It is also likely that the sheer intensity of passion that is so urgent in the older adolescent is attenuated at this earlier age. The tension that is so overpowering in the seventeen-year-old is more like a tickle at eleven and, hence, more easily put aside. However, the eleven-year-old knows that his time is coming and he must prepare for it. (1972, p. 95)

Though *some* females are biologically mature at 13 this is not the norm. Many girls of this age who are capable of reproduction do not even experience sexual desire. Sex does not generate much emotional intensity; and youngsters of this age sometimes claim to feel ''hardly anything at all'' during sexual activity. Sexual behaviour during early adolescence is far and away the least adventurous of the three adolescent phases. Schofield reports that although about one-quarter of the 13-year-olds admit to kissing, less than five percent admit to ''deep kissing'' or what adults think of as passion kissing. Only about three percent engage in minor forms of petting such as breast fondling. Less than one percent admit to having had sexual intercourse. Schofield's data was gathered during the sixties and may be slightly dated. However, most research indicates that the sexual behaviour of young people has not changed dramatically during the past 30 or 40 years even though it is easy to infer that it has because what does exist is more open, and the talk about it considerably more frank and public than in times past. Youth are not "doing less and talking more" rather, doing a little bit more but talking a great deal more.

Middle adolescence is a different matter. The fourteenth and fifteenth year represent a breakthrough in sexual activity. Almost half of the youngsters admit to deep kissing and breast fondling, and about 10-20 percent claim to have engaged in genital play with the opposite sex. (At the age of 16 Rousseau wrote, "My feverish blood incessantly peopled my brain with girls and women." Of course, he *is* recognized as one of the great Romantic writers of his century.)

Though sexual activity is low on an absolute numbers scale, it should not be taken lightly. The number of 14-year-olds giving birth increased during the early seventies, as did the number receiving abortions. Thus, even though the percentage which is sexually active is small, the consequences are significant.

Boy-girl pairings do take place. However, they rarely lead to substantial intimacy relationships, and they are irritated by an even greater abundance of petty issues than are later pairings. It is the age when the rules of courtship are experimented with, when the intricacies of romance are hinted at, and when the pains of shared egocentrism are first interned. It is an apprenticeship which is outgrown. Even among young couples who engage in sexual intercourse, the bonds between them do not take on the existential depth characteristic of older couples. The self is not yet ready for bonding.

Home and Family

The home remains the psychic and physical frame of reference. Conflicts with parents are frequent but not fundamental. The surge for freedom typical of adolescence is so hampered by financial dictates that youth of this age rarely think about leaving home for good, and even more rarely actually do so. *Serious* runaways almost always are fleeing a painful or abusive homelife.

In middle-class families, the children usually help with house or yard work, and sometimes hold mini-jobs such as paper routes. Except in households where the parents are physically abusive, the norm ranges from mutual tolerance to genuine love and affection between parent and child. Flare-ups tend to be brief. Bickering is more frequent than genuine hostility.

Sometimes the peer group is seen as taking away from the importance of the family. It is more accurate to view both peer group *and* family as holding major importance for the early adolescent, because each plays a vital role in the growth process at this age. Consider this.

> The early adolescent wants many friends, for he needs peers to help him sculpt his beliefs, verify his new conclusions, test his new attitudes against an alien set in order to evaluate their hardiness, and obtain support for his new set of fragile assumptions. *However, he still needs his family, for it has several important psychological functions,* even though the helplessness of childhood is past. The family provides the child with a set of arbitrary standards that give structure to his motives and actions. They provide models for identification which, if exploited, help establish a self-concept. The family provides the first set of adults who communicate their estimation of the child's worth. And many pre-adolescents still require this evaluation, because youth continue to award the family a special wisdom and legitimacy. (Kagan, 1972, p. 103)

Practical as well as developmental reasons contribute to the fairly stable home-family relationship of this age. Consider a few of the more salient. Child-adolescents have almost no way to support themselves outside the family. Neither do they have a place to live. They can be detained by the authorities if they fail to attend school. These shackles, however, are not as restrictive as they appear once the nature of the early adolescent is taken into close measure. For example, few youth of this age strongly desire economic independence, and few as yet despise school enough to choose from the few available options. Most youth retain strong emotional ties with their parents and find them more comforting and humane than virtually any other adults in their social world. These ties are not strained excessively by conflicts of interest. Parents and children usually don't find too much to fight about. Parents don't worry too much about the sexual habits of their children. Automobiles are not yet an important part of their social life, neither is liquor or drugs. Exceptions abound, to be sure, but in only mild degree when compared with those of the upcoming years. Of the three ages of adolescence, the greatest home-family harmony exists here. The bases for intense disagreements have not yet surfaced, and the bonds of familial attachment remain sturdy. Daniel Offer, who has conducted what is possibly the best research to date on *normal* adolescents, notes that the "generation gap" is not as bad as is commonly thought, and that for the most part adults and their teenage children get along fairly well. His research indicated "that for the majority of teenagers we have studied there is no major gap of understandings and communication between the generations".(1969, p. 204)

The Future

Life goals and ambitions are hazy. Youth realize that when they reach adulthood they must obtain a job, or at least find some way to secure a continuous income. They recognize that they probably will marry and raise children. They know the norms of their society and assume that, in one way or another, they will live within their framework. For all intents and purposes, however, the demands of immediate day-to-day living take priority over preoccupation with the future demands of adulthood. The role of the future has a much greater impact on *late* adolescents, forcing upon them a struggle with identity far beyond the imagining of the early adolescent.

Most youngsters assume that they will fare well in life, although considerable differences are found in what faring well means. A 13-year-old ghetto boy believes that he will be a successful dealer or runner or merchant; his middle-class counterpart assumes that he will be a shrewd lawyer or a prosperous executive. Neither of them, however, has come to grips with the specific skills inherent to success in these areas, nor have they thought much about the probability of failure. Their egocentric nature inclines them to think that whatever is best for them will happen. The greater realism of middle adolescence forcefully blunts this Mitty-ism.

Very few youth escape the media influence. The younger the adolescent, the more likely he will be taken by the mystique and fiction of popular culture. Thus media heroes are their heroes, and cultural myths are their myths. This is not all bad. It provides a base for stacking myth against reality, but sorting one from the other does not take place in earnest until late adolescence. This is one area where parents and teachers can make genuine contributions if they encourage youngsters to think about what they are seeing, to assess its validity, and to evaluate the motives of the people who produce it.

Survival

The growing person's first obligation is to self, and the blueprint of human development is such that this duty is usually obeyed. Consequently, during periods of rapid development, growth becomes a duty unto itself. In a sense, child-adolescents are subservient to their growth. The expanding body requires more calories, greater nutrients, increased minerals, more exercise and more space. Other intense demands come from the need for *social* growth: the need to obtain interpersonal competence, to deal with peers, and to cope with a forcefully emerging self.

The entire psychology of the early adolescent is influenced by growth demands. The more powerful they are, the less time and energy remain for outside investments. Thus youth first learn to deal with peers; *then* they begin to assess the desirability of particular mates. Youth first learn how to get recognition; *then* they decide whether they most want it from this person or that person. Youth first belong to some group; *then* they become selective of the particular group to which they will give their allegiance. The skills of *survival* always come first; afterward individuals sort out the kinds of people and the types of pastimes with which they will become involved. As a general rule, the mechanics of social competence are learned during early adolescence and are given their touch of individualism during middle and late adolescence. During these latter stages, matters of moral principle, self-identity, and personal commitment exert a commanding presence on the growing personality.

For these reasons the child-adolescent is less discriminating in choosing companions. It is not surprising, therefore, that many middle adolescents discard their former friends, or leave their original gang. Once they have learned to make do, they try to do it in a way which suits them. In this regard they are like the junior executive who first learns the ropes of his organization and *then* begins to twist them to suit his unique personality, even making pulleys of them for his own escalation within the organization.

Moral Outlook

Moral outlook and religious belief tend toward the conventional. Most youth adhere to the religious denomination of their parents (if they have one), and accept matter-of-factly the moral precepts upon which it is based. Differences of opinion exist, but they are founded more frequently upon dissatisfaction with rules than upon a basic difference in metaphysics or axiology. Existential puzzles (such as the purpose of life) do not register deeply on the early adolescent because the mental capacities required for such contemplation are not fully developed, and because the intellect has all it can handle with day-to-day matters.

Religious experiences do not carry the emotional significance evident in middle adolescence. What clergymen call "genuine" religious conversions rarely take place at this age. Religion is viewed somewhat like the government: it is there, it is adhered to by parents, and it should be respected. Youth of this age are incredulous of adults (or peers) who claim to be atheists because this makes them at odds with established authority, and also because a God-less universe is incomprehensible to most of them.

Church-going is difficult because it taxes one's social nature rather than because it contradicts a moral principle. Youth at this age talk a great deal about hypocrisy, but show only an impoverished understanding of it. They rarely recognize it in themselves, and for the most part, it is a scapegoat term employed to show dislike for the conduct of another person. This is a difficult age for understanding the subtle nuances of adult interpersonal exchange. Since most youth lack the experience to understand first-hand what they see, they do not possess the mental dexterity to comprehend behaviour which does not fit their expectations. They continuously find themselves in situations where they don't like what they see or resent what they are expected to do but are unable to put a finger on the precise reasons. This is frustrating to them and they soothe their anxieties by thinking adults hypocritical.

Mortality

The four leading causes of death among youth aged 10-14 are (in order of frequency): accidents, malignant growths, congenital disorders, and influenza-pneumonia. Accidents, however, are far and away the major cause of death, accounting for 50 percent of all age 10-14 mortality. Among the 15-19 year-olds a different picture appears. The four leading causes of death, in order of frequency are: accidents, homocide, malignant growths, and suicide. Of the four leading causes of death less than seven percent are accounted for by natural causes. Accidents, homocide and suicide accounted for about 70 percent of all the deaths at this age. This probably is a conservative figure because so many suicide deaths are recorded under less stigmatic labels. (Katch-adourian, p. 172)

At this age the average boy or girl is not overly introspective. Mental energy is expended on the outside world more so than on the inner personality. The exceptions are found most commonly among 13-year-olds, who hover near the growth advancement of middle adolescence.

Early adolescence is the least introspective of the adolescent stages for two decisive reasons. First, the mental skills required for introspection are not refined, the ability to make hypothetical assessments about oneself, the ability to think propositionally, and the ability to escape egocentrism. Second, the practical demands of day-to-day living monopolize the intellect and leave little energy for reflective contemplation. This contrasts sharply with succeeding stages when introspection is a staple in the intellectual diet.

Postscript

What then are the dominant traits most closely associated with the period of life we here call "child-adolescence"? First and foremost, this is a period of significant growth. Puberty is the particular growth reality around which it gravitates. Puberty influences how youth think about themselves, their bodies and their appearances. It also influences their interest in the opposite sex.

Social growth is likewise important. The peer group increases in power, and one of the most important life requirements is to cope effectively with it. Youth of this age go to school and their social life is inseparable from it. "Fundamentally, for most American twelve-year-olds, school is where it's at. School occupies the time and concerns of all the people you know — your friends, your parents, people you meet." (Martin, 1972, p. 189) The home is equally important and it has not as yet become the source of conflict typical of later adolescence. The bulk of one's social energy is spent learning to become competent enough to cope with peers on some kind of equal footing. The larger society is not an overly important concern; of greater importance are the mini-societies to which one belongs.

Intelligence is blossoming but it is not as sophisticated as the youngster believes. The ability to make sound judgements, to hypothesize cogently, and to detach from selfish interests are poorly developed when compared with middle or late adolescence.

Personal identity is not firmly crystallized because in some areas it is still in the trial and error stage; in others it lacks first hand experience. The future is thought about but not excessively. The present monopolizes mental energy.

Puberty ushers in the capacity for sexual intercourse, but lack of sexual passion leaves this potential largely untapped. Masturbation is more common than sexual play with others. Girls mature sooner than

30

boys and as a result look to older boys for social companions for the first time in their lives. Sexual interests are more social than endocrinological. Little one-to-one romance exists even though its heyday is only a year or two away. The need for personal intimacy is weak and does not govern sexual interests with the authority it shall shortly acquire.

The body remains fairly healthy despite its prodigious growth, and even more significantly, the child-adolescent abuses it considerably less than do older adolescents. Suicide is rare, as is homocide. Pregnancy is infrequent. Social pathology and mental breakdown are not as yet major problems; they await further aging. By middle or late-adolescent standards it is a remarkably trouble-free time of life.

If one were to divide human life into three broad categories: childhood, adolescence, and adulthood, this period of life, more than any other, is a mixture of the first two. Thus its name. These years are somewhat difficult because in them childhood imperceptibly blends and overlaps with adolescence. Boundaries are not clear, definitions are not crisp, body impulses are not precise, and social patterns are not constant. The single world which encapsulates its spirit is *transition*. The stability of childhood vanishes, replaced by the uncertainty of teen existence. In the early adolescent years, one bids farewell to childhood and begins the arduous trek to adulthood. One writer put it this way:

> In the space of three years the change is drastic. At twelve (usually seventh grade) they are clearly on one side of limbo, at fourteen on the other. I always saw my high school students as people becoming adults. They had the size and shape of adults, the physical and mental abilities of adults; they were clearly becoming someone. Early adolescents are a different story. They are also in the process of becoming, *but they move erratically back and forth between the world of childhood and the world of adolescence*. (Martin, 1972, p. 187)

Early adolescents experience their share of stress. Fortunately they not only *learn* from the stress inherent to their age, but time and again significant transitions do not commence *until* promoted by developmental pain. From every developmental pain, however, springs an offsetting pleasure. Physical growth brings the exuberance of new body sensations and impulses; mental growth brings the awe of seeing the world more comprehensively; social growth ushers in the thrill of peer community and a sense of comradeship; psychological growth allows adolescents to see themselves as primary persons, not merely as the reflection of social expectation. Understanding this period of life requires that we weave the

31

sometimes tragic, sometimes comic mixture of stress and joy which inevitably comes with growth.

The youngster wastes few tears on a farewell to childhood; the growth needs are too powerful. Just as the preschooler feels no remorse about leaving toddlerhood, neither does the early adolescent grieve the loss of childhood. Dreams, fantasies, and ambitions centre on the emancipation of age rather than on the burdens and responsibilities which accompany it.

What tasks face children as they grow into early adolescence? They prepare to be less dependent, to make their own decisions and have the fortitude to stand by them, to select friends, and to decide upon moral viewpoints. The childhood years afford shelter from the hardships of social living inasmuch as the community of children is limited and well-protected. The community of adolescents is extended, with few specific borders, and few privileges of protection. During childhood youngsters learn to look out for their physical self, but now they have new vulnerabilities and weaknesses. They must learn to protect their self-esteem, their sense of belonging; they must learn to adjust to group demands without losing individuality.

The *child* likes to be popular and accepted but is not dominated by these impulses. Peer rejection does not wound excessively. During early adolescence popularity achieves lofty prominence. Peer rejection results in so much trauma that for many 13-year-olds a sense of *accomplishment* is felt when an evening with peers brings no ridicule or rejection. Few experiences are more important than peer acceptance, and few more painful than peer rejection. When teenagers bid farewell to childhood, they leave behind a time of life when peers are secondary.

All in all, child-adolescents are more social than philosophical, more impulsive than reflective, more experimental than cautious. Their sense of self is not well-defined because they are in the process of discovering what they like and dislike, what they are good at and bad at. Their morality is based more upon what they have absorbed from their culture than from thoughtful rumination. Their conscience is more pragmatic than ideal, and certainly more egocentric than altruistic. Their most important social goals are to learn the skills which will allow them to survive with a decent amount of recognition and esteem; their temporal concerns are immediate rather than distant. They are not brutal in the Hobbesian sense, but closer to it than most modern psychologists are willing to admit. (William Golding's portrayal of children in *Lord of the Flies* is reasonable.) They are not naturally as cooperative as some of the "man-is-good" anthropologists such as Ashley Montagu would have us believe, but they are capable of genuine sharing — under the right conditions. Like all humans, they are malleable, and like other animals they are equipped by nature to look after themselves and to avoid those things they do not like. They are *easy* to teach because they believe in the power of authority, because their thought process is more geared to assimilate than to analyze, and because they have limited ability to disagree with ideas or facts beyond their range of experience. They are *difficult* to teach because they think they know more than they do, because they question better than they understand, and because their powers of inference and induction are not on a par with those of adults. They do not comprehend relationshis evident to a more astute mind.

Summary

The dominant characteristics of the early-adolescent period of life include the following:

1. The body experiences fast-paced and consistent growth. Virtually all girls and boys begin their pubertal growth; some girls actually finalize their growth and undergo no further physical growth advances during the adolescent period. Sexual maturity approaches its final stages, although finishing touches await middle adolescence. Body appearance changes drastically. Increased production of androgen precipitates secondary sexual changes for boys, whereas increased production of estrogen triggers secondary sexual changes in girls.

2. As a result of rapid body transformations, the youngster tends to experience considerable body consciousness and body shyness. This, in turn, heightens mood fluctuation.

3. The peer world exerts tremendous influence. To survive socially depends on the ability to interact effectively within the peer group. Most early adolescents spend a great portion of their social energy simply learning to get along with others in such a way that they will be accepted and esteemed. The peer world is the arena in which sex role learning is experimented with. Acquiring "appropriate" sex roles is a major social task of this age. All peer relations are transacted by a highly egocentric personality which has considerable difficulty understanding (or appreciating) the viewpoints of others. Of the three ages of adolescence this unquestionably is the most egocentric, and all interpersonal exchanges reflect a certain amount of childlike egocentrism.

4. Most early adolescents are ethnocentric and authoritarian. Their

sense of social justice is underdeveloped and remarkably concrete. They tend to think in terms of the present rather than the future, and their understanding of social problems is dominated by immediacy rather than long term solutions.

5. Interest in the opposite sex is more social than endocrinological. Sexual intercourse is rare. Sexual passion is weak and underdeveloped, the exceptions being found among girls far more consistently than boys. At this age youngsters are still in the process of completing their sexual growth. They are not sure of themselves, partly because their "selves" are incomplete.

6. The home and family remain (as they were during childhood) the most important social and emotional facts in the life of the adolescent. The peer group is competing for allegiance, but remains secondary. In our society there are virtually no options other than to live at home (no matter what the emotional climate), and virtually all youth do.

7. The future carries less impact than during either middle or late adolescence. Interests and concerns are essentially short term rather than long range. This temporal restriction impinges on the early adolescent analysis of philosophical issues and dampens interest in larger metaphysical issues.

8. Moral outlook is a mixture of conventional and authoritarian. Many early adolescents disapprove of eccentricity or divergence from the norm. Religious experience tends toward the shallow.

9. Accidents are the leading cause of death, but of the three ages of adolescence this witnesses the *least* amount of violent death. In terms of emotional stability, early adolescence is certainly the least troublesome of the adolescent period.

The picture I have painted of the early adolescent leans toward the childlike. This deserves a word of caution because developmental psychologists are aware that the maturity of a person is assessed from two distinctly different viewpoints. The first is in terms of where the person *has been*. In this regard, the early adolescent is more mature, more sophisticated and less childlike than ever before in the life cycle. For those readers who view early adolescence from this perspective you will find my assessment limited and perhaps even patronizing. I hope your judgment will be reserved because my major concern with adolescence more strongly favours the second viewpoint which concentrates upon where the adolescent *is going*. Compared to how they will think, feel, react, and judge in the forthcoming years early adolescents are essentially juvenile. The great surges toward adulthood are yet to be lived. The comparison, however, is relative, and each reader is entitled to view it in the manner he or she sees fit.

Chapter Three

The Middle-Adolescent Period: Adolescence

The time of life I refer to as middle adolescence more closely than any other resembles our contemporary cultural image of the adolescent. It is a time when the childlike features of early adolescence are outgrown, when the body begins to really look adultlike, but it also is a time when the personality features of adulthood are not yet finalized. During middle adolescence, one is neither child nor adult — one is in between. The term "adolescent" suits perfectly. They are much closer to adulthood in the areas that count — body maturity, and intellectual ability. In fact, if those are the indicators one uses to measure "adultness", most adolescents would be considered adults. However, there is more to adulthood than a body which is able to reproduce and a mind which is able to calculate swiftly or to reason systematically.

In terms of chronological years, middle adolescence occurs during the ages of 14, 15 and 16 for boys and 13, 14, 15 and 16 for girls, the earlier age for girls being accounted for by their precocious growth through puberty. Quite obviously some youth do not fit these age gradings, especially unusually early- or late-maturers. As a general index of the human cycle, however, this is a suitable age breakdown. In this chapter I shall present some of the important landmarks which help us better understand the phenomenon of adolescence in North America. I will place special emphasis on some of the basic differences between the early adolescent and the middle adolescent, while at the same time try to point out some of their similarities. Middle adolescence is only the second stage in the total adolescent period, therefore, considerable growth remains in store. The late-adolescent period, which I shall overview in the next chapter, represents the culmination of adolescent growth.

Overview

Physical growth loses some of its punch. It doesn't possess the person as it did during early adolescence. It's there, to be sure, but it is less evident.

Youth feel more confident about their bodies. For girls, physical growth is almost complete. Boys continue to grow into late adolescence, adding weight, muscle and some height, but like girls, they experience almost no fundamental changes in any important subsystem, and they do not undergo a qualitative change in their body profile. They are what Gessell calls "bigger and better" versions of the same basic product. The important point to be made is that for the majority of boys and girls the body has reached its adult shape and proportion by the end of middle adolescence. In terms of the physical shape and size they *are* adults.

Increased body maturity brings about a richer sexual drive, and inclines the person to act upon it. (Aristotle, in writing of adolescents, says, "Of bodily desires, it is the sexual to which they are most disposed to give way.") The biological impulse is accompanied by a deeper sense of interpersonal relationship and a stronger drive for intimacy with the opposite sex. The implications of human sexuality become more significant at this age because the incidence of pregnancy increases, as does its medical termination; marriages also increase, as do their legal termination. The number of "illegitimate" children increase and a great many of them are taken care of by the State in one way or another. Consequently, for the first time in the life cycle, the government takes an active interest in the sex habits of its pre-adult citizens.

Social problems aside, sexuality becomes emotionally deeper and more passionate than it was during early adolescence; not for *all* youth, to be sure, and not for as many as will be the case in late adolescence. But the difference is noticeable and, as William James was fond of saying, "It is a difference which makes a difference." For most youth, middle adolescence is the time of life when they first experience sexual passion. It is a much more passionate stage than early adolescence.

The peer group modifies quite a bit from its early adolescent structure, most noticeably in its boy-girl composition. Groups are more mixed and each sex is more likely to admit to the worthwhileness of the other. Dating increases as does couple-bonding. Friendships are durable and outlast considerable bickering. Family relationships may or may not worsen but as a trend, parents recognize in various ways their child's inching toward adulthood and make concessions to the fact that childhood is slipping away.

Significant strides are made in intellectual habits. The thought process shows commendable improvement and not only becomes more thorough, precise, and analytic, but also more profound at examining itself, correcting its own errors and looking within the personality of its owner. (Plato described mathematical and scientific studies for adolescents because they suited the mental skills of this age). Intellectual growth is so important that it merits top billing with physical growth. It creates several fundamental changes in the total life-style, most noticeably a greater preoccupation with self-analysis, an increased interest in the laws which regulate society and the systems which govern the universe. Middle adolescents do not become the philosophers that some psychologists claim, but they are without question more reflective and intellectual than ever before.

The moral outlook is recast partly because of increased experience, but even more so because of the advances in mental capacity. Middle adolescents see moral issues from perspectives previously unavailable. They are also able to analyze moral beliefs with analytic prowess beyond that of a few years before. To say they undergo a revolution of morality is to overstate the case. The expansion, however, is so significant that it is hard to miss. Moral outlook becomes more tolerant, more realistic and less absolutist, and more concerned with justice than with wrongdoing. A special section in this chapter will highlight many of the moral growth trends of middle adolescence.

Social life revolves around the school for the vast majority of adolescents. They are isolated and segregated from the rest of society with alarming finality, and except for what they read in their books, see on TV or hear on the radio, they probably know less about the *world of adults* than any generation in North American history. Because they spend virtually all their daylight hours in school, and because most of the people they interact with are about the same age, they have evolved a peer world which rivals the family for personal allegiance. It marks the first *genuine* threat to the family as the centre of emotional life. The matter of youth isolation and segregation are taken up elsewhere in this book.

From my perspective this is the great age for growing up. It is the "coming of age" age. In cultures where the luxury of protracted adolescence is not possible, this is when adult roles can be assumed with reasonable aptitude and with good chance for success. (Napoleon was a captain at age 16. But equally significant to the theme I shall be drawing is that he was a military genius at 22.) Coming of age, important as it is, is not the *attainment* of maturity; rather, it is the age at which successful interning may commence and the roles expected of adults can be reasonably met. It is worthwhile to keep in mind that society does not always allow adult roles to be assumed merely because the adolescent is ready to assume them. Equally important, however, is the fact that merely because society says a youngster is ready to assume a role does not mean that he or she is able to do so effectively. This relationship between social roles and the readiness to assume them is central to understanding the contemporary adolescent because in some instances they are expected to assume roles for which they are not ready (such as early dating or early career decisions) and in other instances they are expected to avoid roles which they are able to carry out effectively, such as productive work in the community.

The Body

During the adolescent period the body continues to grow, although the *rate* of growth is lower for both boys and girls. By the fourteenth year girls have achieved about 98 percent of their adult height, whereas boys only about 90 percent. Both sexes continue to add weight for the next several years; however a great proportion of this weight gain is represented by muscle volume for males and by fatty tissue for females. The *accelerated growth spurts* characteristic of early adolescence are not typical (especially for girls) but growth does continue.

The most impressive body changes are related to puberty, and include the following: (1) Acceleration and expansion of skeletal growth which results in the body proportions and physical profile characteristic of early adulthood. (2) Altered body composition with a greater abundance of muscle for males and increased fatty tissue for females. During this period, males become measurably larger and stronger for the first time in the life cycle. (3) Increased maturity of the circulatory and respiratory systems leads to increased strength and endurance; as a result there is considerable increase in athletic capacity. (4) The development of the gonads, the reproductive organs and the secondary sexual characteristics. For both sexes these changes are noticeable and unmistakable. The vast majority of youth become capable of reproduction, and a great many exercise this capacity. Finally, all of these body advancements contribute to the general physical appearance of adulthood.

In recent years it has been hypothesized that the differences in the amount of fatty tissue between boys and girls is largely a result of environment. Boys are encouraged to play sports whereas girls are encouraged to be spectators. Consequently, (the argument goes) boys are more muscular and athletic. The evidence does not support such a view. By age one year, girls tend to have slightly more fat than boys, and even though the build-up of subcutaneous fat is slight during early childhood, by about age seven most children begin to accumulate more of it. With the onset of the growth spurt occurs a gradual loss of fat, especially in the arms and legs. This loss results in a "negative fat balance" (a loss of fat) for most boys but rarely so for girls. "As a result, the average teenage girl enters adulthood with more subcutaneous fat than does the average teenage boy, especially in the region of the pelvis, the breasts, the upper back and the backs of the upper arms . . . Consequently, women's bodies are more rounded." (Katchadourian, p. 29) This difference in fatty tissue affects the physical appearance of males by making their muscles bulge more prominently, whereas even in girls with well developed musculature it softens the overall appearance. In ordinary times these points would not need to be emphasized, however, current thought is so dominated by environmentalism that it is necessary to emphasize when a human reality is almost totally dictated by species traits. Such is the case with the adolescent body and the way it looks and why boys are different from girls at this age. It is a species trait in which environment (assuming it provides minimum growth requirements) plays almost no significant role. Tanner provides further information on this matter:

> Before adolescence, boys and girls are similar in strength for a given body size and shape; after, boys are much stronger, probably due to developing more force per gram of muscle as well as absolutely larger size, a higher systolic blood pressure, a lower resting heart rate, a greater capacity for carrying oxygen in the blood, and a greater power for neutralizing the chemical products of muscular exercise such as lactic acid. In short, the male becomes at adolescence more adapted to the tasks of hunting, fighting, and manipulating all sorts of heavy objects . . . . (1972, p. 5)

For boys and girls alike, growth in height tends to reach its adult level at this age. In this respect the demands of growth which monopolized the early-adolescent period remain fairly strong. Important differences, however, are worthy of mention. In the first place, *early* adolescents are growing from one body appearance to another. They are changing from children into an adolescents. Their changes are more than merely quantitative; they are not merely "bigger and better" versions of their previous selves. In essence, they grow into another body — or at least one which is radically different in proportion, density, and, of course, appearance. Of greater import, it is a body which is becoming capable of reproduction. Therefore, the changes which take place between the ages of 10 and 14 are more fundamental than those which occur between 14 and 17. The psychological toll is less in the older years if for no other reason than one has had time to accustom oneself to the growth process.

In recognizing the significance of early adolescent growth we need not minimize the importance of middle-adolescence. It has its own impressive traits. In girls, the internal sexual organs grow dramatically. The ovaries are more capable of producing mature ova. The vagina becomes larger and its lining thicker. The menstrual flow becomes more predictable, often reoccurring in 28-32 day intervals. For boys genital growth reaches adult maturity, and viable sperm are produced in ample volume. This is the sexual coming of age when the body finalizes its readiness for repeating the birth cycle.

Body proportions move progressively toward the adult norm. The *early* adolescent is easy to spot because features are tinged with childish traits; the middle adolescent much more closely resembles the adult, though not as precisely as during late adolescence. The face appears more adultlike because the bones of the face grow faster than those of the cranial vault; thus the prominent nose and the angular jaw (especially in boys) present themselves. Sex differences become much more visible. The male forearm, which is larger relative to body height than the forearm of the female, is more conspicuous. Boys are distinguishable by their larger shoulders, their relatively narrower hips, and their larger legs relative to trunk length. Girls are more adult-like in appearance because breast development is almost complete, skeletal growth has almost stopped, thus leaving the girl with her adult body proportions if body weight does not increase too much. In primitive cultures where age is not counted in years, girls are expected at this time to begin child bearing.

The image of the middle adolescent as a non-stop eater has some basis in biological fact. Of the first twenty years, the greatest caloric requirement for sustaining growth is witnessed during this time. At about age 14, girls are at the peak of their daily requirements, about 2,800 calories per day. Boys at age 14 require about the same amount; however, by age 17 they require almost 3,400 calories per day in order to sustain their *normal growth*. Sound nutrition remains a crucial growth necessity as much as during the tremendous growth years of childhood and early adolescence (Barnett, 1972). Abuse of nutrition is common, often resulting in obesity. Many adolescents consume more calories than they need for growth, adding considerable weight. Obesity is directly related to socio-economic status; it's "six times as common among women of low economic status than among those of high status". A similar rate applies to men. (Katchadourian, p. 153)

The Intellect

The mental processes which characterize adolescence do not suddenly appear. They surface during early adolescence with the advent of what Piaget calls "formal" thought. Many traits are described in this section rather than in the child-adolescence section because in middle adolescence they achieve a utility in day-to-day living which far surpasses their impact in early adolescence, and because the emotional and moral implications of these mental advances become more prominent. During middle adolescence, the *consequences* of mental advancement are unmistakably present, whereas during the previous age they are not.

Six general trends dominate mental ability during adolescence. I shall review them briefly to clarify adolescent intellectualism, and to indicate how it influences moral and emotional experiences. Keep in mind the implications of these mental capacities for two important aspects of adolescent life: moral outlook (the way one makes moral decisions) and, introspection (the way one thinks about one's own personality).

In adolescence thought becomes more abstract. The facility for dealing with hypothetical and theoretical ideas expands. The *formal thinker* (I am using Piaget's description of formal though to describe the adolescent) does not require a premise which coincides with one's understanding of the world as does the child. For example, consider the following question: "If three-legged turtles can fly twice as fast as a Boeing 707, which has a top speed of 650 m.p.h., how long would it take such a turtle to fly 1,500-distance from point A to point B?" This question is beyond the comprehension of most pre-adolescents but within the grasp of most adolescents for two reasons: (1) The initial premise, though false, is seen by the adolescent as incidental to solving the problem; one accepts the premise and proceeds to solve the problem. (2) Solution of this problem requires that the individual retain several facts in mind simultaneously, including: (a) the speed at which the turtle is able to fly, (b) the speed at which the airplane is able to fly, and (c) the distance from point A to point B. The adolescent is considerably more adept at keeping track of these variables than is the younger person.

Abstract thought fosters a greater interest in the *ideal,* the *probable,* and the *nonphysical;* therefore, thought becomes less bound to the narrow parameters of earlier years. Willingness to think about nonphysical concepts such as soul and life after death is common. Even more pronounced is the tendency to think in terms of the *ideal* as well as the real.

The second feature: *Thought becomes more comprehensive.* One distinction between formal and pre-formal thought is the tendency of the latter to deal with only *some* of the possibilities when solving a problem. Children do not recognize that an unexplored possibility may be just as correct as the more obvious possibility or, that one cannot *have confidence* in a solution *until* all possibilities have been analyzed. Adolescents are more thorough in their thinking; they look at more sides of an issue, and are less likely to be duped. Their thought is more comprehensive, and less susceptible to errors of omission.

The third feature: *Thought becomes the object of its own action.* The adolescent discovers that conclusions do not come into existence on their own, but that they result from preceding mental processes. Because thought is increasing in *comprehensiveness* as well as in powers of *hypothesizing,* adolescents apply these skills to their own thought process. They review the product of their thought to see how it stacks up, to see if it is consistent, and if it does justice to the problem.

Thinking about one's own thoughts is an emotional experience which often gives rise to confusion and bewilderment, and in this regard, intellectual advancement contributes to emotional difficulties. The adolescent world is filled with inconsistencies and incongruities. Adolescents note with surprise the opposite emotions (such as love and hate) which exist side by side within them; they notice that one day they behave one way, another day another way. They also recognize inconsistencies in others. The 14-year-olds in many ways, are "amateur psychologists" who hold an "intuitive grasp of their own psychological being". They see traits in their parents which before went unnoticed, and, if they hold them in realistically high esteem, the pedestal upon which they stand is likely to collapse.

The ability to think about one's own thought process is a significant mental breakthrough. It allows greater precision of thought and increases the opportunity to detect mental errors. On the other hand, it causes a certain amount of self-doubt by requiring that ideas be examined from more than one point of view. It deprives adolescents of the mental dogmatism they became accustomed to during childhood, forcing upon them the burden of intellectual freedom. The mental process which permits scientific thought is the same process which introduces the anguish of self-analysis.

A fourth feature: *Thought becomes more propositional.* A proposition is anything capable of being believed, doubted, or denied; it is not true unto itself; rather its truth (or falseness) must be determined by other means. In short, propositional thought deals with *statements about reality* rather than reality itself.

Propositional thinking allows one to consider possibilities far beyond the realm of reality as *presently* understood. It allows manipulation of facts, and freshness of viewpoint. It increases insight because it engenders a greater number of solutions. These mental advances hold far-reaching implications. Adolescent political thought, for example, undergoes important changes because of the increased ability to analyze issues. It has been observed that:

> Ordinarily the youngster begins adolescence incapable of complex political discourse . . . . By the time this period is at an end, a dramatic change is evident; the youngster's grasp of the political world is now recognizably adult. His mind moves with some agility within the terrain of political concepts; he has achieved abstractness, complexity, and even some delicacy in his sense of political textures; he is on the threshold of ideology, struggling to formulate a morally coherent view of how society is and might and should be arranged. (Adelson, 1972, p. 106)

A fifth feature: *Thought becomes less egocentric.* During adolescence one becomes increasingly capable of thinking from points of view other than one's own. This should not surprise us since the adolescent is pretty good at propositional *and* theoretical thought, each of which requires a certain detachment from self.

Adolescents are most likely to think egocentrically when the object of thought is close to their emotional centre. An adolescent boy may be reluctant to believe things about his girl friend which would be painful, or, an adolescent girl may be irrational in her beliefs about her parents. However, the girl may be able to see clearly what the boy will not and *vice versa.* They are too emotionally involved in their own situations to view them objectively; each, however, can see the situation of the *other.* In areas of *minimal* ego-involvement, egocentrism decreases. Thus, when applied to mathematics, for example, the adolescent mind is amazingly free of egocentrism.

A sixth feature: *Thought becomes more future-oriented.* Inevitably the future works its way into the thought patterns of adolescents because, as they approach adulthood, they face decisions which influence the balance of their life. Their ability to hypothesize allows them to consider a wide variety of possibilities, and the ability to think propositionally allows them to assess their plausibility.

Because of these mental advances, adolescent thought undergoes several vital changes:

1. it goes beyond the real to deal with the ideal;
2. it goes beyond the physical to deal with the hypothetical;
3. it goes beyond fragments to deal with wholes;
4. it goes beyond what *is* to deal with propositions which ask "what if"?;
5. it goes beyond the present to examine the future.

All of these capacities exist in one form of another during earlier years, but during adolescence they coalesce into a global mental strategy and achieve a much greater measure of consistency.

All mental activity becomes more complex during middle adolescence and yields thought products unavailable to the mind governed by simpler processes. New realms of insight open, and the world becomes more complex because the mind is able to grasp a greater number of relationships, infer a greater number of possibilities and conceptualize richer combinations of ideas.

The *child* thinks primarily in terms of the *real* rather than the *ideal*; therefore is more a realist than an idealist; the child thinks of present time more than future time, therefore does not share the adolescent's concern for long-range events; the child spends little energy trying to determine whether information is correct, therefore, is much more likely to accept as true what parents say. Adolescents question the *source* of knowledge and disagree openly with parents and other authority figures.

Other differences exist between the intellect of the child and that of the adolescent. Childhood thought is *fragmented* and does not deal well with totalities; the ability to formulate hypotheses is weak, whereas among adolescents, it is strong. Adolescents are able to think *philosophically* as well as *scientifically* while the child can do neither with much proficiency. The intellectual breakthroughs of adolescence make obsolete the rigid vision of childhood. The adolescent intellect tackles sources and origins and, thus, in one sense of the word, they are critics of just about everything. They outgrow attitudes toward life which can be sustained only by the narrow, receptive mind of the child; they are thrust into a world infinitely more complex which requires more contemplation, and, perhaps most difficult of all, a world which demands decisions when clear-cut solutions are unavailable.

Some Psychological Responses to Mental Growth

A subjective component accompanies all forms of growth. During adolescence the increase in mental abilities creates several *psychological responses* which impact overall behaviour. Here I shall overview five general trends which typify the middle-adolescent response to increased mental growth. It should be emphasized that similar responses do occur among early adolescents and late adolescents as well but usually not with the abruptness or forcefulness characteristic of the middle-adolescent experience.

1. *Expanded external awareness.* The narrow, confined world of childhood explodes during adolescence. Increased intellectual powers bring into focus aspects of the social and physical world which heretofore were pretty much ignored. Political, economic, social, and moral systems are seen from a perspective which becomes possible only with the loss of childhood egocentrism and the onset of adolescent formal thought. Adolescents are rarely content merely to observe new discoveries; they apply propositional and hypothetical thought in their direction and, as a result, gain insight as to why and how they came into existence. As they also recognize the imperfections of what they discover, they are forced to deal with the ugly aspects of reality from which they were previously sheltered. The wonder of discovery is blunted by the fact that some of the discoveries are difficult to assimilate into their idealistic minds. Confusion, sometimes disillusionment, is the result. The net effect of expanded external awareness is twofold: (1) the adolescent becomes involved in discovering the systems upon which one's social and physical world operate and, at the same time, becomes less involved in oneself, and (2) the adolescent discovers (via formal thinking) that much of what one discovers is imperfect and needs improvement. When idealism is punctured, adjustments are required by the growing self. Some adolescents accept matter-of-factly that things are not as ideal as they could be; others are emotionally shaken; others become apathetic and detached and, as a result, outward expansion is stifled. Psychologists are not in agreement as to whether these

"symptoms" are normal growing pains or indicators of the inability to cope with life stress.

2. *Expanded internal awareness.* All the basic skills of formal thought can be applied inwardly as well as outwardly. Thus, adolescents become obsessed with *introspection.* They probe their inner resources eagerly. They want to know about their social strengths and weaknesses; they want to know how they stack up. They thrive upon "instant replay" of daily events. Before falling asleep at night they may in their mind's eye run through an event of social importance a dozen times.

Preoccupation with self does not stem only from curiosity; it is a matter of psychological survival. The self does not wait to be discovered; it asserts itself in the form of feelings, desires, resentments and insecurities. The rational mind attempts to cope with these realities, but in no way is it completely responsible for their existence. The rational mind (what Freud call the "ego") is the mediator of impulses and desires which sprout during adolescence.

Introspection serves three major functions: assessing social acceptability; assessing personal acceptability; and assessing self-impulses. A brief look will help clarify these three important mental tasks. (1) Assessing social acceptance involves thinking about how behaviour can be modified so that "I" am more fully accepted by those people I most want to impress. Thinking about social acceptance is a requirement of social living during every developmental stage; with adolescence, it merely becomes more cognitive and strategic. (2) Assessing personal acceptance involves thinking about the quality (goodness) of my behaviour in terms of my own standards. The adolescent cannot live indefinitely on the acceptance of others. One must also be acceptable to oneself. Much adolescent introspection deals with this matter. It reaches its most complicated form when social acceptance contradicts personal acceptance. This occurs in two ways: (a) the adolescent is socially rewarded for behaviour contrary to what is personally acceptable; (b) the adolescent is socially punished for doing what is personally acceptable. Virtually no conflict exists when social reward corresponds with personal acceptance or when social punishment corresponds with personal non-acceptance. The adolescent must sort these matters without losing sight of the basic needs for acceptance, belonging, and esteem. It is not an easy task; for the most part, solutions are reached via extended self-analysis, conversation with others, and trial and error. (3) Assessing self-impulses involves thinking about the viability of impulses which contradict both personal and social acceptance. Sexual impulses often necessitate this kind of introspection. The adolescent may be personally convinced that premarital sex is improper. However, one's own sexual impulses still exist; they are factual. Therefore, adolescents must cope with impulses which they believe they have no right to possess. Other examples are easily detected. Feelings of inferiority, which plague virtually all normal adolescents, often contradict social and personal assessment. In other words, adolescents may say to themselves that they have no reason to feel as they do, their peers may concur, but the feeling still persists. Feelings of hostility and resentment follow similar patterns.

Thus, mental growth permits the complicated form of internal exploration necessary for the identity crises of adolescence. Mental power does not *account* for such crises; it is merely the tool by which the personality attempts to understand its own inner workings.

3. *Coping strategies become more systematic.* One conspicuous result of formal thought is that it results in a greater ability to understand the principles upon which other people (or objects) operate. Adolescents look after their own vested interests and apply this knowledge to their advantage. They learn from experience that the school principal can best be dealt with when addressed as ''mister'', when respect is shown, etc. They *anticipate* that what worked for principal A probably will also work for principal B, as well as for, say, policeman C. Coping strategies result in more diversified social behaviour.

When callously applied, coping strategies set the stage for deceit and hypocrisy, and few people are more adept at this than adolescents. They have offsetting virtues, to be sure, and they are not dominated by these negative skills. They do, however, use them more systematically and with greater premeditation than during any previous developmental stage. Because mental skills are still highly egocentric when *applied to oneself,* adolescents are not as impressed with their own hypocrisy and deceit as they are with that of others.

Coping strategies, of course, are not always used selfishly. Adolescents know that they must deal with six-year-olds differently than two-year-olds and, as a result, they develop better strategies for dealing with younger children. They recognize that employer-employee relationships are not the same as other kinds of adult-adolescent relationships; they recognize that their own behaviour influences how others respond to them, thus, they organize themselves better to procure what they want. In a phrase, adolescent behaviour becomes more premeditated and more strategic.

4. *Idealism is tested.* Adolescents tend to see the world in terms of the ideal, thinking that things are as they might ideally be rather than as they are. When exposed to information which contradicts the ideal, the adolescent becomes frustrated. Sometimes the idealism is little more than childlike *naïveté*, as when parents are thought to be perfect or authority figures exempt from human failings. Other forms of adolescent idealism border on the philosophical and are worthy of serious consideration. Adolescents are likely to demand to know *why* food cannot be more equitably divided among society's citizens. They are not impressed with economic explanations, with tradition, or with political policy. If these do not jibe with what is right, they reason, so much the worse; if they do not accord with what is right (ideal), then they must be changed. (This outlook stands in marked contrast with the more rigid authoritarian outlook of the early adolescent, and contributes significantly to a reduced ethnocentrism during middle adolescence). Examples abound where social facts have been changed because youthful idealism would not compromise with adult "realism". For the most part, however, the established policies of society are more enduring than the idealism of adolescence. The loss of idealism is not accepted gracefully. Bitterness, cynicism, resentment, apathy, and rebelliousness are common symptoms of squelched idealism. Interestingly, adolescents are able to accept *intellectually* the limitations of idealism before they are able to do so emotionally. (One must have a philosophy of adolescence to decide whether this is a strength or a limitation of the adolescent character.) The most noticeable consequences of frustrated idealism occur during late adolescence when philosophical insight apexes.

Despite the negative experiences, many positive effects accrue from testing idealism. Adolescents are forced to sort the naïve from the philosophical; they must realign their conception of how the world operates and recheck their own biases and prejudices, each of which contribute to intellectual expansion.

5. *Self-doubt increases.* One of the major characteristics of formal thought is the ability to countercheck the thought process. This capacity, by increasing the accuracy and decreasing errors in thought, forces the *person* who owns the thought process to doubt his or her own thoughts. The ability to doubt the product of one's own thought process is one of the fundamental differences between the adolescent and the child. It benefits thought, but taxes self-concept. For adolescents, it is an especially heavy tax because they already are burdened with feelings of uncertainty about social acceptance and inferiority about body image.

Adolescents learn to live with self-doubt, just as do adults. However, being inexperienced, they know few ways to escape its full impact. Because self-doubt is soothed by certainty, adolescents crave surety and dogmatism. Their expanding intellectual powers, however, quickly advise them of the limitations of dogma. As a result, adolescents strive for intensity of *emotion,* which is impossible to deny or refute. We thus see one of the major paradoxes of adolescence: increased intelligence helps bring about the need for intense emotionalism.

Self-doubt can be harmful when used as a prod by peers (or adults) to get adolescents to ''prove themselves''. One of the growth requirements of adolescence is to develop a strong self-image while at the same time to cope honestly with pangs of self-doubt. Adulthood brings no respite from this dilemma.

It is obvious that advancements in mental growth create numerous psychological dislocations, and in some instances, considerable anxiety. The ability of the adolescent to cope effectively with them greatly determines the extent to which daily life is filled with the storm and stress so frequently attributed to youth, or the extent to which things are taken in stride and absorbed matter of factly.

Morality

The nature of moral outlook changes considerably as the intellectual basis for making decisions changes. These changes *begin* during the earliest period of adolescence, but reach fruition during the middle teens. Here are some important shifts in moral outlook which influence adolescent life.

Moral outlook becomes progressively more abstract and less concrete. Adolescents expand their frame of reference in moral matters by recognizing alternatives to their own particular beliefs and by realizing that *their* moral viewpoints are not the only ones. They understand better than ever that family morality and institutional morality are variations of morality and do not represent an ultimate ''solution'' to moral questions. They are more tolerant because they identify not only that others have a *right* to viewpoints which differ from their own, but that they are dependable; youth become more relativistic in moral matters and rescind many of the absolutist outlooks of their childhood.

Moral outlook becomes more concerned with justice. Children are more impressed with what they think is wrong than with what they think is right. This is reversed during adolescence partly because of the awareness that what is "wrong" for one person is not always so for another, and partly because of the ability to recognize that all viable ethical systems are based upon the pursuit of the good rather than the avoidance of evil. Adolescents become more impressed with the right-doing of others. A growing awareness of the relativeness of moral conduct allows more tolerance of the "vices" of others. Recognizing that "virtues" require strength of moral character, they are impressed with good behaviour when they see it. Many adolescents brought up in the Christian tradition have boundless respect for the moral conduct of Gandhi, but no inclination whatsoever for his religion; likewise, Martin Luther King was admired by adolescents who in no way shared his quest for equal rights. The adolescent becomes capable of believing simultaneously in the goodness of the person, but the wrongness of that person's beliefs. Such complexity of moral thought is beyond the grasp of the child.

The moral advances brought about by the increased concern for justice are even more important when one considers the extreme authoritarianism characteristic of most *early* adolescents. Adelson claims that authoritarianism is rampant at this age.

> To sum up, the *young* adolescent's authoritarianism is omnipresent. He has only a dim appreciation of democratic forms (for example, he is more likely to favor one-man rule as against representative or direct democracy); he shows little sensitivity to individual or minority rights; he is indifferent to the claims of personal freedom; he is harsh and punitive toward miscreants; his morality is externalized and absolutistic. The decline and fall of the authoritarian spirit is, along with the most rapid growth in abstractness (to which it is related), the most dramatic developmental event in adolescent political thought. (1972, p. 119)

Moral outlook becomes increasingly cognitive. This, of course, is a natural consequence of the increased capacity for hypothetical and abstract thought which emerges during the adolescent period. Most noteworthy is the increased ability to backtrack the origins of one's personal beliefs, to isolate the reasons which most likely caused one to acquire the moral viewpoints one calls one's own. This allows adolescents to have greater confidence in beliefs when they are well founded; however, it increases self-doubt when beliefs crumble before the investigation. Adolescents are more susceptible to reasons, persuasion and discussion than are children. They outgrow the notion that moral rules are fixed like the impersonal laws of the physical universe. They do not

52

discard the rules of their society; they merely investigate them more closely and adhere to them less blindly.

Moral outlook becomes less egocentric. The child has only limited ability to perceive a moral issue. The child thinks in terms of immediate life experience, and makes judgments by the rules which govern it. As one would infer, given these conditions, a child's morality is governed by egocentrism. The adolescent retains a considerable flavour of egocentrism but also outgrows some of its restrictions. The self-centredness and rule-centredness of childhood are replaced by other-centredness and concept-centredness during adolescence. However, egocentrism does not disappear. It merely abates. It is a lessening which inclines youth toward a more mature morality, turning them perceptibly different from their childhood selves.

Moral outlook becomes psychologically expensive. One effect of moral maturity is that morality becomes more emotionally strenuous and personally exhausting. Guilt acquires a new dimension because it now is aroused by failing to live up to personal standards as well as by violating particular rules, and also because it is assessed as to whether it is "deserved" guilt. This change is understood by some psychologists as the difference between Freudian guilt and existential guilt.

From the foregoing it is evident that impressive differences exist between the moral outlook of children and that of adolescents. These differences first appear during early adolescence, but they exert their most powerful influence during middle adolescence. They become further refined during late adolescence but do not undergo any funda-mental revisions. Thus, the differences of morality which separate the adult-adolescent from the middle adolescent are not nearly as basic as those which separate the child-adolescent from the middle adolescent.

Social Living

The social world also modifies. Gangs, cliques and close friends continue; however, changes are evident. Middle adolescents are better at *choosing* their friends, and are less likely to mix with peers only because they are from the same neighbourhood or classroom. They also are better at avoiding self-defeating "friendships" filled with continu-ous bickering; they are better able to deal in a civilized way with the opposite sex whether or not a romantic interest exists. Dating is more common and *may* result in genuinely strong bonds, a trend which rarely occurs during early adolescence.

The peer group, of course, plays an important role in the life of the adolescent, but it is not unequivocal. For example, many youth, when given the opportunity to speak in an open and frank manner, or without fear of reprisal, appraise their peers in way similar to adult appraisals of these same peers. Adolescents ably recognize faults in their friends, admitting, for example, that one girl may be hypocritical and deceitful, while another is forthright and honest. Most adolescents are fairly adept at analyzing their own personality strengths and weaknesses, though for the most part they tend to overplay their weaknesses. When *adults* point out the weaknesses in a friend, most adolescents feel compelled to rally to the defense, pointing out the positive traits which counterbalance the deficiencies. The next day, however, when interacting with another peer, the boy who the night before vigorously defended his friend may gossip about his deficiencies, excluding from the conversation the positive traits he so gallantly paraded before his parents.

Disagreements with parents may focus on *important* differences; therefore, the possibility of genuine conflict increases. But since the middle teen is better able to understand the parent's perspective even while disagreeing with it, this helps to ease conflict. Most youth keep parents from learning about the things they do which will magnify family strife, and locate places away from home to carry them out. Although this makes social living in the household more stable, it creates stormy reactions in the developing moral character. The disparity between what youth are impelled to do and what adults want them to do is the basis for much hypocrisy, contributing to the double standard by which most adolescents live. A special section on adolescent hypocrisy will deal with this phenomenon.

Some evidence points to the fact that boys of this age tend to be "male chauvinists". A study carried out by Entwhistle and Greenberger (1972) using 15-year-old subjects indicates that boys are considerably more conservative in their views of what employment opportunities should be made available to girls. Boys were also much more likely to claim that "girls should not work". It was also found that boys (especially middle-class boys) viewed high achieving girls as "competition" and created dating sanctions and other forms of social boycott against them. High-achieving girls often encounter considerable pressure as a result of their achievements whereas this rarely occurs merely because of sex to high-achieving boys. Entwhistle claims that even though the middle class is thought of as the most liberal of the social classes, it is among them that some of the strongest pressure to thwart female career aspirations and ambitions exists. In fairness to males, and to the research here reported, some changes in male perceptions appear to have taken place since this study was conducted (1972), but it is nevertheless fair to say that many middle-adolescent boys fit well the concept of "male chauvinist".

This is a critical age for adjustment to school. Those youth for whom school is *not* socially rewarding, or for whom the learning does not improve job prospects, are more likely than ever to withdraw from school. (In our society dropping out or staying in school represents the single most important decision of middle adolescence.) Youngsters to whom school offers social rewards *and* provides the credentials for future "success" rarely drop out. For them school is the most important fact of their social lives, outranking even the family.

The dropout rate from the public school accelerates remarkably during middle adolescence because this is the age at which youth are no longer forced to attend school. Dropouts tend to have high unemployment rates, to acquire debts greater than they are able to pay, and to end up on welfare. Whether this results from deficiencies within *them* or within our social institutions is not clear. In either case, leaving school is invariably the single most important factor in the social life of dropouts. It changes the nature of their peer group, their socializing habits, their day-to-day activity, their nightlife, and it also alters their relationship with their parents, usually for the worse.

In terms of social pathology, virtually all areas of self-destructive behaviour show an upswing during middle adolescence. The suicide rate continues to escalate as does the incidence of homocide and physical assault. Death from accidents increases, with automobiles leading the fatality list. Drug-related deaths, especially drug "overdoses", and suicides while under the influence of drugs or the depression induced by them, also increase. The more severe psychiatric ailments such as depression, schizophrenia and paranoia also demonstrate a significant increase over figures for the early adolescent years. Common to all of these difficulties is the fact that they will increase during the coming years, and that the suffering they exact will likewise continue. With virtually all forms of personal and social pathology there exists a gradual increase throughout the adolescent period, with early adolescents exhibiting the least, late adolescents the most, and middle adolescents in between.

The "Moratorium"

When describing the social life of the middle adolescent (and to an increasing extent, the *late* adolescent) it is imperative to deal with Erikson's concept of moratorium. Erikson believes that during the adolescent years a period of time should be set aside when the adolescent is expected to experiment with different roles, to investigate many facets of personality and to be exempted from making important life decisions. The moratorium is essential for two reasons: first, the adolescent cannot be expected to make wise decisions vital to adult functioning without having a reserve of experiences upon which to base them; second, middle adolescents, in many regards, simply are not mature enough to assume adult roles, therefore they should be granted time for growth and expansion.

Erikson has more to say on the purpose of a moratorium during adolescence:

> A moratorium is a period of delay granted to somebody who is not ready to meet an obligation or forced on somebody who should give himself time. By pyschological moratorium, then, we mean a delay of adult commitments, and yet it is not only a delay. It is a period that is characterized by a selective permissiveness on the part of society and of provocative playfulness on the part of the youth, and yet it also often leads to deep, if often transitory, commitment on the part of youth, and ends in a more or less ceremonial confirmation of commitment on the part of society. (1968, p. 157)

Of the three ages of adolescence, middle adolescence is the most appropriate for the "moratorium". Early adolescents are busied with learning the ropes of interpersonal competence, and late adolescents are preoccupied with acquiring the skills which make decision-making during adulthood possible. In our society middle adolescence is the moratorium period, and in terms of developmental priorities, this is probably the ideal time for it.

Sexuality

The nature of human sexuality modifies considerably during the second phase of adolescence. Sexual feelings are more likely to be experienced as genuine sexual arousal and they are more capable of stirring sexual passion than during early adolescence. Since most girls have completed their sexual growth a large percentage are biologically able to conceive and bear children. Most boys are also able to perform sexually and are capable of siring children. Boys are still growing in height and weight and remain somewhat in the clutch of a growth stage, whereas girls have, for the most part, completed their biological growth and have attained their adult body size. Virtually all aspects of heterosexual behaviour increase over the preceding period, including not only the incidence of sexual intercourse but also all forms of sexual interplay which adults are likely to call "foreplay" when referring to themselves, but "petting" when referring to their adolescent children.

Several interesting features present themselves in the sexual attitudes and habits of youth at this age. Addy (1977) points out that research conducted in the United States and Canada supports the ideas that adolescents take their sexual behaviour seriously. Most girls, for example, do not approve of "casual" sexual encounters; they prefer that their partner has known them for a while and considers them important as a person. Most girls of this age also believe that sexual intercourse between couples who are not "in love" is wrong. More frequently than is the case during early adolescence, marriage is entertained as a future possibility with a sexual partner. In fairness, it should be pointed out that often it is envisioned in a romantic or unrealistic way; however, the point is that commitment and sexuality become linked.

Many sexually active youth are what Sorensen calls "serial monogamists" which means they are having sexual relations with only one person over a length of time. This is the *expected* norm for adults in our society, and is close to being the *actual* norm for youth. Sexual adventuring occurs, to be sure, just as it does in all life stages. It is likely to be taken more seriously than before, however. Youth resent a partner they feel has exploited them sexually, or who is interested in them only as a source of sexual pleasure. The "sexual adventurers", as Sorenson calls them, must learn to deal with the emotional side of the partner more so than during early adolescence when sexuality was a social-experimental phenomenon which did not dye as deeply into the emotional fabric.

Sexually active adolescents are remarkably poor at avoiding pregnancy. About 20 percent of all girls who have intercourse during adolescence become pregnant (Sorenson). This is due to the fact that they rarely use contraceptives, that they often do not understand the biology of pregnancy, or that they simply "believe" that they cannot get pregnant. In the entire arena of adolescent behaviour it is difficult to find parallel examples of such poor thinking. In the chapter on adolescent sexual behaviour we shall examine the reasons for this loss of reason.

Statistics released by the State of Oregon are fairly typical of the trend throughout North America with regard to teenage pregnancy. In 1975 the babies born to mothers 19 years of age and younger broke down like this: one child was born to a mother age 12 (in every state and province of North America a small percentage of all live births are delivered by mothers in the 11-13 age bracket; therefore this single birth in Oregon is not a biological anomaly unique to a particular year or place); 8 children were born to mothers age 13; 58 children born to mothers age 14; 132 to mothers age 15; 612 born to 16-year-olds; 993 to mothers age 17; 1,501 age 18; and 2,029 age 19.

The tremendous percentage increase between 15 and 16 is typical and due to the fact that 14 or 15 is the age at which these girls are most likely to have experienced their first intercourse.

The statistics for abortion during the teenage years follows a proportion pattern similar to the pregnancy trends: few abortions for ages 12-13, a consistent increase at age 14 with a spectacular increase for girls age 15 and 16, followed by a consistent increase through the final teen years. Once again the statistics from Oregon are fairly representative of the North American trend. They report that in 1976 the number of abortions for each age was as follows:

10-year-olds: 1
11-year-olds: 1
12-year-olds: none
13-year-olds: 36
14-year-olds: 127
15-year-olds: 423
16-year-olds: 814
17-year-olds: 977
18-year-olds: 1,219
19-year-olds: 1,058

The incidence increases with age. The decline among 19-year-olds is most consistently explained by the fact that this is an age where marriage is a likely outcome of pregnancy. (Oregon data quoted in *The Oregonian*, May 9, 1977)

Youth became more sexually active during middle adolescence. They also become more emotionally complex, and their sexuality becomes more integrated into this complexity. They rarely experience sex neutrally as they sometimes did during early adolescence, but at the same time, sexual impulses are not as powerful as they will be in late adolescence.

Intimacy strengthens during middle adolescence partly because the self is more secure and better able to interact with others in a deeper and more genuinely personal way, and partly because inner feelings are less satisfied by mere affiliation. Intimacy is experienced differently than it was during childhood because it now requires a sensitive awareness of the intimacy partner. Childhood intimacy requires only that one be immersed in affection or warmth; during adolescence it requires an awareness of the partner as a person. Harry Stack Sullivan believed that the emergence of *heterosexual intimacy* is one of the dominant features of adolescence, not because intimacy did not exist in earlier years, but because its sexual component was different. He notes that:

> The change from preadolescence to adolescence appears as a growing interest in the possibilities of achieving some measure of intimacy with a member of the other sex, rather after the pattern of the intimacy that one in preadolescence enjoyed with a member of one's own sex.'' (Kiell, p. 111)

Intimacy and romance go hand in hand, although either is possible without the other. Likewise with intimacy and sexuality. By adult standards the intimacy of the adolescent is more mature than that of the child-adolescent; however, it continues to grow as the self deepens and as life experience gathers. It reaches the zenith of its existential urgency and of its day-to-day significance during adult-adolescence. We shall deal more directly with it in the next chapter.

Introspection, Self-Doubt and Anguish

The adolescent's interest in *other* people prompts a great deal of inner searching. The need for acceptance, belonging, and recognition is so pressing that adolescents constantly look from the vantage point of those they are trying to impress. They think (and worry) about appearance; they evaluate their social ''performance'', as would a movie director, filtering those actions which bring praise from those that bring neutral or negative reactions. These internal efforts to construct an identity are essential to the middle-adolescent period of life. Erikson makes the following observation on the mental gymnastics deployed in identity formation:

> . . . identity formation employs a process of simultaneous reflection and observation, a process taking place on all levels of mental

functioning, by which the individual judges himself in the light of what he perceives to be the way in which others judge him in comparison to themselves and to typology significant to them; while he judges their way of judging him in the light of how he perceives himself in comparison to them and to types that have become relevant to him. (1968, pp. 22-23)

The inward journey is a distinguishing trait in these years. The journey takes an emotional toll which even the sturdy, resilient teenager cannot take completely in stride. Recuperation periods are necessary; solitude and self-imposed isolation are evidenced in a way never observed during childhood. Parents are perplexed to see such apparently bizarre actions; subject to feelings of inferiority (just like their adolescent children) parents assume that they are to blame for the seclusive, moody patterns, but this usually is not the case.

The journey inward is necessary because inner emotions explode, sending shock waves through the personality; they demand attention and receive it. Inner feelings, however, cannot be capriciously paraded outward; one must journey inward and deal with them on their own territory. Sometimes these feelings respond to logic and common sense; often they do not. Sometimes inner emotion harmonizes with family expectations, but not always. Sometimes inner passion leads to joy; periodically, it leads to anguish.

Adolescence is a time for being on display. Like the novice actor striving to earn a dramatic role, the adolescent parades before peers, authority figures, and even younger children in hope of earning their recognition, acceptance, and praise. Recognition because it is the first step in being acknowledged; acceptance because it confirms that the self has been recognized and, that it has been "taken in" by another person; praise because it represents *proof* of recognition. The more desperately adolescents need recognition, the less concern they have with whether praise is honest; the more secure the adolescents, the more likely they are to insist that praise represent true feelings and that it comes from an individual considered worthy.

The awareness of others so punctuates daily experience that Elkind claims adolescents live much of their life as though performing for an *imaginary audience*. Youth sense that all eyes are upon them and that their every move brings critical praise or rebuff. Every feature of appearance, every gesture or mannerism is detected by the audience. Nothing is missed. Elkind describes the imaginery audience:

And, since the audience is of his own construction and privy to his

60

own knowledge of himself, it knows just what to look for in the way of cosmetic and behavioral sensitivities. The adolescent's wish for privacy and his reluctance to reveal himself may, to some extent, be a reaction to the feeling of being under the constant critical scrutiny of other people. The notion of an imaginary audience also helps to explain the observation that the effect which most concerns adolescents is not guilt, but, rather, shame, that is, the reaction to an audience.

The adolescent strives for popularity for the same reason as does the junior executive: popularity indicates approval. The adolescent, also like the junior executive, matures with time and sets limits on the kinds of things performed to receive approval. *Before these limits are set,* however, the pressure to conform is very strong and the internal substance to resist is weak. One of the basic differences between early adolescents and middle adolescents is that the former are more susceptible to peer manipulation because they have a less developed moral outlook and because they lack experience in handling peer pressure.

The adolescent parade is *not* a charade. Motives are earnest because approval really *is* desired. The parade is not joined merely because everyone else is doing it. In some respects, it is *not* a parade because it is a natural manifestation of a developmental period; therefore, it has more authenticity. To the outsider, however, it has all the markings of a social ritual, making it easy to think of as a mere parade.

Adolescents are vulnerable to *feelings* of failure and rejection because they are so powerfully motivated to achieve success and acceptance. Their social world is neither gentle nor protective; therefore, they often receive full force the trauma of ridicule, rejection and ostracism. This is a time for learning the *skills* required to cope with sorrow, anger, depression, fear, grief, hostility, jealousy, panic, and all experiences associated with social rejection. This is not the age when these experiences are first encountered; it is, however, the time when the individual comes to grips with the *inescapable* nature of these emotions and cultivates habits and defence mechanisms which allow them to be incorporated into one's life-style. As Kohlberg says, this is a time "of intensified emotionality whether experienced as sexual or not".

During *early* adolescence the most intense anguish relates to peer disapproval and rejection. The reader should not interpret this to mean that during middle adolescence social disapproval is taken lightly; it *never* is taken lightly. However, by age 15 the adolescent has a greater capacity to place social rejection into a perspective which makes *certain kinds* of rejection less painful. He or she is freed from the indiscriminate anguish commonplace during the years when peer approval was overpowering.

Most adolescents experience considerable *self-doubt.* The reader who does not recognize this fundamental fact never will understand completely adolescent psychology. Adolescents doubt their social skills, their personal tastes, their reservoir of knowledge, their inner potential, and their future. Doubt is not crippling, but it is restrictive. It accentuates normal inferiority feelings and restrains one's sense of adventure. It decreases self-pride and depletes the reserve of strength necessary for coping with life problems.

Adolescence also is a time of discovery and, for all healthy humans, discovery reaps joy. What does the adolescent discover? In a very real sense, one *discovers oneself.* One discovers inner feelings, inner personality, and inner moral structure. The fact that these continually change and grow does not dampen the excitement of discovery any more than parental love dissipates as the newborn grows and matures. The adolescent *discovers intellect,* discovers that thought can be organized, manipulated, analyzed, and transformed. Word games and wit games exist in all youth cultures because they are irresistibly impelled to exercise what nature has given them. To be sure, they do not play these games with the composure and etiquette of adults but, nevertheless, they are played. The adolescent *discovers sexuality* — growth through puberty assures it. There are male adolescents and there are female adolescents, and never before in the life cycle has the difference made such a difference. Each sex is genuinely influenced by the other in a way which did not exist during childhood. To discover the opposite sex is also to discover one's own sex. During adolescence sex roles become significantly more than mere imitation; they become integral parts of how one defines and understands himself or herself. Sex roles become existential facts by which self is measured and evaluated.

The joy of adolescence is not restricted to discovery. Much of it is found merely in *being.* Much of the frivolous, carefree enthusiasm of childhood lives within the adolescent. He or she frolics, laughs, ridicules, satirizes, quips, mimics, scoffs and every now and again comes very close to making life appear ridiculous. High school teachers daily observe students convulsed with laughter, desperately clasping their stomachs, gasping their breath, pausing only to replenish exhausted oxygen, and then ripping out again in total laughter. Life is vibrant and vital and the adolescent rejoices in it, cresting a tide of adventure, driven by the thrill of newness, innocently reckless, daring fate to bring bad news.

Philosophers must decide whether man, in a state free from worry and responsibility, is inclined by nature to be happy. If they are serious in their attempts to solve this mystery they would be well-advised to study humans other than adolescents because, if they observed the pranks, petty truancies, and bizarre oddities which fill the absurd theatre of adolescence, they could infer only that man is inclined not just toward happiness but, more precisely, toward a touch of wholesome madness.

Summary

1. Of the three adolescent periods, middle adolescence most closely resembles what we typically think of when using the term "adolescence". The childlike features of early adolescence weaken while the adultlike features of late adolescence strengthen. All trends are definitely toward the adult and away from the child.

2. Physical growth continues in noticeable and forceful ways, but not with the accelerated pace of early adolescence. Height reaches the adult level for most youth. The skeleton expands and assumes its adult form; males add considerable muscle volume, especially to the upper body; strength and endurance increases because of growth advances in the circulatory and respiratory systems; the reproductive organs mature and secondary sexual traits appear. Athletic skills increase dramatically because the body increases in strength, coordination and stamina. Boys, for the first time in the life cycle, are conspiciously larger than girls and are able to perform feats of muscular strength, and physical endurance beyond the capacities of most girls.

Girls are more capable of reproduction because the ovaries are better able to produce mature ova. The menstrual flow becomes more predictably cyclic.

3. Differences between the early and the middle adolescent are considerable. The early adolescent has been out of childhood for only a short while; child traits permeate his or her personality, tastes and inclinations. Middle adolescents come to grips with a new body and, as a result, perceive themselves as adults rather than children. The early adolescent displays weak skills in dealing with members of the opposite sex, and the middle adolescent is considerably better not only in dealings with the opposite sex, but with adults as well.

4. Mental growth witnesses dramatic improvement even though *initial* breakthroughs took place during early adolescence. Six general trends highlight intellectual growth: thought becomes more abstract and less concrete; thought becomes more comprehensive and less fragmented; thought becomes more propositional and analytic; thought becomes less egocentric; and, thought becomes more future oriented.

Each of these trends represent an improvement over their early adolescent character and produce a more scientific and philosophical thought mode. The end result is that thought becomes more idealistic, more theoretical and more semantic.

5. Mental growth influences the personality in several ways. First, it makes the individual more aware of the outside world, and fosters awareness of political and social systems which previously were unnoticed. Secondly, it creates a keener awareness of the inner workings of the personality; it encourages introspection and self-analysis, and indirectly, self-doubt and self-criticism. Thirdly, it permits coping strategies to become more systematic. Social activities are negotiated with greater premeditation and with more emphasis on pragmatic outcomes. Fourthly, the idealism of early adolescence is contested by new information and improved patterns of intellectual analysis. Fifthly, self doubt increases when the dogmatism of childhood has been punctured.

6. *Moral outlook* undergoes several significant changes brought about by increased mental ability and by greater exposure to the outside world. They include the following: moral outlook becomes more abstract and less concrete; it becomes more concerned with justice and rightdoing as contrasted with wrongdoing; it becomes increasingly cognitive and decreasingly egocentric; finally, moral issues become genuinely expensive in that they taken an intense emotional toll.

7. The social world undergoes significant change, primarily in the direction of greater self-autonomy, increased interest in the opposite sex and more complicated relationships within the family unit. Same-sex groupings are less popular than during early adolescence, but nevertheless remain the dominant medium for interaction with peers. Mixed-sex gatherings provide the experimental arena for establishing deeper relationships. Forming couples, dating and going steady are more common than during early adolescence, but not nearly as predominant as in late adolescence.

The peer group exerts less *direct* pressure, and is less able to blackmail or coerce. However, it is powerful because it contains the nucleus of the individual's social life. Adolescents are "climbers" in their willingness to elevate social ladders and achieve greater recognition; peers are vital to their sense of achievement and accomplishment.

Parental conflict tends to *lessen* in the area of *minor* skirmishes and disagreements, but for many youth, conflict in the major areas increases. Moving out of the house becomes a viable option for the first time in the life cycle. Dropping out of school also becomes a viable option for the first time.

8. School dropouts are an important fact in the social life of many youth. When close friends drop out of school it radically realigns the nature of the peer world. The adult world in which dropouts find themselves holds considerable allure to the adolescent's growing sense of adultness and, for many youth, it confirms maturity.

9. Many psychologists, most notably Erik Erikson, claim that at some period during the adolescent years a moratorium should be declared when youth are free to experiment and gather insight into their personality. In our society this moratorium usually takes place during middle adolescence.

10. Middle adolescence is a period of dramatic sexual change. Physical changes are noticeable, but more importantly, the *desire* for sexual experience, (and the *passion* which accompagnies it) reach a peak never attained during early adolescence. All aspects of heterosexual involvement escalate; sexual fondling and intercourse increase considerably. Boys and girls alike tend to disapprove of casual sexual episodes, and for the most part, sexual activity is taken seriously. Sexually active middle adolescents are not successful at avoiding pregnancy. Their contraceptive habits are poor, as is their knowledge of the ovulation cycle. Of the three adolescent ages, this is when a sexually active girl is most likely to become pregnant. (Late-adolescent girls make better use of contraceptives, and early-adolescent girls are frequently too immature to carry through a full pregnancy). Sexuality becomes interlaced with intimacy. Romance and falling in love occur for the first time for many individuals.

11. The combined effects of increased mental growth, expansion of moral outlook, reorganization of the social fabric, and the introduction of sexual interchange, creates a considerable amount of turmoil and anguish. Inseparable from this is introspection and self-doubt. Therefore, the adolescent journeys inward and becomes self-analytic. This is made difficult by the high emotions of the age, by changing standards of acceptance, and by a self which continually changes its assessment of itself.

Chapter Four

The Late-Adolescent Period: Adult-Adolescence

During the final years of adolescence the individual changes from a full-fledged adolescent into an adult-adolescent; youth assume features we associate with "adultness" and outgrow many we associate with adolescence. In terms of mental and physical growth late adolescents *are* adults; in terms of psychological growth they are rapidly becoming adults; in terms of assuming active social roles, however, they remain essentially adolescents. I have written about this predicament of being excluded from social roles although sufficiently mature to handle them in *The Adolescent Predicament*.

In terms of chronological years, the adult-adolescent period includes ages 16, 17, 18 and 19, and in a few cases where social circumstances or personal choice have prevented the youth from assuming adult roles, 20 and 21. The age distinctions are less attached to perceptible physical growth; therefore, they do not have the landmark traits of the earlier two periods.

I am reluctant to refer to late adolescence as a developmental stage because so little physical or mental growth occurs. Others have taken a similar posture, such as Kimmel, who writes, "Perhaps the most striking characteristics of young adulthood in America today is that somewhat aritificial way in which it was created as a stage in human development." (p. 79) It is without question, however, a *unique* age because important strides are made beyond the composition of the adolescent personality and a much tighter link with the adult personality is established. Before getting into the specific topics of this chapter, I would like to discuss briefly these "links" with the adult personality.

From Adolescence into Adulthood

One of the most striking traits of this age is the *absence* of physical growth. This is the first period in the human life cycle where the body does not grow measurably in height, width or depth, or where the skeleton does not enlarge. A similar "absence" exists with regard to mental growth; with the exception of a few mental skills which improve with experience (such as word fluency) — little evidence indicates that mental skills increase during this age. As with physical growth, this is the first time in the growth cycle that this holds true. Thornburg represents the consensus in developmental psychology when he asserts that "between ages of 15 and 17 the adolescent reaches his full intellectual growth potential and has a capacity similar to that of the adult." (p. 70, 1975)

If the body has ceased its growth, no such comment can be made about the ego, which is rapidly expanding its boundaries, bolstering its weaknesses, and becoming considerably more consolidated and forceful. Youth become more self-reliant because they are more sure about "who" they are; consequently they are less susceptible to peer manipulation. During *early* adolescence identity was largely dependent upon how one was assessed by peers; now peers are more likely to be assessed in terms of one's ego identity. The situation is not completely reversed, but the balance of power definitely shifts from outside to inside.

During late adolescence each person improves in perceiving personal uniqueness, and at coming to grips with "the way I am". Negative traits such as unattractiveness are assimilated into the personality in a more matter-of-fact way (though not in a way which makes the person feel *good* about being unattractive). Positive traits, such as reliability or industry, assume greater prominence because the person realizes that in the next few years, competence skills and general abilities will determine the future. Facing up to one's personal uniqueness does not encourage raging eccentricity, but simply discourages the adolescent wish to please all people, or to flatter invariably when putting one's best foot forward. As Robert White points out, the ability to accept uniqueness within oneself also helps to accept the uniqueness of others and disclines us not to force parents, relatives, or teachers into narrow expectations.

Some interesting changes within the psychological need structure take place during late adolescence. The nature of self-importance modifies. One is less likely to regard oneself highly *only* because one is regarded highly by family or peers; one develops personal standards and private ambitions by which to assess one's own struggle toward *genuine* importance. Self-importance becomes more linked with *competence:* one feels important when one can *do* something important. "Fonzie" is a myth the adolescent can love and identify with because he commands the attention and affection of his peers. However, *late* adolescents note that Fonzie cannot *do* anything; he holds virtually no *important* competence, and his life is remarkably devoid of substantial intimacy. For the early and the middle adolescent he is identified with and perhaps even admired. For the late adolescent he is escapist fare.

Robert W. White describes several *growth trends* which flavour the transition from adolescence into young adulthood. He claims that at this age greater *stabilization of ego identity* occurs, whereby one's sense of identify becomes more clear and "more consistent and free from transient influences"; as a result it is more inclined toward commitment. Youth become more consistent in their perceptions of themselves and more acceptant of their nature. A second feature: Youth of this age become more adept in *perceiving the unique personhood of other individuals,* forcing them less than they did as adolescents into predesigned patterns. They see more clearly the individuality of parents and relatives. And for this reason adults find them, as a rule, easier to get along with than middle adolescents who still lack insight into the adult personality. Keniston describes in greater detail this process:

> *Relationships with elders* may also undergo characteristic youthful changes. By the end of adolescence, the hero worship of the middle adolescent has generally given way to an attitude of more selective emulation and rejection of admired to disliked older persons. In youth, new kinds of relationships with elders become possible; psychological apprenticeships, then a more complex relationship of mentorship, then sponsorship, and eventually peership. Without attempting to describe each of these substages in detail, the overall transition can be described as one in which the older person becomes progressively more real and three-dimensional to the younger one, whose individuality is appreciated, validated, and confirmed by the elder. (1975A, p. 17)

A *deepening of interests* is another trait of late adolescents. The trend is away from short term interests or fleeting involvements toward greater attraction to durable or continuous investments. This is in response to increased cultural demands for long term decisions, such as job and marriage, but also in response to an ego which is becoming more secure in itself and more clear in what it thinks meaningful in the long run. This deepening of interests also inclines the late adolescent to have greater interest in basic religious issues, give more earnest consideration to marriage and to think about things in life worthy of personal commitment. White claims that a general *humanizing of values* also takes place at this age. Kimmel says "they are creating their value system out of their growing understanding and synthesis of their own feelings . . ." and as a result they respond "with more empathy to the needs of others while at the same time they are creating their own unifying philosophy of life." (p. 93) The fifth trait characteristic of late adolescents is an *expansion of caring,* as witnessed by growing empathy with others and a greater concern for their feelings.

In essence, White claims that during the time of life we here call late adolescence the person becomes more stable in ego identity, that (partly because youth know better "who" they are) they are freer in relationships with others and increasingly skilled at recognizing others as unique individuals who are not forced to live up to "my" personal expectations. Interests and involvements deepen, yielding greater existential commitment. More so than the middle adolescents, late adolescents *identify themselves in terms of their involvements.* In the Sartrean sense, one *is* one's choices. Values tend to be more humanized, and care for others deepens.

The future grows in importance to late adolescents. They are less intrigued by immediacy (unless their future is bleak) than during early or middle adolescence. Their thoughts are more likely to live in the future than in the past. "Making a difference" becomes such a viable force that in many ways it appears as a need itself.

Uniting with the sexual impulse to give it even more force, intimacy acquires a raw strength not before experienced. Youth acquire greater reliance upon heterosexual relationships for self-confirmation and a sense of personal worth, and depthful alliances with close friends become more meaningful than scattered social engagements. This represents a complete reversal of early-adolescent patterns, but only a continued swing started during middle adolescence.

Sexuality becomes more genital, more passionate, and at the same time, more personal and intimate. The sexual impulse is stronger than during adolescence and the passions it excites and the desires it creates are experienced more fully. It is a sexual age even for the celibate. It also is an age for marriage and childbearing. Of all the pre-adult ages, this one unquestionably is preeminent for coupling and bonding.

This also is an age when the person brings into sharper focus the differences between himself or and herself and society. Paul Goodman says that in this period people recognize the struggle between themselves and the dominant society. Of course, not all youth see the struggle the same way; the distinguishing trait, as far as I am concerned, is their capacity to view society as more than something to adhere to blindly.

Keniston, using the term "youth" for late adolescents and early adults, concludes that one of the major differences between *youth* and adolescence is the tendency for youth to experience tension between themselves and society, and to be less inclined to accept passively the limited offerings of society:

> Perhaps the central conscious issue during youth is the *tension between self and society*. In adolescence, young men and women tend to accept their society's definitions of them as rebels, truants, conformists, athletes, or achievers. But in youth, the relationship between socially assigned labels and the "real self" becomes more problematic and constitutes a focus of central concern. The awareness of actual or potential conflict, disparity, lack of congruence between what one is (one's identity, values, integrity) and the resources and demands of the existing society increases. ("Prologue: Youth as a Stage of Life".)

This tension is partly a function of growth: "The *adolescent* is struggling to define who he is; the *youth* begins to sense who he is and thus to recognize the possibility of conflict and disparity between his emerging selfhood and his social order." (1975, p. 9) As the adolescent achieves greater emancipation from the family the tension between self and society "comes to constitute a major area of developmental work and change".

Keniston's analysis is especially insightful in focusing upon an essential transformation in the life of young adults — the metamorphosis from the familial to the societal. In adolescence the real focus of conflicts is "on the family and all of its internal psychic residues". With youth, however, it is society-at-large. On the other hand, Keniston's analysis, in many instances, leads to a misinterpretation of youth if it is concluded that *all* youth are preoccupied with social tension; in fact, most youth are loyal and committed to their dominant society.

The at-odds posture about which Keniston, Paul Goodman and Edgar Friedenberg have so brilliantly written is far from universal among North American youth. Throughout the generations, outright rebellion has been a minority response and it likewise is today. I neither praise nor condemn the young man or woman who defies the larger society; I merely point out that rebellious youth are neither morally nor psychologically superior to those who are not, and that social betterment is guaranteed by neither the dissenter nor the conformer. I stress the point because some of our most brilliant writers have glamourized the role of dissenting youth, and have romanticized youth's ability to understand society and its relationship to the integrity of the person. Consider, for example, an observation made by Edgar Friedenberg on this topic.

A youngster who has abandoned the task of defining himself in dialectical combat with society and becomes its captive and its emissary may be no rarity; but *he is a casualty.* There is not much more to be said about him: *one can only write him off* and trust that the world will at least feed him well if it cannot keep him warm. The promise of maturity must be fulfilled by those who are strong enough to grow into it at their own rate as full bargaining members.

Must there be conflict between the adolescent and society? The point is that adolescence *is* conflict — *protracted conflict — between the individual and society.* There are cultures in which the conflict seems hardly to occur; but where it does not, the characteristic development of personality which we associate with adolescence does not occur either. (1965, p. 32)

Our understanding of how adolescents come into greater awareness of their society is not restricted to the writings of social commentators such as Goodman and Friedenberg — some psychometric data is available on the topic. For example, Mussen and co-researchers (1977) obtained information from 500 high school students in grades 9, 11 and 12 in an attempt to determine if *opinions about political and ideological issues* changed during the teen years. Questionnaires were administered to the students dealing with such topics as civil rights, equal opportunity, taxation, criminal treatment and the power of labour unions. The major findings of the study were:

1. Attitudes about critical current events continue to change until at least age 18.
2. With increasing age there is less acceptance that the present government is the best governmental system.
3. There is a shift toward greater "liberalism" between the early and later years of high school.
4. Anti-authoritarianism is greater during the later years of high school.
5. With greater maturity comes greater awareness of the complexity of issues and a rejection of simplistic explanations.

The researchers conclude that the differences in outlook toward political issues results primarily from the broader range of social experience and the higher sophistication of the late adolescents.

This data tends to support the notion that youth experience tension between their personal outlooks and societal solutions to political issues during the adolescent years; however, it does not establish the ways this tension manifests itself, nor does it indicate whether in time the adolescent comes to accept or reject those aspects of society towards which he or she holds major disagreements.

Our treatment of late adolescents is radically out of line with their nature. Physically, they are adults, yet they are treated as adolescents. Sexually, they are adults, yet there is no socially sanctioned opportunity for sexual intimacy. Mentally, they are adults, but society offers virtually no opportunity (except within the isolated school) to exercise their mental competence. Psychologically, they are ready for adult experience, but they are encouraged to continue involvement in trivial adolescent rituals and to spend their money on juvenile-trade items. Morally, they are capable of adult response to moral issues, but they live in a world where the exercise of moral judgment in any significant way is almost impossible. "Millions of young people today are neither psychological adolescents nor sociological adults," Keniston claims. "They fall into a psychological no man's land, a stage of life that lacks any clear definition." (1975, p. 3) His observation that youth are neither "psychological adolescents" nor "sociological adults" rings true because the social rituals and personal exchanges vital to the middle adolescent no longer carry much impact despite the fact that few significant *new* social roles are available. This is part of the reason why I agree that for many youth this age is a "psychological no man's land".

Throughout the life cycle we prompt youth to grow. As infants we stand them upright in anticipation of their first step; in toddlerhood we strive to get them toilet trained, to teach them words and manners; in the preschool years we impose social maturity upon their egocentric nature by insisting that they follow group rules; we teach numbers and letters when these growth advancements are relatively difficult; during childhood we reward them when they act "grown-up" or "behave like adults"; during early adolescence parents encourage dating before the desire comes into existence; in middle adolescence we encourage all kinds of experimentation so that when adulthood comes youth will be ready for it. With late adolescence, which for all intents and purposes *is* adulthood, we suddenly slam on the brakes and make a sudden about face. We require youth to live below their developmental capabilities in every important way. We make it difficult for them to show their aptitude, except in adolescent ways, to voice their opinion, to show their adult capacities. We perceive adult-adolescents as though they were still adolescents. Consequently, they are under-evaluated, their talents are under-assessed, and their integrity undermined.

The Body

Late adolescence is the first period in the life cycle when significant body growth is *not* evidenced. Were it not for significant transformations in social and psychological makeup, it would be pointless to refer to it as an "age" of adolescence. This age is unique because the demands of physical growth are so weak that the personality is free to concentrate on personal and social realities. The body no longer is an unfolding mystery. It simply "is". For better or worse it is "mine". The issue changes from curiosity about what the body will be, to facing up to how it has turned out.

By age 16 boys have, on the average, reached almost 98 percent of their adult height, by 17, over 99 percent of their adult height; girls, who reach their adult height earlier than boys, achieve over 99 percent of their adult height by age 15, and very few grow any taller during late adolescence. Growth in weight shows a similar trend. Girls average only about two pounds gain between ages 16 and 18, while they gained over 15 pounds during the three-year period previous to that. Boys gain only about 11 pounds between 16 and 18 while they gained about 26 pounds in the previous period of the same length. From the most obvious indicators of growth — height and weight — it is clear that late adolescence is not a period of substantial change.

Neither does the general appearance of the body change much. The adult profile for both boys and girls is well formed by 17. If one does not add excessive fatty tissue during adulthood the body build he or she has at 17 will be the same at 30.

The growth process can be divided into four general patterns — *general* growth, *neural* growth, *lymphoid* growth and *genital* growth. A brief inspection of these patterns as they relate to late adolescents will demonstrate the nature of growth at this age. *General* growth, which deals with "the skeleton and musculature as a whole, the respitory and digestive organs, the kidneys, the spleen, various parts of the cardiovascular system, and blood volume", is steep during childhood but levels off between the ages of five and ten, and then rises again sharply during puberty. By age 16 it has reached over 90 percent of its maximum. *Neural* growth is even more quickly attained, with almost complete

74

adult maturity being reached by the onset of puberty. The *lymphoid* tissue is even more advanced, reaching almost complete adult maturity by the age of 12. Of the four major growth patterns, *genital* development is the slowest to reach adult status, but as previously indicated, sexual maturity for the vast majority of young people is completed during middle adolescence. (See Katchadourian, 1977, p. 24-26 for amplification of human growth patterns).

The respiratory system undergoes important changes during puberty as the size and capacity of the lungs increase — especially for boys. The amount of air that can be taken in increases markedly in boys (not so much in girls), and the exchange of oxygen in the lungs also becomes more efficient. These growth advancements, however, take place during early or middle adolescence — by late adolescence little natural respiratory growth occurs.

The cardiovascular system also registers remarkable growth during puberty. The weight of the heart nearly doubles, systolic blood pressure rises steadily and attains adult values after the puberty period. "Blood volume, hemoglobin, and red blood cells increase markedly in boys, but not in girls. Adult women have about one million fewer red cells per millilitre of blood than do men." (Katchadourian, p. 46) I must stress, however, that all of these cardiovascular changes are associated with puberty — not the post-puberty years of late adolescence.

For almost all youth, the ability to reproduce is determined either *before* late adolescence or during its first year. Late-maturing boys constitute the majority of exceptions to this general developmental fact. The brain reached 95 percent of its adult weight by the age of ten, so little growth occurs there. Caloric requirements peak at about age 14 for girls and about age 17 for boys.

By virtually every conceivable criteria, little physical growth is evidenced during this period of life. The energy liberated by the absence of physical growth is absorbed by psychological and social growth, thus making late adolescence the first period in the life cycle where body growth is not quantitatively increased in a significant way. This is one reason I call this the adult-adolescent age.

Even though body growth is approaching the adult form, late adolescents are nevertheless body-conscious and concerned about their appearance to the opposite sex. Lerner et. al. (1973) studied the importance of physical attractiveness and self-concept among a group of late adolescent college students and surmised that "chubby" youth have poor attitudes about this physique and their feelings of how attractive they are to the opposite sex, whereas those with average physiques tend to have positive feelings. The study also showed that late-adolescent males and females are consistent in their ratings of the importance of physical attractiveness to the opposite sex. Lerner claims, for example, that both sexes agree that "hips, shape of legs and thighs" are more important for girls than for boys, whereas "width of shoulders and height" are more important for boys than for girls. In summary, this study contends that self-concept, physique, and one's sense of attractiveness to the opposite sex are inter-related during the late-adolescent years.

The Intellect

Most writers agree that intelligence does not show any significant gains after the adolescent period. Although adults benefit from increased experience they probably employ no superior mental processes in doing so. Late adolescents utilize the abilities of formal thought which they acquired during early and middle adolescence in a more sophisticated way than formerly, but this is largely due to practice and does not result in significant improvements upon the *kinds* of thought processes they employ.

The parallel to physical growth is evident: early and middle adolescence are periods of rapid and significant growth while late adolescence is a period of consolidation, synthesis and improvement. Evidence of this growth format is obtained by investigating the relationship between adolescent and adult intelligence. Conger reports that *preschool* and adult IQ's correlate about .65 whereas *adolescent* and adult IQ's correlate between .80 and .85. He also notes that, "In general, adolescent measures of IQ appear to be fairly good predictors of adult IQ's" (p. 135, 1973).

The IQ is only one measure of intelligence, and as the recent controversy on the validity of the IQ instruments (especially their tendency to favour middle-class youth and to discriminate against non-white and/or lower income youth) points out, an imperfect one. Different components of mental ability mature more readily than others. Mental abilities which reflect biological capability, such as perceptual speed, tend to develop more rapidly than those influenced by experience — such as word fluency. Nevertheless, the overall conclusion is that during late adolescence and early adulthood the improvements in mental ability are not monumental and certainly they are not of the qualitative significance of those which take place during early or middle adolescence when formal thought becomes part of the intellectual process.

Psychological Makeup

The inner workings of the late adolescent are similar, in some respects, to those of the early and the middle adolescent. The need for approval, acceptance and belonging remain strong and motivate a great deal of day-to-day behaviour. The desire for reassurance, contact comfort and encouragement exist within the personality just as during earlier years. The importance of having peers recognize your competence and think you are "special" persists — as it will through adulthood.

To understand the late adolescent we must recognize that the fundamental psychological needs of achievement, independence, belonging and role experimentation during *all* adolescent ages. With late adolescence, however, they undergo changes which alter the volition of the personality, making it more intent on achieving certain goals at the expense of others, experiencing certain sensations, and establishing different kinds of security. The child-adolescent's need for peer acceptance ebbs considerably, because the need for affiliation comes more directly under the supervision of the ego; choices are made in a more straightforward manner and are left less frequently to chance and circumstance.

Many of our ideas about adolescence in general do not hold true for late adolescence. Late adolescence is much more an adult age than most psychologists believe. Consider the following statement by Anna Freud which is thought by many psychologists to be an honest description of the adolescent experience because it embodies the diverse nature of youth and points the polar extremes to which they are attracted. Please read it carefully.

> Adolescents are excessively egoistic, regarding themselves as the centre of the universe and the sole object of interest, and yet at no time in later life are they capable of so much self-sacrifice and devotion. They form the most passionate love-relations, only to break them off as abruptly as they began them. On the one hand they throw themselves enthusiastically into the life of the community and, on the other, they have an overpowering longing for solitude. They oscillate between blind submission to some self-chosen leader and defiant rebellion against any and every authority. They are selfish and materially-minded and at the same time full of

lofty idealism. They are ascetic but will suddenly plunge into instinctual indulgence of the most primitive character. At times their behaviour to other people is rough and inconsiderate, yet they themselves are extremely touchy. Their moods veer between light-hearted optimism and blackest pessimism. Sometimes they will work with indefatigable enthusiasm, and at other times they are sluggish and apathetic. (1937, p. 149-150)

Some psychologists (myself included) are not impressed with this assessment. As far as the *late* adolescent is concerned it is genuinely misleading. Very few late adolescents, even those receiving psychotherapy, behave in a way which would incline an observer to assume that they think of themselves "as the centre of the universe and the sole object of interest". The dominant trend at this age is a concern with "outside" realities, the nature of society, and the pull of the future. The narcissism Anna Freud describes is more representative of childhood, or at latest, the child-adolescent. Several years of modestly reliable research have well documented that few adolescents, before the age of 16, "form the most passionate love relationships"; the norm at this age is limited sexual interchange and weakened passion. As Offer, in his study of *normal* adolescents confirms, most youth are not raging rebels, they do not alternate between "blind submission to some self-chosen leader and defiant rebellion against any and every authority". They are neither blindly submissive nor defiantly rebellious; they are much more bent upon "moderation". Whether adolescents in our society "throw themselves enthusiastically into the life of the community" is not known because virtually no opportunity exists for them to do so. Therefore, I find Anna Freud's description of adolescence out of sync with the late-adolescent experience. If any age of adolescence comes close to fitting this description it is middle adolescence; for late adolescence or early adolescence it is totally inappropriate.

In many respects Anna Freud's misrepresentation of adolescence is typical. It is not unusual, for example, that school administrators think of all adolescents as being bound to the limitations of personality described in the previous quote. Likewise, many government officials perceive youth to be considerably more juvenile and child-like than is the case. As a result many government programs offer trivial involvements for adolescents when, in fact, they are capable of sophisticated and advanced workmanship. (For a further elucidation of this concept refer to "The Incompetence Myth".)

Intimacy

During late adolescence the person acquires a stronger sense of personhood, becomes more stable in ego identity, and less monopolized by egocentricity. One comes to know oneself better, and to know more about the strengths and weaknesses of one's personality. The desire to share oneself with another person and to have that person reciprocate becomes an eminent trait which exerts more influence here than during middle or early adolescence. It encourages romantic and sexual bonding as well as close friendship and sharing.

Intimacy is experienced at all ages, but with late adolescence it springs from a richer emotional base and from a more crystallized identity. The intimacy of *childhood* is based upon closeness and contact. It fills the person with pleasant feelings, and these feelings, in essence *are* the intimacy. Adult intimacy also has these childlike qualities — but much more, especially a commitment to the partner as a person, and an awareness of oneself as a person. This "putting oneself on the line" makes intimacy a scary proposition; therefore, its avoidance is as important to some youth as its fulfillment is to others.

Intimacy may or may not lead to sexual relationships. In our culture it tends to do when the partners are of the opposite sex, when they feel they love each other, or when either partner genuinely desires sexual relations. When the intimacy partners are of the same sex, close friendship and togetherness are the most common expressions. Whatever the sexual arrangement, however, intimacy occurs only when both persons are fairly secure in their own identities, or at least know themselves well enough to represent themselves authentically to the partner. As Erikson points out, "It is only when identity formation is well on its way that true intimacy — which is really a counterpointing as well as fusing of identities — is possible." This is a primary reason why intimacy, in the sense presently used, is not much evident in the earlier periods of adolescence. Erikson goes on to indicate that "The youth who is not sure of his identity shies away from interpersonal intimacy or throws himself into acts of intimacy which are promiscuous without true fusion or real self-abandon." (1968, p. 135) "True fusion" and "real self-abandon" are vital to our understanding of intimacy for they convey the intensity and genuineness of the relationship, and also give a feel for the merging of two personalities.

For the late adolescent to live without intimacy is more difficult than for either the early or middle adolescent. Both ages have their corollary experiences (for the early adolescent it is comradeship at the peer level and parent-love at the family level; whereas for the middle adolescent it is friendship and romance) but these necessitate personalities more involved in the process of *identifying themselves* than of genuine *identity-sharing*. Intimacy is not an easy topic for the psychologist to research, but some data is available which suggests that intimacy is more forceful during late adolescence. Douvan and Adelson interviewed adolescent girls individually in an attempt to discover their feelings towards their friends. One of their findings was that preadolescent and early adolescent girls were not overly interested in the personal qualities of their friends; rather, they were more concerned with the opportunity to share activities with them. When asked to describe "what a friend ought to be like" the *early* adolescent girls mention considerably fewer personal qualities than do older adolescent girls. In summarizing the findings of Douban and Adelson, Galatin notes:

> With older adolescent girls, however, Douvan and Adelson observed something approaching the intimacy that Sullivan ascribes to preadolescent chums. Both in middle and late adolescence, girls defined their friendshps in terms of virtues like loyalty, the ability to keep confidences, emotional support, and common interests. The researchers concluded that *these older subjects were much more capable of establishing a relationship with another person, of truly sharing experiences and being responsive to their friends.* (1975, p. 127)

The counterpart of intimacy is what Eirkson calls "distantiation", which is "the readiness to repudiate, isolate, and, if necessary, destroy those forces and people whose essence seems dangerous to one's own". Within most individuals the need for distantiation thrives when intimacy fails, when self is too long unacknowledged or prevented from asserting itself. The result of distantiation is "the readiness to fortify one's territory of intimacy and solidarity and to view all outsiders with fanatic overevaluation of small differences between the familiar and the foreign." (1968, p. 136)

Inseparable from intimacy is *caring,* and, in our culture, from caring springs *commitment.* Thus intimacy is a more powerful social reality than one may think. In romance it preserves itself by demands of fidelity. People expect the intimacy partner to know and understand their inner workings better than an outsider, and they entrust their most sensitive moments to the partner. The intimacy partner becomes one of the most important people in the phenomenological world.

Personal Growth and Social Roles

More so than any of the other adolescent ages, late adolescence is a *social* rather than a biological fact. The major restraints which hold back youth are social convention rather than any inherent growth deficiency. Flacks stated it well when he said: "Puberty is a biological fact, but youth is a social one. There is no biological imperative to reinforce the idea that for several years after puberty young persons should continue to be segregated from adults and prevented from assuming adult sexual, economic, and social roles." He then goes on to point out one of the important themes which I am trying to emphasize in this chapter. "By age 18, *at the latest,* virtually everyone is physiologically adult, having reached sexual maturity and the peak of physical and mental capacity. Thus, the segregation and categorization of young people is unknown in many cultures; furthermore, it is a very recent development in western civilization." (1971, p. 9) This segregation from society at a time when the body and the psyche are ripe for contribution is a major *societal* predicament for our culture.

That the late adolescent is biologically, psychologically and emotionally ready to assume adult roles does not surprise anyone with a sense of history. Less than three generations ago it was expected that early and middle adolescent youth would assume many adult roles. Listen to the first-hand account of a man who recalls his teenage years lived on the Canadian Prairies at the turn of the century. First, a childhood recollection.

> Of course there was the water to bring in, and a milk pail full of water is pretty heavy for a five-year-old. I mind how at first I'd have to carry that pail with both hands and the pail banging between my legs against my knees and the water slopping all over. I was so small I couldn't get it up to put it in the stove reservoir — my mother would do that.

> When I was seven or so, there I was, winter or summer, milking my one cow, and then it got to be two cows and three, until by about nine I was doing a man's job with the cows, milking, carrying the pails to the house, getting the De Laval separator turning.

Work roles are assumed when they have to be. Necessity dictates. If work is to be done, and only children are available to do it, they will do it. The absence of necessary work (which by definition is also worthwhile work) simply makes work less necessary. Some positive benefits accrue from having important work to do.

I didn't mind it so much. One thing in those days, and maybe still now, you were proud of your strength, proud you could work like a man even though you were just a boy in years. But actually you were a man because by the time you were 13 or so and had the knack for farming, which you would pretty well have, there wasn't much you didn't know around the place.

It is not comfortable to deal with adults on equal footing, but without question it can be done — or at least tried. "At 13, you pretty well considered yourself a man and certainly old enough to tell your old man how he was running the farm wrong. That's when you sure found out fast that you weren't as big as you thought you were."

Like the youth of today, interests ran to considerably more than work and family, and also like youth of today, they would make do where they could.

At 16 you'd start courting or sparking around the district, usually in your own shiny buggy with your own horse because that was something like a car for a young fellow today. A young fellow in those days liked to have his own rig. Gave him mobility, you might say, like taking the Benson girl on a Sunday evening down the road along the creek, something like that. Or there was a lot of visiting too on Sundays. Maybe 10 or 15 young people would get together at one place and sit around and laugh. They've done it enough at our old place. It all depended on how the old folks looked on such goings-on. If they were the kind that would go to prayer meeting on Wednesday night, choir practice on Thursday, and church twice on Sunday — if there was church twice on Sunday — then the chances were you never went to that farm. (All quotes taken from Broadfoot, 1976, pp. 183-185)

The quotes do not *prove* anything, they simply indicate that in times past youth assumed important roles in their family, and as a result they *were important*. This is not to glamourize work or make it appear as though youth categorically like it. It is only to point out that in our society work is the primary means by which self-importance and self-worth are gained and that when youth are denied access to it they find alternate means, and that much of the pathology inherent to our youth culture is based squarely upon their poor track record at finding alternate means. Rollo May makes this point in *Power and Innocence:* "No human being can exist for long without some sense of his own significance. Whether he gets it by shooting a haphazard victim on the street, or by constructive work, or by rebellion, or by psychotic demands in a hospital, or by Walter Mitty fantasies, he must be able to feel this I-count-for-something and be able to *live out* that felt significance'' (p. 37). His options for achieving significance I find intriguing, especially if viewed within the context of adolescent psychology. If you take ''or by constructive work'' out of this quote you are confronted with the variety of pathologies our society's children use to gain their sense of personal significance.

Sexuality

By every important indicator, sexual activity and sexual passion increase during the late-adolescent years. For couples who are going steady, sexual play is the norm. By age 19 more than half of the girls have experienced sexual intercourse, and the incidence for girls who are ''going steady'' is considerably higher. Sexuality has a more intense nature than it did during early and middle adolescence, and the person is more likely to develop a strong romantic link with the sexual partner, and to think in terms of marriage. This, of course, does not hold true for all youth because many are able to engage in ''recreational sex'', which is essentially genital in nature and does not require real personal involvement with the partner and because many youth are not interested in marriage as a life-style. It differs from the shallow sex play of the early adolescent in that the genital pleasure is more intense and the sexual passion is more fully experienced, even though the treatment of the partner may be similarly superficial.

Pregnancy is a major concern at this age since, according to Sorenson, over 20 percent of the sexually active girls become pregnant during adolescence. A closer look at teenage pregnancy will be taken in a later chapter.

In terms of the growing person, *three distinguishing traits characterize adult-adolescent sexuality* which are substantially less prevalent in earlier ages. First, the physical desire for sexual activity increases. The subjective sensation of the sexual impulse is stronger than ever before in the life cycle. Second, the psychological need for intimacy becomes intertwined with sexuality more so than at any previous age. Third, the individual, having weathered the social internship of early adolescence, and the courtship ritual of middle adolescence, is simply *more ready* for the interpersonal difficulties associated with sex. The end result is that youth of this age are more sexually active, more easily aroused by a sexual partner, experience their sexuality more intensely, and are more likely to think of marriage and forming couples than during earlier adolescent years.

Rollo May claims there are four kinds of love in the Western tradition. It is interesting to evaluate them within the context of developmental age, especially as far as the early adolescent and the late adolescent are concerned. The first is *sex*, "or what we call lust, libido". The second is *eros*, "the drive of love to procreate or create", what the Greeks called the urge toward "higher forms of being and relationship". The third kind of love is *philia*, which is friendship or brotherly love. The fourth is *agape*, "the love which is devoted to the welfare of the other". From my point of view, each of the kinds of love May refers to are within the emotional grasp of the late adolescent. For the middle or early adolescent, however, this is not the case. Egocentrism is not as yet replaced with altruism, and libido is not the "seething cauldron" that Freud thought it to be. Virtually all relationships deepen during late adolescence and early adulthood, not only because one's sense of identity becomes more established and the capacity for intimacy enriches, but also because many self-conscious inhibitions weaken to permit a deeper flow of experience. On this final point Symonds claims that one of the reasons young adults are better at dealing with intimacy problems is that "the things feared in adolescence *are less fearsome after they have been experienced*".

Whether adolescents are more active sexually now than they were in past decades is not clearly established. Some researchers claim that sexual behaviour is relatively constant from generation to generation, while others disagree. The issue is compounded by the difficulty of gathering sound empirical data, and the tendency for researchers to find different results. Among the most respected investigators of adolescent sexual behaviour are Professors Melvin Zelnik and John Kantner currently (1977) of the John Hopkins School of Hygiene and Public Health. Their 1976 research indicates that unmarried teenage girls between the ages of 15 and 19 are more sexually active than the same age group of 1971. For example, they report that about 18 percent of the 15-year-olds have had sexual intercourse, whereas for the 1971 group only about 13.8 percent of girls this age admitted to having had sexual intercourse. For 17-year-olds the difference is even more noticeable, with 41 percent of the 1976 sample having intercourse, compared to only 27 percent of the 1971 girls. The trend toward a greater percentage of girls having experienced sexual intercourse continues for the 18- and 19-year-old girls as well. Zelnik and Kantner claim that their data "represents clear evidence that more young women today are engaging in premarital intercourse than in years past".

In addition to their findings on the incidence of sexual intercourse among adolescent and late adolescent girls, the following items highlighted their research. The median age for first intercourse dropped to age 16. Half of the young women participating in the survey reported to having had more than one sexual partner. The teenagers' knowledge of the risk of pregnancy remained poor, as only 41 percent knew the point in the menstrual cycle when pregnancy is most likely to occur. This supports most existing data on young girls' knowledge of *when* conception takes place. "But their knowledge of pregnancy risk and other fundamentals of sexuality remained poor overall, and, as in 1971, contraception is often not initiated *until after an unplanned pregnancy* has occurred." They also found that most sexual activity takes place in the home of either the girl or the home of her partner.

Zelnik and Kantner's data indicate that sexual activity among the teenage girls in our society is increasing. They are more sexually active than were girls of the same age in 1971, and they are more open in their discussion of sex in general. Whether this trend will continue is matter for conjecture.

Attitudes of the female toward sexual play change considerably once she is "going steady" with her partner. Collins points out that the "very marked change that takes place in the behaviour of females when they are going steady clearly supports the contention . . . that adolescents going steady typically believe they are in love and that going steady can add acceptability to heavy petty and intercourse." Collins also notes (as do most researchers of adolescent sexuality) that the evidence "supports the contention that extensive lovemaking is engaged in only with steadies and not with just casual dates". (1974, p. 325)

Sorenson, whose research is among the most widely cited in North America, reports some interesting data on why adolescents *do not* engage in sexual intercourse. The three major reasons given by youth who have never had sexual intercourse are:

Because I'm not ready for it;
Because I haven't met a boy/girl I would want to have sex with;
Because I haven't met a boy/girl who wants to have sex with me.
(1973, p. 166)

He also found that almost 70 percent of the boys and 55 percent of the girls affirm that "So far as sex is concerned, I do what I want to do, regardless of what society thinks.'' But at the same time the majority of adolescents tell their parents only what they will accept in matters of sex. Sorenson supports that adolescents are serious about sexual behaviour, a point which virtually all research confirms; they do not take their sexual experiences lightly, nor do they approve of (or secretly admire) those who do.

Gordon's research on the sexual habits of teenagers in the United States indicates that socioeconomic differences are a factor. ''Youth from low-income homes tend to have earlier . . . and more frequent sexual experiences than youth from middle-class homes.'' He goes on to report that in a ''typical'' Upward Bound program made up of 16- and 17-year-old youths, ''about 80 percent of the male students and 55 percent of the female students had had sexual intercourse more than a few times prior to their association with the program''. (1973, p. 17)

The sexual impulse is strong for late adolescents *as a group*, but not necessarily for all *individuals*. For example, Jense's statement that ''Sex urges come upon them like a 10-ton truck. The urges are inescapable; something must be done with them'' (p. 142), unquestionably is an overstatement. So is Anna Freud's belief that with adolescence the ''relation established between the forces of the ego and the id is *destroyed*, the painfully achieved psychic balance is upset, with the result that the inner conflicts between the two institutions *blaze afresh*''. (1936, p. 158) (taken from Offer, p. 177). What Jense and Freud say holds true for some youth but it is not universal. However, it is sufficiently important to be given consideration.

The pregnant teenager is drawing considerable public attention in the late seventies because of the growing trend for unmarried teenage mothers to keep their babies rather than to place them for adoption. Because many of these mothers draw social assistance or welfare they have become the focus of governmental interest and are studied more than they used to be. With regard to the sexual habits and preferences of adolescent girls who become pregnant some interesting information has been gathered. For the most part, the sexual patterns of teenage girls who get pregnant are about the same as those of teenage girls who do not get pregnant but who do have sexual intercourse. The girls who get pregnant are not more promiscuous, do not have significantly more sexual partners, and do not begin their sexual activities at a much earlier age than other girls who have sexual intercourse during adolescence.

Carol A. Cowell provides some interesting data based upon 1,000 pregnant teenagers who came to the Teenage Pregnancy Counselling

Clinic at the Hospital for Sick Children in Toronto. She found that the average age that the pregnant girls *started dating* was 13.5 years, and that the average age for first going steady was about 14.2 The first sexual intercourse took place at about 15 and the first pregnancy at 16.5. Of the girls involved in the study the majority had only one partner in their sexual career; and, only about 15 percent had more than three partners. In this regard, girls who get pregnant show sexual habits and partner preference similar to teenage girls who engage in sexual intercourse but who do not get pregnant. (Data reported by Addy, 1977).

In North American society, late adolescents are the most likely to become sexually involved. The endocrinological immaturity of the early adolescent years has been outgrown and the social timidity of middle adolescence has been partly worked through. Strong sexual impulses blend with and gather strength from the blossoming need for an intimacy partner. Virtually all girls and boys of this age are capable of reproduction; therefore sexually active youth who do not use contraceptives, or who do not understand well the ovulation cycle, run a high risk of pregnancy.

Sexual impulses register forcefully, but by no means do they control the person. Many youth are *not* sexually active. Although some of them wish they were, many of them say that they are not yet ready for sex, and "when things are ready they will happen". Their attitude is not one of indifference, but rather one which is based upon the realization that sexuality involves more than sexual behaviour. It requires a partner with whom one has some confidence, with whom a certain pattern of personal intimacy has been established, and with whom one can lower personal defenses without fear of exploitation.

Summary

During late adolescence several distinguishing traits highlight the growth process, including the following:

1. In most features of the personality, the individual makes significant strides toward adulthood, and in many important ways is outgrowing the juvenile traits of early and middle adolescence. The growth traits of this age period are not nearly as noticeable and definable as those of earlier adolescent periods. The individual becomes more self-directing, and less a product of peer manipulation. Self becomes defined more in terms of adult competencies.

2. Several growth trends are evident in personality development. The ego becomes more stable in its identity; the personality is better able to perceive the uniqueness of other individuals and less inclined to view them merely as "outsiders" or as stereotypes; interests deepen and a greater interest in metaphysical issues begins to manifest itself; values become more humanized; and, commitment becomes more focalized.

3. During late adolescence the person perceives more acutely the split between *personal needs* and the *vested interests* of society. For some this results in an alienation from society or pervasive cynicism toward it.

4. The body does not evidence significant growth in height, weight, depth, skeletal alignment or general appearance. This is especially true for girls, with boys more suceptible to increased growth during this age.

5. The intellect does not undergo any significant increase in power, however, it does benefit considerably from experience and from greater consolidation.

6. Late adolescents tend to be *more* stable than some psychologists, such as Anna Freud, believe. They also tend to be *less* rebellious and less anti-establishment than some commentators, such as Paul Goodman, Kenneth Keniston, and Edgar Friedenberg, believe.

7. Intimacy increases in strength and becomes a more powerful life force than it was during middle or early adolescence. It also becomes more integrated with sexuality. Intimacy requires a stabilization of ego identity not frequently found during earlier adolescent periods. The intimacy *partner* also assumes a progressively more important role in the life of the adolescent.

8. Even though the body and intellect have achieved most of their adult growth, and the personality is quite adultlike in its outlook, few social roles of any significance are available to late adolescents in our society.

9. Sexuality increases in activity and passion. The physical desire for sexual play increases; the need for intimacy increases; and, the individual is better equipped to handle the interpersonal complexities of sexuality than during earlier adolescent years.

Chapter Five

Further Observations on the Adolescent Experience

In this chapter I shall overview some important topical matters which heretofore have been either omitted or glanced over too briefly. In some respects this chapter will serve as an enlarged "summary", however, new information will be added in order to more fully encapsulate the substance of the adolescent years. Some topics are dealt with in a more complete manner in forthcoming chapters, and the reader will be so advised when this is the case.

Parent-Child Relationships

Even though youth are moving toward adulthood during the adolescent experience, they also are children. They have parents, and as a rule, their parents think of them as "their" children. Traditionally adolescents think they are more mature than they actually are, while parents tend to think they are less mature than they actually are. This disparity of outlook creates considerable tension in many households.

Frequently it is the early adolescent who has the most difficulty with parents. They are still close to childhood and their parents think "childhood" when dealing with them. However, the early adolescent is serious about proving how much he or she has grown up lately and resents being treated as a younger (which to them means inferior) person. Early adolescents tend to bicker and shout a good deal, and to be argumentative over matters which the middle or late adolescent learns to take in stride. They are not gifted at avoiding the behaviour which irritates parents and teachers, in fact, many seem to derive a mischievious pleasure from irritating adults. On the other hand, middle adolescents tend to engage in less outright argumentation with parents, but when they do argue, the substance of the disagreement is likely to be more serious than during early adolescence. This derives from the fact that middle adolescents are more fully developed physically and perceive themselves as genuinely adult in *some* ways; they are more sexual, more independent, more capable of finding pastimes outside the family home, have greater access to automobiles and cash, and, in general, they are more mobile and self-directional, therefore, the opportunity for significant disagreements with parents increases.

Late adolescents represent an unusual mixture because they understand their parents better than they did as younger adolescents, and they possess a more realistic appraisal of parental strengths and weaknesses. At the same time, however, they are more firm in their personal identity and know their own self in a more matter-of-fact way than in earlier years. This permits them to realize that they have fundamental or even irreconcilable differences with regards to their parents. In our culture this typically includes matters relating to school (whether to stay in or drop out); work (whether to maintain a part-time job in order to sustain a cash flow); sexual involvements, especially with regard to abstaining from sexual intercourse (particularly important in many parent-daughter relationships); drugs and alcohol use; and preparation for future employment. Many youth learn to live compatibly with their parents in the midst of these disagreements whereas others live a day-to-day truce with flare-ups occuring whenever tempers run short. Many adolescents realize that when high school ends it will be time to move out of the house.

On the whole, however, there does not exist between parent and adolescent a glaring generation gap. And though adult-adolescent relationships are stormy they often are less turbulent than the relationship between husband and wife within the same household. (The issue of "generation gap" is dealt with more fully in Part Three).

Interestingly, it is early adolescents who do the most overt complaining, but they are linked emotionally with parents more powerfully than either the middle or the late adolescent. The late adolescent does the least outright bickering but is less bonded to his parents in an emotional sense. The middle adolescent, as is true in so many important growth matters, straddles these two peramaters of parent-child love.

Why do adolescents rebel? Adolescent rebellion has long been observed not only in the North American family, but throughout the world. Of special interest to psychologists is the extent to which the rebellion indicates "normal" adolescent growth as contrasted with disturbed inter-family relationships. Balswick and Macrides (1975) studied this issue and found some rather interesting results. In a group of college students whose average age was about 20, they report that about 14 percent of the males and about 21 percent of the females claimed that they *did not go through a period* of rebellion during their adolescence. However, 65 percent of the males reported that what they went through a period of "slight rebellion" and 21 percent asserted that they went through a period of "extreme rebellion". Of the females in the study, 56 percent went through slight rebellion and 23 percent were extremely rebellious, according to their perceptions of their adolescent behaviour.

Balswick and Macrides also report that the parent-child relationship significantly influences adolescent rebelliousness. For example, youth who see their parents' marriage as unhappy are more likely to rebel than youth who feel that their parents get along well. High rebellion is associated with unhappy parent marriages *and* with upbringing habits which are either extremely permissive or extremely restrictive. Females are more likely to rebel under very restrictive child-rearing practices than are males. The research also pointed out that the greatest amount of rebellion is likely to take place in households where *either* the mother or the father is seen as having much more authority than the other, and more rebellion occurs when it is the mother who has the greater authority.

It is hypothesized that very restrictive home situations create an atmosphere where the adolescent can gain independence only by going through a drastic break with parents. This is usually interpreted by the parents as a gesture of extreme rebelliousness or as an act of aggression. In either instance, the relationship between parent and child deteriorates and increases the possibility that whatever the adolescent does it will be interpreted negatively by the parents.

In summary, it appears that adolescent rebellion is a "normal" phenomenon; however, its incidence and the form it takes is greatly influenced by the parent-child relationship, with hostile or punitive relationships increasing the likelihood of adolescent rebellion.

Runaways

Each year hundreds of thousands of North American youth "runaway" from home. Many of these flights represent attempts to gain attention, others reflect a serious disturbance within the family, and others fall somewhere in between. Running away from home has a respectable tradition in North American folklore because there existed in time past the opportunity for energetic, ambitious youth to leave home and find constructive work or at least playful adventure. Those days are no more. With the advent of compulsory schooling, and with nation-wide communication networks it is extremely difficult for youth to engage in what Fritz Redl calls "a therapeutic runaway".

In an attempt to discover more specific facts about runaways in contemporary times, Justice and Duncan (1976) undertook an investigation of youth who have run away from their home. They found in their sample of 12-17-year-olds that about 10 percent of the boys and about nine percent of the girls had run away at least once. Multiple running away occured among about three percent of both boys and girls.

According to Duncan and Justice runaways have more contact with police than non-runaways and they also have a higher incidence of drug abuse. Interestingly, runaways are exposed to drugs and crime more *after* they have run away than when they were at home. There also is evidence to suggest that once runaways are apprehended by the police and brought under "corrective influence" of the juvenile system that their delinquent behaviour increases rather than decreases.

Runaway youth are not restricted to any particular parental income bracket, however, their homelife tends to be characterized by high levels of parent-child conflict, by intense disagreements about personal conduct of the adolescent especially with regards to dating, manner of dress and other personal matters. The researchers of this particular study feel that runaway youth pose a serious problem to themselves and to society and that the problem is widespread.

As is characteristic of most adolescents who get into trouble with the law, or who experience considerable stress in their personal lives, *negative perceptions of parents* exist among runaways. Wolk and Brandon (1977) studied runaway adolescents' perceptions of their parents and of themselves and their findings were:

1. Runaways saw their parents as less supportive and more punishing than did youth who have never run away.
2. There was no difference in the *amount of control* exercised by the parents of runaways and non-runaways.
3. Runaway girls received more parental control than any other group, whereas runaway boys received the least. It appears that for girls, running away is a reaction against excessive control and a punitive or restrictive family environment.
4. Runaways tend to be anxious, critical of themselves and highly upset by their family circumstances. They tend to be less trusting of others, more restless, and have less interpersonal skills than non-runaways.

Thus, the adolescent runaway, at least in modern times, is typically a youngster who experiences a restrictive and punitive home environment, and who has rather low self-esteem.

These studies, however, do not tell us about those youth who run away from home, who later return to their families, and apparently make up their differences. This represents a large number of youth, however, it is virtually impossible to obtain reliable statistics about them because they usually are not reported to the police, they tend not to end up in crisis wards or youth centres, and they tend to have greater interpersonal coping skills than "hard core" runaways.

Egocentrism

It is impossible to get a "feel" for youth, to make sense out of their self-conscious vitality, or to come to grips with their helter-skelter style without taking into account their egocentrism. The self is such a preeminent fact of youthful existence that it tends to become involved with every action and experience. The self intrudes into events and spaces where it often does not belong. Adolescents tend to believe that people are watching them when they are not; they overreact to minor social errors; in general, they are keenly preoccupied with themselves, they are dramatically self-conscious, and they tend to personalize almost everything. The constant energy overflow which typifies many youth is heightened during any kind of personal encounter. In a very literal sense they are centred in their own ego, and this ego-centredness influences in visible ways their conduct and behaviour.

In the first place, they tend to view most differences of opinion from their own frame of reference. Among early adolescents, for example, it is typical for two boys to exchange ideas for an hour after which neither has understood the point of view of the other. Late adolescents, however, are less monopolized by egocentrism and it shows in many ways. They are better able to appreciate moral outlooks or political opinions which differ from their own, and they are better able to think about realities far removed from their own personal experience.

Adolescents live an extraordinary percentage of their lives in a state of elevated self-awareness. They censor themselves and analyze their actions much the same way as does an adult being interviewed for a job who is in a situation where it is important to always put forward one's best effort or to shine whenever possible. This state of "social anticipation", as one might expect, is an energy consuming phenomenon. Equally important, it is easy to mock or take lightly a person who exudes such self-preoccupation. Many adults succumb to this temptation and, as a result, incur the anger and resentment of youth who take themselves seriously even if they do so in a self-conscious, fidgety manner.

The egocentrism of youth virtually guarantees that they are interested in any topic which has to do with themselves. An adult who prefaces a comment to an adolescent with "I noticed that you . . ." invariably finds a good listener. If the adult is complimentary or flattering to the adolescent the adult may be surprised to find how quickly the so-called "generation gap" dissipates.

In summary, a cardinal rule of adolescent phenomenology is this: the consciousness about one's self and the intensity of experiencing one's self is a weighty and forceful fact of adolescent experience through which virtually all day-to-day experiences reverberate and magnify. Therefore, the self rarely takes itself lightly, and does not take kindly to being taken lightly by others.

Moodiness

Adolescents are far more susceptible to mood swings and emotional ups and downs than are children. Several factors contribute to this unpredictability of mood some of which are social-environmental and some of which are grounded in the internal growth process of the personality.

Although it is universally recognized that youth are prone toward topsy-turvy emotionalism, it has never been firmly established that they are more so than many adults. I mention this to avoid the image of adolescents as frenzied creatures who vascillate in and out of "normal" behaviour. At the same time, to better appreciate the quirks of adolescent behaviour it is worth keeping in mind that mood shifts and periodic emotional upheavals are not terribly unusual.

Thirteen is the age when parents and teachers most consistently report noticeable change in the emotional patterns of youngsters. This is probably related to their growth through puberty, the remarkable changes taking place within their body, and the constellation of perplexities encountered by the ego in its attempt to understand its changing nature. Moodiness, however, is also greatly influenced by advances in mental power which allow one to think about oneself and to introspect within one's personality in a more sophisticated manner than was available as a child. Moodiness is enhanced because adolescents are more capable of self-doubt and more sensitive to their inner workings and are better able to examine and criticize themselves.

The increased richness of emotional growth also contributes to adolescent moodiness. With advancing maturity the individual registers emotions more deeply, therefore, psychological skirmishes really do hurt more than they did during earlier years. Likewise, the capacity for intimacy deepens during the adolescent years, making the person's most sensitive emotional centres more accessible and responsive to pleasure as well as pain.

As self-identity becomes more established one takes oneself more seriously therefore, encounters with people who do not treat the adolescent with respect tend to elicit reactions which previously remained dormant. As a result, temper flare-ups, verbal outbursts and other behaviour which appears bizarre to the detached observer become more typical during the adolescent years.

Solitude is more and more important to adolescents because they need time to sort the relevant from the non-relevant in their life. (This is an important developmental task because youth encounter so many facets of life for which they have little experience that it is difficult for them to decipher what in the experience is important and what isn't). To the outside observer — especially parents — youth who request "to be left alone" appear to be "moody", whereas, their motivation often is merely to seclude themselves so they can give personal thoughts total priority.

Moodiness is a more powerful life force during adolescence than during childhood, and taking all factors into account should be treated with greater tolerance. However, many adolescents recuperate from their low mood swings with remarkable abruptness, and may shift from apathetic lethargy to their normal fast-paced, light-hearted standards in ten minutes. Equally possible, however, they may remain moody and inaccessible for hours, sometimes days, before phasing into a more social posture.

It frequently is asked if drug use and emotional mood are related during the adolescent years. Paton and Kessler (1977) investigated the relationship of depression and drug use among adolescents in an attempt to better understand this issue. Their research concentrated on the role of separate drugs including marijuana, hashish, LSD, various am-

95

phetamines, opiates and inhalants. The general findings were that depressive moods are related to drug use, especially drugs other than marijuana. It appears that marijuana does not cause depression, nor does depression cause marijuana use. Marijuana users tend to be more stable in their use of the drug than users of other illicit drugs. Girls tend to be slightly more depressed than boys. In summary, a clear link between drugs and depression does not exist during adolescence, though one may contribute to the other.

The Peer Group

Adolescents live in a peer world partly by choice and partly by necessity. Peers are vital to personal growth because for many youth the peer group exerts greater influence than does the family or the school — which is saying quite a bit.

The actual role played by the peer group during the adolescent experience is greatly influenced by age, by the importance of parents in the life of the adolescent, and by the ability of the youngster to become involved in meaningful activity with people of varying ages.

Gangs, cliques and other units of cohesive youth are found in every culture. Ours is rather extremist in that youth spend most of their day in the presence of people their own age. (This issue will be set aside for now, however, a special section in Part Three is devoted to it).

The early adolescent is monopolized by the peer group more than other adolescents because this is an age when youth know very little about themselves, when they rely heavily upon the opinions and judgements of others, and when their own sense of self-identity changes so frequently that they truly do not know "what to think of myself".

Day-to-day survival skills are learned in the peer group. Sex role ideas and habits are greatly determined by peers, as are clothing styles, hair styles, musical interests and a host of other matters that preoccupy the adolescent mind. The criteria for acceptance and popularity stem from the peer group; likewise, the treasured reward of praise, recognition and admiration flows from the human reservoir of emotion inherent to the group. A good deal of adolescent conformity emerges from the desperate attempt to belong, to affiliate, or simply to be a member of the group. (The reader does well to keep in mind that in our culture the adolescent without a peer group is a comparatively abandoned person. Think about youth you know from personal experience who do not belong to a group of comrades. As a rule they are lonely youngsters).

The peer group is the lifeline to crucial realities. It is a good place to learn about sex, about jobs, about cars, about the world-at-large. Each adolescent discovers in his or her own way that what one learns from the peer group may or may not stack up well in reality. As middle adolescence approaches, youth become more impressed with what the peer group does *not* know, and a stronger sense of self-reliance sets in. A gradual separation process begins: adolescents slowly shift their psychological allegiance from the peer group to themselves. It is perhaps the most dramatic individuation process in the entire adolescent period because it comes about only when the self has acquired a measure of genuine autonomy and assurance. "Know thyself" is becoming a reality rather than merely an empty platitude.

Of course, no one is completely exempt from the influence of peers. (Significant findings in the social sciences during the past twenty years document how thoroughly influenced *adults* are by their "peers".) The general trend, however, is that the power of the peer group lessens as the adolescent ages. Its power often is shifted to a single partner — frequently of the opposite sex, but not necessarily. By late adolescence, intimacy emerges as a life force which openly competes with the need to belong to a group, a gang or a clique. Many youth, however, satisfy both needs rather well. (Although it rarely is mentioned in textbooks, the integration of intimacy needs with belonging needs is one of the fundamental developmental tasks of early *adulthood* and represents one of the major psychological problems faced by university students).

The peer group serves numerous important functions. It lets me know what I am good at. It gives me practice in handling others. It teaches me about aspects of my personality which I did not know about. It is where I learn to cope with ridicule, rejection and candidness. It is where I discover that I'm attractive, or witty. It is where I learn about parts of me I can't find out about as well elsewhere.

It is a vital fact of the adolescent experience; though certainly not the only vital fact.

The Psychology of
the Adolescent
Part Two:

Chapter Six

The Psychological Needs
of Adolescence

The needs of adolescence are different from those which govern childhood. During the adolescent years the need for *status and acceptance* (especially from peers) grows in strength such that, for the first time in the life cycle, peer acceptance may be more important than parental acceptance. The need for *independence and self-assertion* peaks; the need for *achievement* becomes focused more precisely; and the need for *role experimentation* impels the adolescent to sample social roles and to broaden social relationships with others.

It is not accurate to claim that these needs are experienced *only* during one phase of adolescence, however, at particular times they exert greater influence than at others. The needs discussed in this section have the greatest impact on the lives of *early* and *middle* adolescents. In the next section the needs of late adolescence will be our focus.

Status and Acceptance

The ability to interact effectively with peers, to cope with social expectation, to take care of oneself in a social setting — each relate to securing social status. In this regard it is difficult to separate social competence from social acceptance. During the first years of adolescence, social competence is required for effective peer-group functioning. The youngster unable to respond to rapidly changing group codes and behaviours is likely to be left out of the whirl. Likewise, the youngster unable to cope with ridicule or belittlement may find that the only role among peers is as a jester or as the brunt of debasing jokes. (It is intriguing to note the number of boys and girls willing to assume such status in the peer group.)

For some adolescents the need for acceptance is so powerful that virtually nothing interferes with its pursuit. When the need for acceptance becomes the strongest focus in a person's life, other needs become subordinate; therefore, in the attempt to satisfy this need, the individual engages in behaviour he/she otherwise would not. Fourteen-year-olds *dominated* by the need for acceptance will participate in almost any behaviour they believe will lead to group acceptance. On the other hand, the 14-year-old for whom acceptance is only *one of several* important needs is less chained to the unqualified demands of peers. Youth dominated by the need for acceptance are more easily manipulated and exploited than those for whom acceptance is "held in check" by other needs such as autonomy or independence.

Social status during the first years of adolescence is linked with skills valued by same-sex peers; during the middle adolescence, social acceptance is determined largely by social skills valued by both sexes. This change accounts for the large number of youngsters held in high esteem by peers during one period of adolescence, but not during another.

The adolescent quest for acceptance is not blind and relentless — it has its own built-in restrictions. Normal adolescents will not consistently violate their own values merely to gain peer acceptance. When strong conflict exists between personal codes and social acceptance, adolescents are as likely to follow their own codes as those of the group. This is especially true for the adolescent whose sense of worth is based upon *more than* peer group acceptance. Teenagers who know that other sources of acceptance are available to them (parents, other peers), are reluctant to go against their own inclinations; they are less susceptible to group blackmail.

Adolescents do not accept status randomly. Like adults, they prize status received from "significant others" more highly than that received from ordinary people. Praise which comes from important peers is valued no matter what its content; therefore, good feelings swell within adolescents when they receive any compliment from an important friend. The same compliment from a less-valued person may bring a mere shrug of the shoulders.

In summary, the need for status and acceptance during adolescence is strong but not unqualified. During *early* adolescence the individual is dominated by the need for group acceptance more so than during other developmental stages; this becomes less intense as the individual recognizes the extent to which group domination infringes upon personhood.

Independence

Despite adolescents' striving for independence, in several areas of their life they remain *dependent*. Since few avenues exist for earning money, adolescents remain economically dependent upon their parents.

During the middle and early stages of adolescence, parents are not genuinely interested in their child assuming independence. As Josselyn puts it: "Parents want him to be independent as long as he does what, by their criterion, he is supposed to do. They want him to make decisions, but to decide as they feel he should decide." (1971, p. 16)

A more precise use of terminology would incline us to say that the adolescent has a strong need for *self-assertion*. In social groups, in personal living, in fantasy, it is self-assertion that the adolescent craves — not true independence. Independence has too many complications and requires too much responsibility. Adolescents want the chance to prove themselves, to be important members of their families and school, to be socially acknowledged and made to feel important, to be accepted, recognized, and esteemed. All of these, when summed up, do not equal independence; rather, they equal a more general need — the need for self-assertion.

Since total independence is not possible, the adolescent is impelled to exert independence whenever possible. *Dislike* for authority often blossoms at this age because it allows release of built-up tension generated by parental authority; *suspicion* of authority increases because adolescents resent infringement and are easily convinced that adults are devising ways to increase their infringement. Interestingly, *respect* for authority also matures at this age because the adolescent observes that some adults are more adept at handling authority than others, indicating that *competence* is essential to its proper execution, not merely age. The adolescent fascination with competence forces them to acknowledge expertise — even when it comes from authority figures.

During *late* adolescence the matter of independence must be faced more directly. From 15 to 20, the basic skills of adult autonomy must be refined. Unfortunately, by this age many adolescents have adjusted to dependence and resigned themselves to relinquishing their sense of independence and self-assertion. Unwittingly, many parents (and school systems) condition autonomy out of the person by rewarding conformity and by stifling innovation and eccentricity.

When choice can be expressed in two different yet equally attractive directions, we have what is called an independence-independence conflict. When adolescents must choose between two undesirable courses — going to school or working all day at home — they experience a *dependence-dependence conflict*. Numerous conflicts centre around the adolescent need for independence, most of them compounded by the impulse for self-assertion, but also by his or her "nonimpulse" (in some cases, inability) to cope with the responsibility of total independence. The adolescent battle cry for independence is really only a plea for less restriction, not a cry for true independence.

The adolescent need for independence also is manifested in the various ways by which the individual becomes liberated from the peer group. Research conducted by Bixenstine and co-workers (1976) indicates that with increased age most youngsters command a greater ability to avoid peer-group activities which they consider wrong, or activities which will be opposed by their parents. In their study four separate age groups of young people (grades three, six, eight and eleven) were surveyed to determined their values, their judgment of right and wrong, and their *readiness or resistance to misbehave*. Of special importance for our concerns is the extent to which young people's willingness to "misbehave" is influenced by factors other than peer group pressure. Bixenstine derived the following results from this particular study:

1. Children who expected their parents to review their statements they made during the experiment *resisted peer pressure* more than those youngsters who had no one to find out what they reported.
2. Children who expected peers to review their statements were *more conforming*.
3. Females were more resistant of going along with peer misbehaviour than were males.
4. Children continue to succumb to peer pressure up until about the eighth grade, where greater independence begins to assert itself.
5. Eighth-grade students and eleventh-grade students *who held adults in high regard* were less likely to go along with peer misbehaviour. (This important point will be dealt with at greater length in part three under the heading "The Peer Group Myth".)
6. The more unfavourably youth perceived adults, the more likely they were to go along with peer misbehaviour.

The implications of the foregoing research are considerable. First, it indicates that the need for independence exists not only in relation to gaining greater autonomy from adults, but also from peers. Second,

102

conformity to peers is greatly influenced by the quality of relationships that adolescents have with adults. Third, with increased age there appears an increased ability to resist peer pressure when it contradicts personal beliefs.

Achievement

The *specific* definition of "achievement" varies from culture to culture, and from individual to individual within a given culture; however, it usually refers to the need to accomplish, create, master, build, finalize, or originate. Achievement is one of North American culture's most prized goals, and few individuals reared in this culture escape its influence.

The adolescent need for achievement is moulded from four sides: parents, peers, society, and self. As the need for achievement results from a blending of these four forces, it commonly has contradictory elements. During adolescence one must sort out the nature of one's own achievement need — a task requiring not only trial-and-error but also a good deal of introspection and self-analysis. *Parents* may encourage achievement efforts towards college preparation or vocation; *peers* may encourage involvement in athletics; *society* may suggest that owning a sporty automobile is a symbol of personal achievement; *self* is understandably confused as to what achievement really is. An example of the conflict between achievement and acceptance is noted by Gordon, who claims:

> There is inherent contradiction between acceptance and achievement in that some of the most visible forms of achievement (such as making high grades in school) rank quite low as grounds for popularity, and peer group and dating activities (beginning ar around thirteen or earlier) that engender and maintain popularity take large segments of time and attention away from studying. (1972, p. 39)

The adolescent need for achievement is not treated seriously in most technological societies; consequently, it is frustrated more often rather than satisfied. Meaningful constructive behaviour is rarely available to the adolescent, thus forcing the achievement impulse into less important activities and encouraging *peer-based* rather than societal-based achievement.

The adolescent, uncertain as to how the need for achievement should

103

be directed, is often lured into achievement patterns simply because they bring peer praise and acceptance. A 15-year-old boy may concentrate his need to achieve in rebuilding automobiles because he is talented in this activity and because it lends peer acceptance and recognition. Parents who feel their son's talents for mechanics could be profitably employed by training to become an aeronautics mechanic are dismayed to observe him spend day after day in a backyard shed tinkering with a broken-down Chevy.

Role Experimentation

During adolescence the search for identity becomes complicated. Identities which served well during childhood (son, daughter, sibling, "good boy", "good girl", helper) no longer suffice. A more complex identity forms which demands that individuals have some idea of *who* they are, *what* they are, and *why* they are. During childhood the first two forms of identity are acquired; the "why" of identity is the dilemma of adolescence. It is instructive to note, however, that a sense of personal identity is virtually impossible to acquire without sampling and experimenting. How can an adolescent girl establish a sense of feminine identity without interacting in a variety of ways with other girls and boys? How is the adolescent boy to establish a sense of masculinity without testing himself in a variety of social settings? How can any adolescent cultivate a sense of personal worth without experimenting with different activities which have the *potential to produce feelings of worthwhileness?* Identity demands experimentation and sampling, and adolescence is the time when a good deal of it takes place.

As we have already pointed out, early adolescents have strong needs for status, acceptance, independence, and achievement which can be satisfied only when they are able to assume different roles. Adolescents may discover that they are not well-accepted by peers when they assume a dominant role, but they are even less acceptable when acting passively or wishy-washy; in time, they comprehend that their peer group prefers people who are firm in their beliefs, but not forceful in obliging others to behave as they do. The same adolescents, in another group, may discover that peer acceptance is accorded *only* when they assume a subservient role. Recognizing one's place in a group comes about only after considerable role playing and role testing.

Role experimentation is particularly important in four general areas: 1) gender roles, 2) competence roles, 3) social roles, 4) independence roles. *Gender roles* refer to patterns of behaviour which suit the adolescent's concept of appropriate sex behaviour. Girls learn to express what they consider feminine (adolescent girls change their viewpoints about femininity as a result of sampling different roles, discovering that some of their ideas are fictitious, or at least, unrealistic); boys learn patterns which permit expression of their sense of manliness. Gender *ideals* are absorbed from the outside culture; thus, one of the primary developmental tasks for youngsters of this age is sorting out *cultural* stereotypes which are *personally* inappropriate. Adolescents not trained to think for themselves have difficulty accepting the fact that they may be trying to be something (or someone) their personality is not suited for. *Competence roles* are those which permit the exercise of skills the adolescent is attempting to master; athletics, drama, debating, etc. are provided by the school system on the assumption that participation in these activities promotes important competencies while at the same time offering social exchange and self-expression. *Social roles* represent patterns of interaction which allow the individual to discover how it feels to express different aspects of one's own personality in a social setting, for example, playing a dominant role in one situation and a compassionate role in another, or being first antagonistic and whiny and later supportive and affirmative. During the early adolescent years the teenager learns the give and take of social exchange, but can give and take only to the extent of social competence. *Independence roles* relate to patterns of behaviour in which the individuals decide for themselves what they will do, with full realization that the price for doing so is to be answerable for the consequences.

The Late-Adolescent Need Structure

No reason exists to think of the needs discussed thus far as exclusively adolescent. The psychological need for acceptance, achievement, independence, and role experimentation are needs which, to a considerable degree, characterize the *entire* life cycle. Their prominence during adolescence is credited to the fact that during this period these needs are given special significance in constructing one's self-definition and in preparing the person for adulthood. In addition to the needs discussed thus far there also exists another set of needs which assume considerable importance during late adolescence.

In this section I shall outline six general traits of the adolescent experience which achieve prominence during late adolescence and exert a tremendous impact on day-to-day living habits, and the subjective experiences of youth. These include: the need for self-importance, the need for significant contribution, the need for introspection and self-analysis, the need to sample identities, the need to make a difference, and the need to focus on the future. These life forces are not *needs* in the rigid sense of the word, but their influence is sufficiently powerful that the term "need" is used to convey their impact on the adolescent personality.

Self-Importance

All youth are filled with a desire for *self-importance* so intense that it can be understood as a need. Self-importance is among the most powerful adolescent impulses and blends with the needs for self-assertion, intimacy, belonging, and esteem. To be important means: to be essential; to be well thought of or held in high esteem; and, to be missed when away. It also means to *do* things of relevance, to contribute to the significant events in one's peer group or family, and to achieve goals thought important by oneself or one's close associates.

The need for self-importance is not usually experienced in a conscious, rational way. Rarely do youth actually say, "I am important," or, "I feel important today," or even, "I wish I felt more important." As with all subjective needs, satisfaction may or may not become the object of rational thought. The search for self-importance is a dominant theme of youth fantasy. It symbolizes the purpose behind much of their daily striving and their personal ambition.

Self-importance provides the confidence which permits investigation and exploration of life opportunities; the absence of such confidence fosters acquiescence. Self-importance provides a *reserve of psychological strength* which allows one to cope more adequately with anxiety and frustration. It also makes the appraisal of new people or novel situations less threatening. Finally, a sense of self-importance means that the young person is not at the mercy of contrived rituals or invented customs designed to *prove* one's importance. Self-importance reinforces self-reliance by instilling confidence, and opposes the blind conformism which derives from the desire to attain importance at the expense of individualism.

Certain *actions* such as building useful products, asserting oneself *because of* personal beliefs, and establishing love or intimacy relationships create feelings of self-importance. Certain *reactions from others* also instill feelings of self-importance, such as being held in special esteem, being judged as possessing desirable character traits, being thought capable of making sound judgements, and having one's opinion carry social weight.

The quest for self-importance closely resembles what Rollo May calls "the cry for significance". It does not always assume extroverted form: significance may derive from internalized ideas or beliefs. ". . . significance may not be extrovert at all but may be shown (and achieved) by meditation or other introvert, subjective methods. It is nevertheless *experienced by the person as a sense of power* in that it helps him integrate himself and subsequently makes him more effective in his relations with others" (1972, p. 35).

For the majority of youth litttle opportunity exists to *do* things which generate feelings of self-importance. Little opportunity arises to construct useful products which contribute to the improvement of the environment; little opportunity exists to assert oneself in a positive and wholesome manner because the areas of life in which youth actually make a difference are minimal; *some* opportunity exists for love and intimacy and, for many youth, this represents the only way to feel important. Because the social formulae governing adolescent action tend to oppose importance derived from *actual* work or *real* love, most youth turn to their peer society for a sense of personal importance. This, in turn, makes them manipulable, highly preoccupied with the assessments of their mates, and imprints the tendency to *pursue importance in terms of how it is defined within the immediate peer setting.*

2. Significant Contribution

All those things a family must *do* in order to actualize what it wants is *significant work*. All the work which, in large or small measure, contributes to the significant work of the family is called *significant contribution*. In North American society, especially in the middle economic classes, the significant work of the family is monopolized by the parents.

The inability of youth to contribute to essential work proves two things. First, that they have not learned how "things" work. Second, that they are unable to make a difference within the environment. The failure to make significant contribution (however defined) causes adolescents to question whether they are ready for adulthood.

Developmental and social factors both contribute to the emergence of significant contribution as a dominant adolescent theme. Adolescents are living a life phase when competence is highly regarded. They are also facing up to the demands of time, recognizing that adult roles soon will befall them, and their ability to handle the roles will, in great measure, determine the quality of their adulthood years. Therefore, they intuitively know that their ability to engage in worthwhile work, that is, to make a significant contribution to whatever it is that they want to do, is part and parcel of self-definition. As the ability to make significant contributions increases, so also does self-esteem; conversely, when significant contribution *declines,* so also does self-esteem.

Perhaps we should caution against *overstating* the adolescent need for significant contribution. It does not exist as a straightforward biological impulse as does, for example, the need for food or exercise. Nor does it exist as a primal impulse which forcibly asserts itself as does the need for autonomy. Rather, it exists as a *by-product* of a variety of needs and developmental requirements. Its existence is based upon needs for competency, involvement, self-assertion, esteem, and acceptance.

Our notion of work as a form of penance has blinded us to the fact that, at certain times in the life cycle, "work" is not really work at all, but a way of satisfying needs which require building, forming, creating, and, in general, doing. Adolescence is one such time. In young children we pay attention to these needs because they can be actualized by what adults mistakenly call "play". It is not play at all. It is growthful work which, because it is natural and essential to full human development, produces feelings of pleasure.

Introspection, Self-Analysis and the Future

No alternative exists to youth's need for periods of introspection to analyze their own personality and the mysteries which fill it. Youth answer not only to their peers and to adult authority figures but also to themselves which is no easy task since self is inconsistent and somewhat unpredictable. The adolescent often does not know for sure what (or who) "self" is, especially in novel or unusual situations.

Some psychologists give the impression that adolescents "discover" themselves. Thinking of self as a thing to be discovered, or as an entity which matures on a predesigned schedule, is an inaccurate view because it denies the fact that, in many instances, self is *invented.* They make up a self, try it out for a while to see how it fits, and then determine whether it is worthy of further development.

No one understands precisely how the human mind evaluates, analyzes, and investigates itself. Nor does anyone know clearly how the people come to accept one part of their personality and reject another. What *is* known, however, is that the process involves considerable anguish and introspection. Probably at no time during the life cycle is a greater portion of psychic energy consumed in self-analysis. The evolving self has reached a juncture in its history when life-choices are influenced by the impulses of inner-self and, therefore, one must be certain that one is reading them correctly and that they are legitimate yearnings, not merely short-term desires.

Few people take the Socratic maxim "Know thyself" more earnestly than adolescents. However, knowing thyself is no easy business; it requires pensive concentration. For youth not inclined toward such cerebral exercises, this requirement is especially painful but, nonetheless, essential. Adolescents with low intelligence (as measured by IQ tests) are introspective just as their more intellectually-gifted comrades; the main difference between them is that brighter youth tend to talk about their thoughts and conclusions more adeptly. Because of this difference we sometimes lose sight of the self-analysis typical of less intelligent youth, inferring incorrectly that introspection is for gifted youngsters only.

Thinking about oneself and coming to conclusions about how one *is* as well as about how one ought to be requires solitude. Casual forms of introspection may take place anywhere but the "dark nights of the soul" take place only in isolation. Solitude is required if the process is to be lived honestly. Encouraging youth to fear isolation, to doubt the legitimacy of loneliness, or to feel something is amiss when inner feelings demand expression is to encourage self-alienation.

Understanding adolescent introspection forces us to recognize how much the young people actually create and formulate themselves. They actively strive to *cultivate* particular skills, interests, likes and dislikes; they actively strive to *stifle* certain feelings, desires, and ambitions. They coddle those parts of their personality which need assistance. They take pride in character traits which bring praise and affection and, conversely, they doubt "weaknesses" which bring ridicule or rejection. They constantly appraise, investigate, decelerate this desire, accelerate that habit, modify this tendency, and stabilize that impulse. Like the master architect who redesigns a building by altering the facade in favour of a more substantial foundation or changing one wing to add greater appeal and beauty to the edifice, so do adolescents continuously realign their personality blueprints by striving to bring inner feelings into harmony with outer actions.

Adolescents are not all introspection and self-analysis — the rest of their makeup precludes such monotony of character. They snap out of their introspective spells, sometimes with deceptive quickness.

The need for introspection is deepened by the role played by the future because self-analysis is the primary means by which the ambiguities of self are integrated into the uncertainties of the future.

Future Pull

Youth do not, and cannot, live entirely in the present. This is especially true for late adolescents. They visualize and anticipate their future, assessing in their own minds the nature of what it holds for them. This assessment of the future, which is an intrinsic and inevitable consequence of human intelligence, represents one of the most important factors in the lives of young people.

The ability to tolerate pain, cope with stress, and endure anxiety is related to one's perception of where one is going. The more optimistically and openly one faces the future, the greater is the ability to cope with adversity in the present; contrariwise, the more negatively and fatalistically one faces the future, the more overpowering is present pain. For youth, the formula is elementary: when the future is painted brightly, filled with promise and high expectation, the turmoil and anxiety of everyday living is reduced and placed in perspective; when the future holds little promise for personal growth or self-assertion, the anxiety of present time becomes the central fact of life; nothing cushions its intensity and no feeling of future liberation relieves the distress.

Youth are pulled toward the future by their *biology*. They are growing, unfolding, and expanding; therefore, to know oneself as an adolescent is to know that the future is essential for completion of the bodily self. Youth are biologically incomplete and they know it; the future holds their biological maturity and this fact is acknowledged by preparing for it.

Youth are pulled toward the future by their *psychology*. The need for intimacy increases during late adolescence; thus, the search for an intimacy partner is essential for psychological fulfillment. "I-ness" is gradually being replaced with "we-ness"; until the transition takes place, self is not complete. Youth are pulled toward the future because

110

without it they are only part of what they can be.

Youth are pulled toward the future by their *morality*. Understanding the moral world is a predicament encountered by youthful souls. Shedding the moral dogmatism of childhood, they search for viable explanations and viewpoints; uncertain as to what is right and what is wrong, they formulate moral codes which balance impulses and justify actions in order to keep their own equilibrium. Youth tire in their search for moral guidelines and lapse into periods of comparative amorality, but they inevitably come around and realize that amoral existence is self-defeating and self-debasing. The pull of the future is the only hope for reconciling moral dilemmas; therefore, if morality is to exist in a meaningful way, youth must look to the future.

Do not misread the message. Youth are not overpowered by the future. They do not spend every waking moment in its anticipation or calculate every step in terms of where it leads. The message here is more moderate but, nevertheless, crucial. Future time is an essential parcel in the adolescent package; optimal growth cannot take place when the future is feared or when it is thought to be unworthwhile. Youth need to be convinced that the future will not deny them those things most important to their lives: self-assertion, intimacy, productive work, acceptance, esteem, and love. When the future is perceived as holding only chains but never keys, the growth of late adolescence grinds to a halt. The present acquires unnatural power because it has been stripped of the only thing which lends it clemency — the future.

Future pull is not a dominant fact of life in *all* stages of the growth cycle. For infants it exerts negligible influence; for young children its presence is felt, but it remains embryonic; for middle-years children, future pull becomes stronger, but lags behind other growth requirements; with early and middle adolescence the role of the future is dramatic, exerting greater influence than ever before. However, in late adolescence and early adulthood, future pull reaches its peak. It can be mistreated during childhood and even during early adolescence without serious effect; with late adolescence no such latitude for mistreatment exists. At this age the person must respect the future because, more than ever before, it is central to self-definition, self-ambition, self-purpose and self-identity.

The inevitable by-product of thinking about oneself while preparing for the future is the need to formulate a *personal identity*. The key word here is formulate since, in many regards, adolescents do not have an identity; they certainly do not have a crystallized or unified identity —

but then neither do most adults. The quest for identity goes hand in hand with *sampling* various identities.

Sampling Identities

Adolescents do not *acquire* identities. Neither do they *find* their identities. An identity is not a pre-existent reality to which the adolescent becomes hooked in the teen years. Personal identity is formed as adolescents *interact with their environment and introspect within themselves*. An identity is part of the total personality which inclines one toward certain actions or beliefs and away from their opposites. One does not *have* an identity, rather, at any given time, one *is* an identity; during adolescence identity is incompletely formed, therefore, it manifests itself inconsistently and sporadically, not knowing for certain when it is on home ground and when it is on foreign territory.

In general usage, *identity* refers to how one thinks of and defines oneself, taking into consideration one's own expectations of oneself and the roles society assumes one will carry out. Identity refers to the sameness of character which persists throughout an individual's behaviour despite superficial differences in behaviour or mood and, therefore, represents unity of personality over a period of time. By its very nature, identity is *formed* and *nourished* rather than merely *acquired* or *learned*. During adolescence the matter of identity takes on added importance because adulthood demands choices which are difficult to make without a fairly unified identity. Few adolescents (few young adults, for that matter) have a clearly defined identity or experience themselves in completely predictable ways. They undergo "identity crises" because they panic when unable to reconcile the conflicting elements of their changing nature.

Identity crises are also precipitated by the inability to find something to attach oneself to, or to have something to believe in. Erikson describes such an identity confusion:

> For the moment, we will accept Biff's formulation in Arthur Miller's *Death of a Salesman:* "I just can't take hold, Mom, I can't take hold of some kind of a life." Where such a dilemma is based on a strong previous doubt of one's ethnic and sexual identity, or where role confusion joins a hopelessness of long standing, delinquent and "borderline" psychotic episodes are not uncommon. Youth after youth, bewildered by the incapacity to assume a role forced on him by the inexorable standardization of American

112

adolescence, runs away in one form or another, dropping out of school, leaving jobs, staying out all night, or withdrawing into bizarre and inaccessible moods. (1968, p. 131)

Adolescence, of course, is not the only time in the life cycle when crises of identity are experienced; it is merely the first time they are dwelt upon at length and articulated in the presence of adults. Children, for example, experience identity crises because they are constantly changing, continuously being elevated in status, given responsibilities beyond their developmental level, and treated inconsistently. A case can be made that identity crises during the preschool years (when the child first drifts away from household moorings, encounters new authority figures, and runs headlong into the jungle law of peer society) are as intense as those experienced by the adolescent. However, even though the experience of preschool identity crises may be intense, young children have neither the sense of abstraction nor the preoccupation with the future which produce mature identity crises. Age tends to remedy the crises of childhood, but it compounds those of adolescence. The closer one comes to adulthood, the greater the need for personal identity and, therefore, the greater the pressure to find solutions and to sample identities.

The requirements of identity are such that the only way youth can sensibly deal with the matter is to sample, experiment, and dabble with various identities, emotions, and habits.

The quest for identity periodically results in over-identification with heroes or amorphous investment with whoever happens by. Erikson notes that even teenage romance is influenced by identity:

To keep themselves together, they temporarily overidentify with the heroes of cliques and crowds to the point of an apparently complete loss of individuality. Yet in this stage not even "falling in love" is entirely, or even primarily, a sexual matter. To a considerable extent, adolescent love is an attempt to arrive at a definition of one's identity by projecting one's diffused self-image on another and by seeing it thus reflected and gradually clarified. This is why so much of young love is conversation. (1968, p. 132)

Even though the need to sample identities exists within virtually all youth in our culture, it does not follow that *all* youth experience acute identity crises. For some adolescents the path to identity formation is fairly uneventful, or at least, far removed from the turbulent image fostered by the alienated, identity-confused youth. The research of Offer and Offer supports the view that acute identity crisis is *not* the norm for adolescents. Manaster has an even sharper view. He claims that much youthful preoccupation with identity results from their protracted moratorium where they are excluded from work or important life commitments. He concludes that many youth have neither the time nor the inclination for the complicated mental operations required of identity crises.

It may be that dwelling on issues of personal identity is a luxury that comes with an extended psychosocial moratorium. Adolescents who are not pressed into the adult social and occupational world, most probably because they are pursuing courses of higher education, are granted the time, and to some degree are expected, to look closely at themselves and their future.

But not every adolescent by any means is granted this time, or possesses these capabilities. The majority of adolescents come to the end of their schooling with, at most, a high school diploma, and maybe even an additional technical training course of some type. They are pressed into the adult world. They need to find a job. They want to get married and move out of their parents' home. The question for psychologists, teachers, and counselors is whether these adolescents experience an identity crisis, and whether there is any need for them to do so.

It appears to this author that the identity crisis relates to cognitive development, the psychosocial moratorium, and related personal and social variables (such as IQ, SES, etc.) and does not occur for many adolescents, and need not. (1977, p. 123)

Whether one places keen emphasis on the role of identity crises or not, two conclusions present themselves. First, sampling identities is an essential part of the adolescent package. Secondly, for many youth the sampling process is confusing and painful.

Making a Difference

Humans are genetically predisposed to behave in certain ways and engage in certain activities with the net effect of making a difference. Humans of all ages (unless it has been conditioned or punished out of them) are inclined toward developing competency skills to better master the requirements of the environment; they likewise interact with others in such a way that they may be recognized, esteemed, and appreciated; they also build monuments in order to be regarded favourably and thought well of. Humans must make a difference; otherwise, they are without consequence.

All healthy humans, universally and without fail, abhor not making a difference. It is the closest thing to nonexistence one can experience, even though in many respects not making a difference is closer to antiexistence than nonexistence because it not only denies what mankind is all about, it actually opposes what mankind is all about.

People treasure most highly those things and those people that make a difference. People who generate emotion, passion, and conviction make a personal difference. People who build, change, and construct make a tangible difference. People who dance, love and sing make a poetic difference. People cannot be valued or loved unless they make a difference.

Creating a difference in the physical world and experiencing a difference in the emotional world is what adolescence is all about. When all is said and done, *making a difference* is what matters to youth.

After talking with hundreds of adolescents over the course of several years, one cannot help but be impressed with the singular way they describe their favourite high school teacher, their best counsellor, or their most admired adult. Invariably, they claim (after a certain amount of beating around the bush) that these precious adults made them feel (and often forced them to behave) as though they really made a difference — that they were important. The idiom changes with the times, but expressions run like this: "He just made me feel as though I was important"; "I don't know, I just kinda felt he thought I was somebody"; "I like her because no matter how stupid whatever I said seemed to others, she always thought it was worth something."

The best way to ensure that young people get into trouble is to design their environment so that their nontroublesome behaviour does not make a difference. Strip them of the ability to make a difference legally and they will find ways to make a difference illegally. Making a difference is far more important to humans than following rules; it likewise is more important than efficiency, harmony, smoothness of operation, and more important than learning subject matter or writing lessons.

A Humanistic View of the Adolescent Need Structure

Hadley Cantril (1964) put forth his interpetation of basic psychological needs in an essay entitled ''A fresh look at the human design''. Many humanistic psychologists have responded positively to Cantril's outline

115

of human needs, claiming they are more humane than those proposed by other psychologists. Here I have taken the liberty of presenting Cantril's viewpoint from the adolescent frame of reference in order to present a humanistic interpretation of adolescent needs.

1. Adolescents want security in both its physical and its psychological meaning to protect gains already made and to assure a beachhead from which further advances may be staged. Adolescent psychological makeup requires that they be able to perceive the world as somewhat predictable and orderly, allowing for preparation for the future. In addition to the need to perceive a promising future, the urge to demand a somewhat stable present is also part of the adolescent need structure.

2. Adolescents crave sufficient order and certainty in their lives to enable them to judge with fair accuracy what will or will not occur if they do or do not act in certain ways. According to Cantril, people want to be certain that ''satisfactions already enjoyed will be repeatable and will provide a secure springboard for takeoffs in new directions.'' Not only do people crave ''sufficient order'' but they actively embark on activities which will promote and guarantee it. It not infrequently occurs that the need for order and certainty is strong enough to *override other needs*. Thus, for some adolescents the need for order is stronger than the need for novelty or, perhaps, even for freedom. The ability to predict how one will affect others as well as how others will act upon oneself is related to the need for order and certainty.

3. Adolescents continuously seek to enlarge the range and enrich the quality of their satisfactions. Adolescents are not content with past achievement and conquests. Cantril asserts the search for increasing satisfaction takes place at two general levels; (1) learning new methods of satisfying reoccurring needs and (2) developing new needs which require completely new forms of satisfaction. From this perspective, adolescent behaviour classified as unhealthy may be little more than awkward attempts to discover novel ways of gratifying needs for which conventional means have become mundane. The adolescent need to enlarge the range and quality of satisfaction is the forerunner of the adult need for self-actualization.

4. Adolescents are creatures of hope and are not genetically programmed to resign themselves. They reflexively interpet (unless it has been conditioned out of them) future events as holding greater promise than those of the present and they tend to gear themselves for the future with the aspiration of things getting better.

5. Adolescents have the capacity to make choices and the desire to

exercise this capacity. To ask adolescents to live in a situation where they cannot make meaningful choices is to ask them to live contrary to their basic makeup. Not only do they prefer to make choices, they achieve satisfaction from doing so.

6. Adolescents require freedom to exercise the choices they are capable of making. This is the logical extension of the previous posture. Humans require a much greater degree of freedom than other species because of their greater capacity to move about and to engage in a wider variety of behaviour. An environment which does not allow for freedom of choices may elicit behaviour otherwise not expected of the adolescent.

7. Adolescents want to experience their own identity and integrity. Many psychologists tend to overlook this need and many more are reluctant to consider it a primary need. Though it is true that each individual learns various ways of achieving unique identity and integrity, the underlying impulse pre-exists in every person as an attribute which one takes to all social interaction. If the environment affords little opportunity for meaningful confrontation and involvement with other humans, the need is stymied and frustrated, creating a sense of bewilderment and confusion.

8. Adolescents want to experience a sense of their own worthwhileness. Although each person receives satisfaction from achievements and triumphs, one also has the unquenchable desire to be accepted in and of oneself, with no ulterior reasons or motives. One likes, even craves, being accepted as a primary person.

9. Adolescents seek some value or system of beliefs to which they can commit themselves. Sometimes described as mankind's religious nature, this propensity urges people to conceptualize a scheme of understanding and belief which allows for the existence of a reality greater than oneself.

> Commitment to a value or a belief system becomes more difficult among well-informed and sophisticated people who self-consciously try to reconcile what they believe with what they know and what they know with what they believe. In such circumstances, beliefs become more secular and less important as personal identifications. (Cantril, 1964)

Maslow agrees with this premise and feels that failure to recognize it has been one of modern psychology's more serious oversights. He stresses the pathological consequences of not having a system of values:

The state of being without a system of values is psychopathogenic, we are learning. The human being needs a framework of values, a philosophy of life, a religion or religion surrogate to live by and understand by, in about the same sense that he needs sunlight, calcium or love. (1962, p. 206)

10. Adolescents want a sense of surety and confidence that the society of which they are a part holds out a fair degree of hope that their aspirations will be fulfilled. The reader can see that this postulate is a synthesis of several of the previous needs, including hope, order, identity, worthwhileness, and future preparation. As with other needs, an environment which does not allow gratification fosters frustration. The experience of frustration is compounded if the individuals are not cognizant of what their needs truly are, for then they have nothing to attach their frustration to, thus accelerating anxiety.

Unhealthy Adolescent Needs

Psychological needs, when taken to extremes, may become unhealthy forces in the life of the adolescent. The normal need for esteem or belonging, when it becomes overpowering and uncontrollable, may interfere with the development of other normal needs such as autonomy and self-assertion. Normal needs have the potential to become unhealthy when they impede growth.

The distinction between normal and unhealthy behaviour is not easily drawn and requires the insight of a trained psychologist. Our intent here is to point out some of the consequences when normal needs are exaggerated out of proportion and become unhealthy.

Karen Horney is of the impression that neurotic behaviour results from exaggerated manifestations of *normal* needs. Therefore, neurotic needs differ from normal needs in degree rather than kind. The following are the neurotic needs she considers to be of greatest consequence:

1. *The neurotic need for affection and approval.* This need is characterized by the indiscriminate wish to please others and live up to their expectations. The centre of gravity exists outside rather than within the self; self-assertion is dreaded as is the fear of incurring hostile reactions from others. Adolescents are extremely sensitive to signs of rejection or unfriendliness; they are blenders, mixers, conformists whose need for approval dominates their daily lives.

2. *The neurotic need for a "partner" who will take over one's life.*

Adolescents with this need overvalue love and are extremely afraid of being deserted or left alone. Therefore, they crave a partner (a parent, a friend, a leader) who will take responsibility for life crises as well as decision making. Adolescents with such an exaggerated need refuse to live up to their own responsibility, autonomy, and individuality.

3. *The neurotic need to restrict one's life within narrow borders.* This need results in an unreasonable fear of self-expansion — of growing beyond one's present limitations. The adolescent with a need for narrow borders is undemanding, content with little, and prefers to remain as inconspicuous as possible.

As might be expected, these first three trends are often clustered together in the neurotic life-style. They each stress nonreliance, nonresponsibility, and nonassertion. Any one of them may exist in isolation, but frequently they group together and foster a personality minimally capable of coping with the demands of normal growth.

4. *The neurotic need for power.* People with this need crave domination over others; they likewise demonstrate disrespect for others, their individuality and dignity, as well as their personal feelings. The need for power results in an indiscriminate admiration of strength and contempt for weakness. The neurotic need for power is encouraged by a culture which stresses the right to dominate by strength — the "might makes right" philosophy. Adolescents who are afraid to exert power openly sometimes attempt to control others through intellectual superiority or dominance.

5. *The neurotic need to exploit others.* Others are evaluated primarily according to whether or not they can be exploited. Adolescents with this need have a morbid fear of being exploited or made to appear stupid, and will go to virtually any measures to insure this will not happen.

6. *The neurotic need for social recognition or prestige.* All things are evaluated according to their *prestige* value; even self-evaluation is dependent upon public acceptance. There is a dread of humiliation and fear of loss of public approval.

7. *The neurotic need for personal admiration.* Adolescents with this need desire to be admired because they cannot accept themselves unless others overtly demonstrate their admiration. As with the neurotic need for social recognition, nothing is more feared than the loss of admiration.

8. *The neurotic ambition for personal achievement.* This need is characterized by a dependency on being the very best, whether it be lover, sportsman, or scholar.

The needs for prestige, admiration, and personal achievement have in common a more or less open competitive drive toward superiority over others. These characteristics may be clustered or exist in isolation. For example, the need for personal admiration may force the person to temporarily disregard social prestige.

9. *The neurotic need for self-sufficiency and independence.* This need reflects the fact that distance and separateness are the only basic source of security for individuals. They dread needing others or having close ties because this puts them in an anxiety situation in which they are not always successful.

> Having been disappointed in his attempts to find warm, satisfying relationships with other people, the person sets himself apart from others and refuses to be tied down to anyone or anything. He becomes a lone wolf. (Hall & Lindzey, p. 133)

10. *The neurotic need for perfection and unassailability.* This need is characterized by the fear of making mistakes or of being criticized. Adolescents defend themselves against these fears by making themselves "impregnable" and "infallible". They constantly search for flaws in their own makeup so that they may be covered up before they are noticed by others. Their striving for perfection gives them a feeling of superiority over others, the neurotic nature of which is betrayed by the fact that they dread criticism even from those to whom they consider themselves superior.

Each of these needs is moderately characteristic of normal adolescents. Only when carried to such an extreme that they dominate the individuals' lives, their ability to cope with themselves and others, their ability to grow and expand, and their ability to honestly invest themselves in others, only then do these needs become neurotic. Many adolescents go through periods where one particular need (such as the need for affection and approval) exerts tremendous influence over daily life. In such periods it is difficult to determine whether the behaviour is "neurotic" or part of the normal adolescent growth process. Proper diagnosis can be made only by trained personnel.

Summary

The psychological needs which motivate and influence the adolescent have been the focus of this chapter. Although the needs we have discussed are not restricted to the teenage years, they exert considerable impact during this time of life. The following concepts highlight the psychology of the adolescent:

1. During the entire adolescent period, but most noticeably during *early* and *middle* adolescence, the individual is greatly influenced by four pervasive needs:

    a. the need for status and acceptance;
    b. the need for independence and self assertion;
    c. the need for achievement and competence; and,
    d. the need for role experimentation.

Satisfaction of these needs is dependent upon parents *and* peer group. They are the external sources of satisfaction. For these needs to be fully gratified requires maturity of personality and consolidation of ego identity, which, for most youth, takes place during the later adolescent years.

2. An additional cluster of "need" also exerts dramatic influence on the life of the adolescent. I have labeled them:

    a. self importance (the need to affirm self-significance);
    b. significant contribution (the need to contribute to important work);
    c. introspection (the need to analyze and synthesize one's self);
    d. future pull (the need to incorporate the future into one's world view);
    e. sampling identities (the need to give expression to all facets of one's personality);
    f. making a difference (the need to register impact on the social and physical world).

The pursuit of these "needs" motivates a good deal of adolescent behaviour. Emotional stability, in large measure, is based upon their gratification, and anxiety is greatly increased by their deprivation.

3. A humanistic view of the adolescent should take into account the total personality. Hadley Cantril's philosophy of human nature, as applied to the adolescent, well portrays the spectrum of adolescent needs from a humanistic perspective.

4. Normal needs and desires, when carried to extremes, take over the personality. When this happens they acquire many of the self-defeating characteristics of a neurotic coping reaction and therefore, may be considered unhealthy.

Chapter Seven

Stress and Strain During Adolescence

The stress and strain inherent to adolescent life is viewed differently by psychologists. Some psychologists assume that *all* adolescents experience extreme turmoil, that they toil in the relentless grip of alternating depression and ecstasy, and that their day-to-day living is an emotional battlefield. These beliefs have been popular since 1904 when G. Stanley Hall in his two volume classic introduced the phrase *"Sturm und Drang"* (storm and stress) to typify the psychological climate of the adolescent. Hall decided that it was characteristic of youth to vasilate between the extremes of sorrow and exuberance, and to shift unexpectedly from friendly altruism to selfish hoarding. It was Hall's opinion that adolescents were capable of the most intense romantic passion and "Promethean enthusiasm". All in all, they were accorded an incredible range of emotional abilities which they roamed unpredictably.

This image of adolescence remains widely held for several reasons, the most important being that our knowledge of youth is weighted in favour of the emotionally distrubed or socially deviant. The psychiatrists, social workers, and psychologists who treat them are frequently the same who write about the "nature" of adolescence in general. "The adult of our Western culture has apparently learned to expect a state of acute disequilibrium and anticipates the 'storm and stress' in his adolescent child . . . . The expectation has seemingly been incorporated into the literature of psychological development . . . ." (Anthony, 1969, p. 65)

Other social scientists do not agree that adolescence must *necessarily* be a time of storm and stress. Margaret Mead was among the first to observe that in some cultures adolescents live a comparatively tension-free life. In her assessment, *cultural pressures and restrictions* are the basis of adolescent tension more than anything inherent in adolescence itself. Offer and Offer, who perhaps have conducted the most exhaustive psychological research on "normal" adolescents take strong exception to the storm and stress theory. They note that: "Investigators who have spent most of their professional lives studying *disturbed adolescents* stress the importance of a period of turmoil through which all teenagers must pass in order to grow into mature adults. On the other hand, investigators who, like us, *have studied normal adolescent populations tend to minimize the extent of the turmoil."* (1969, p. 180)

It is safe to say that the available research confirms that *all* youth do not experience considerable strain and stress. It, however, does not refute that *many* youth do. A viewpoint of considerable merit has been put forth by the German psychiatrist E. Spranger, who contends that *three* general developmental rhythms characterize growth through adolescence and that young people tend to fall into one of these patterns. The first is the *Strum und Drang* view of adolescence which corresponds with the ideas of G. Stanley Hall, emphasizing the turbulent nature of youth, their dramatic mood swings and their fluctuating sense of self-experience. The second is a growth pattern in which adolescents actively shape their own destiny and show a considerable drive for power, discipline and self-control. They stand in contrast to the "storm and stress" youth who do not know their own minds, who flounder in the face of new demands and who fear the future. Finally, there is a group of adolescents *for whom little turbulence or turmoil is observed.* Development is comparatively uneventful, and day-to-day living, is fairly free of major disturbance. Offer claims that "this division of adolescents into three groups is consistent with our contention that a high level of turmoil is characteristic of *only one route from adolescence to maturity."*

In this chapter, I shall not elaborate a philosophy of adolescence which clarifies whether storm and stress is *inevitable* during adolescence. The empirical evidence is clear beyond any doubt that *many youth* experience considerable anxiety, the consequences of which range from mild uncertainty about the future to suicide. Therefore, the focus of this chapter will be upon the range of reactions to adolescent stress, the consequences which often accrue from them, and the psychological principles upon which they are based.

Age-Related Factors

The stresses and strains to which the person is subject change considerably during the course of the adolescent period. Certain stressors are more likely to appear at one age rather than another. For example,

124

during the *child*-adolescent period the greatest difficulties evolve around peer conflicts, survival within the school, and lack of self-confidence. Turmoil at home is founded upon bickering between parent and child and the tendency for parents to not pay attention to their youngsters; disagreements tend to be based upon specifics of conduct such as when to report home, whom to associate with, achievement in school, and other day-to-day realities, rather than upon major disagreements requiring a philosophy of life. Strain during *middle* adolescence tends to be like *sturm und drang*. Emotional upheavals are more noticeable, romantic feuds more intense, and disagreements with parents more substantial. During these years turmoil leads to more serious consequences both personally and socially. In the *late*-adolescent period stress is experienced as tension with society at large and the future in general. It is adult in composition and resembles the inner torment characteristic of adulthood. Conflicts concerning career plans and separation from parents are also common at this age.

Laufer (1975) has suggested that the "priorities and preoccupations" of the adolescent personality vary considerably. He suggests the following "concerns" as related to the emotional strain of adolescence:

A. Early adolescence:

1. concern over adjustment to the developing body;
2. concern over loss of self-control;
3. concern with newly emerging sexual feelings;
4. concern over the fear of growing older and of no longer being cared for as a child.

B. Middle adolescence:

1. concern over becoming emotionally independent of parents;
2. concern with the maturing body, especially as to whether it is "abnormal", attractive, and how it compares with the bodies of others;
3. concern about masturbation and sexual adequacy.

C. Late adolescence:

1. concern with one's adequacy as a man or a woman;
2. concern with permanence in social and sexual relationships;
3. concern with integrating sexuality and intimacy into life experiences;
4. concern with sexual identity;
5. concern with establishing a stable personal identity.

With regard to the more serious reactions to adolescent stress there is no doubt that middle and late adolescence are more crucial than early adolescence. Neurotic reactions such as *obsessions* and *compulsions* are considerably more prevalent during the later years. The most acute forms of psychopathology such as depression, schizophrenia, and suicide occur much more frequently during the late-adolescent period.

The reasons for the late adolescent being victimized by psychological ailments are numerous. Conflict with parents tends to become progressively more fundamental as adolescence progresses, therefore the bickering and argumentativeness of early adolescence often deteriorates into full-fledged hostility by late adolescence. Loss of a romance partner which causes the middle adolescent only a few days grief may result in prolonged despair and depression for the older adolescent. Likewise, fear of the future, which lingers only as a distant apprehension for middle teens, hangs like a weight around the neck of the late adolescent. Also to be considered is the fact that many youth who have been surviving on a weakened personality find the increased strains of aging too much to cope with. This is especially true for adolescents who rely excessively on defense mechanisms to protect them from harsh realities; who are overly rigid or lack of problem solving skills; who have low tolerance to stress; who have low self-esteem; and, who lack helpers and loved ones in their personal lives.

Defense Mechanisms

During all growth stages, the individual experiences tension, anxiety, and stress. Adolescence is no exception and perhaps, as some psychologists have suggested, it may even be the most stressful of all growth stages. One task of adolescence is to learn to cope with the demands of daily life under stressful conditions. This task is difficult and many adolescents never become very proficient at it. One of the basic ways the adolescent personality protects itself is by the *defence mechanism*. Defence mechanisms are also used by adults and children; however, considerable adolescent behaviour would be difficult to explain if we were not familiar with the mechanisms of defence.

What Is a Defence Mechanism? – protect you,

A defence mechanism is pretty much what it says: a mechanism of defence. More specifically, *it is a psychological mechanism which defends the ego from anxiety or other forms of injury, pain, or disinteg-ration.* Defence mechanisms are considered involuntary because they are activated at an unconscious level. The primary function of all defence mechanisms is to *temporarily* reduce anxiety. Defence mechanisms have the following characteristics:

1. They have a heavy unconscious basis (but not totally unconscious).
2. They are attempts to reduce anxiety or other forms of ego pain.
3. They are involuntary.
4. They are self-deceptive for two reasons: (a) they distort reality and (b) they originate in the unconscious part of the mind.
5. They cannot be negotiated away by logic or preference, tending to go away only after having served their original function, which is to reduce anxiety.

Most psychologists acknowledge Sigmund Freud as the father of defence mechanism theory. He believed that they operated at the unconscious level and became activated when the individual was threatened with ego injury. Freud believed that the mind protects itself from anxiety and that the defence mechanism is *only one means* of pain protection. They are called into use when the individual's adjustive reactions are exhausted and anxiety still persists. Defence mechanisms consist of varying degrees of *denial, distortion,* and *reorganization* of reality and serve the dual function of temporarily decreasing psychological pain while at the same time increasing pleasure. However, in a pinch, either is sufficient justification for deployment of defensive reactions.

For normal adolescents ample opportunity arises for use of mechanisms of defence because of their numerous encounters with anxiety-arousing situations in daily living. The adolescent personality is designed so that it reflectively moves away from excess anxiety. (The word "excess" is critical here because *moderate* anxiety can serve many positive functions, such as increasing general arousal and awareness, which allows one to better confront challenging situations whether they be social or physical.) Frequently, escape is accomplished merely by leaving the source of anxiety; more drastic measures are necessary when it is impossible to completely escape. When it is difficult to escape the *source* of anxiety, the probability of one or more defensive mechanisms occurring is increased.

Defence mechanisms cause the adolescent to *deny, repress,* or *turn away* from some aspect of reality. The negative consequences of defence mechanisms, in the long run, outweight the positive benefits.

They are, by most definitions, antithetical to growth because they prevent accurate perceptions of reality.

For example, a 14-year-old boy may feel awkward or inadequate in his attempts to socialize with a potential sweetheart. His inexperience results in blunder upon blunder. The anxiety is hard to take. Failure is hard to take. He rationalizes, "Girls, who needs 'em?" "Sissies, that's who girls like, well, that ain't for me." By use of this defense mechanism (rationalization) he removes himself from the anxiety associated with heterosexual interaction (virtually a required developmental task in our society) but also makes it more difficult to learn how to deal with the opposite sex. Thus, a potentially growth-fostering situation has been temporarily (in severe cases, permanently) sabotaged by avoiding the anxiety inherent to the situation. Many adolescent experiences are anxiety-producing; therefore, the individual capable of dealing with anxiety at a conscious, open level is more able to cope effectively with such normal stress.

Defence mechanisms generate negative consequences because they fail to deal with the *real causes* of anxiety. By distorting or denying, the true cause escapes detection. For this reason, it is said that defence mechanisms deal with the *symptoms* of anxiety but not its *causes*. Characteristically, they become little more than a form of self-imposed anesthetic which soothes painful aspects of interpersonal relationships.

Defence mechanisms are given special attention in the psychology of adolescence because of their repercussions in day-to- day living. Indiscriminate use of defence mechanisms can lead to vicious circles which increase anxiety. Defence mechanisms employed over a long period of time cause maladaptive behaviours which prevent the individual from confronting reality.

As to whether defence mechanisms can be *growth-fostering* as well as growth-inhibiting, there is some divergence of opinion. The general concensus, which stems from the early Freudian interpretation, is that defence mechanisms generate more negative than positive consequences. However, it is possible that many adolescents described as "normal" benefit from the judicious use of defence mechanisms. The occasional repression of anxiety-producing memories, for example, might prove helpful to a given individual's overall functioning, just as the selective use of rationalization may make one's life more tolerable. Most therapists are unwilling to say that defence mechanisms are categorically unhealthy. The pragmatic emphasis which dominates psychology tends to rule in this matter with the following maxim: if the use of defence mechanism fosters an increase of anxiety rather than a reduction of it, if it limits the ability to interact with one's environment rather than enhance it, and if it reduces the ability to satisfy basic needs, *then the defence mechanism is unhealthy*. On the other hand, the defence mechanism which alleviates anxiety and enhances self-esteem without promoting neurotic behaviour is difficult to classify as unhealthy. During adolescence, it is not easy to determine when defence mechanisms contribute to maladjustment and when they are temporary means of reducing anxiety.

The most critical function of any defence mechanism is to distort stimuli which are anxiety-producing. The degree to which this function is served is the degree to which the defence mechanism is executing its purpose. However, the more successful any given defence mechanism is in excluding anxiety from consciousness, the greater the probability that residual consequences *of a negative variety* will emerge. For example, a young man undergoes the torment of guilt feelings because of sexual activity with his lover. He is torn between the admonitions of his conscience on the one hand and his sexual passion on the other. The frustration of sexual abstinence is taxing but the censoring from the superego (conscience) is even more so. Finally, he can no longer cope with his anxiety. Something has to give. In response to this predicament, the young man *represses* his sexual desires — he (to the best of his ability) shuts off his experiential connections with his sexual impulses. This involuntary mechanism, invoked to rescue the ego from anxiety, also pushes memories out of awareness. In short, the adolescent boy has *repressed* the conscious aspects of his sexual drive, as well as the memories of previous sexual behavior.

This example must be viewed from at least two perspectives. The first is the immediate, short-term consequences. Often there occurs an immediate reduction of anxiety and, consequently, a greater ability to deal with the external environment. Friends might comment on a more relaxed, easy-going manner. The second consideration is for the long-range implications. The sex drive will remain. Therefore, energy must be expended to keep sexual impulses out of consciousness. Presumably, other situations will arise when the young man is "tempted" by sexual behaviour and he will have to form intellectual opinions concerning sexuality. But how is he to do this when he cannot experience sex without guilt and tension? Each of these realities must be faced without the resource of honest self-awareness. All in all, the short-term benefits prove to be a meager exchange for the long-range complications.

Summary

Defence mechanisms are ways by which the ego protects itself from anxiety. Defence mechanisms usually cause more problems than they solve because they distort reality in order to shelter the person. They are employed by all types of people, both neurotic and healthy, and become progressively more serious the longer they are used and the more they distort reality. Even when defence mechanisms prove effective in dealing with anxiety they seem less adaptive than rationally-based solutions. Most psychologists agree on the following characteristics of defence mechanisms:

1. They are usually involuntary psychological reactions.
2. They have a heavy unconscious basis but can be understood by the conscious mind.
3. They are attempts to reduce anxiety or other forms of ego pain.
4. They are self-deceptive because they distort the perception of reality and they originate in the unconscious.
5. Although they can be understood by the conscious mind, they are not controlled by it and cannot be talked out of existence.

Now that we have acquired some definitional criteria, we would do well to take a look at some specific defence mechanisms, especially those related to adolescent adjustment.

Repression

Repression is the process whereby a thought, wish, or memory is pushed from the conscious part of the mind into the unconscious. In many respects, it is the most important defence mechanism because several others are built upon it or result from it. *The function of repression is to push anxiety from the conscious mind.* Freud, who originated the concept, described repression as ''the process by which a mental act capable of becoming conscious is made unconscious and forced into the unconscious system''. When an idea, wish, or memory is pushed into the unconscious mind it continues to seek expression and will directly manifest itself in dreams, fantasies, or symbolic acting-out.

Regression

Regression is the act of *adopting behaviour patterns which were successful at an earlier age but considered inappropriate for one's current age*. It involves moving backward to a more stable, more secure, time of life. Regression usually results in shrugging off responsibility or an unwillingness to assume responsibility. An example is the renewal of bed-wetting by a six-year-old who has been a non-bed-wetter for several years. The addition of a new sibling frequently brings about this regressive behaviour. Temper tantrums are also a form of regressive behaviour, usually carried out when the individual is exposed to stress he or she cannot handle. Temper tantrums are not unique to any particular age level. They begin at about 12 months and, for certain individuals, last through adulthood.

When carried to an extreme, regressive behaviour leads to the childish life-style characteristic of psychotic behaviour. For the most part, however, regressive outbursts are temporary escapes from stress. Most adolescents experience stress which they cannot cope with, hence, they employ regression to circumvent it.

Rationalization

Rationalization is the tendency to explain or understand reality in such a way as to enhance one's own self-esteem. Rationalization is the most frequently used of all defence mechanisms. When using the defence mechanism of rationalization, the adolescent *automatically accepts explanations or ways of viewing things which maximize positive self-concept or self-evaluation*. Rationalization is not necessarily unhealthy; it may even be *correct*. A student who just failed a mid-term exam retorts: ''I would have done much better except I stayed up all night studying another subject.'' In actual fact, this may be true. This example represents *rationalization* because there are many possible explanations for failure on the exam, of which staying up all night is but one. Other possible explanations include: (1) insufficient intelligence, (2) insufficient knowledge, (3) insufficient skills at test-taking, (4) insufficient ability to prepare for the type of exam which was taken, and (5) inability to work under pressure and strain. Any of these could ''explain'' failure. Because most of these ''theories'' are contrary to self-esteem and self-concept, they are not chosen. The explanation chosen, though not complimentary to self-esteem, is less ego-deflating than its options, thus becoming a rationalization.

When rationalizing, individuals often describe their thinking as ''common sense'' and preface their statements with, ''It is obvious that . . .''. This reflects two important considerations with regard to rationalization: (1) individuals rarely recognize that the purpose of thought is to enhance the self; (2) individuals usually do not understand why their point of view is not readily accepted by everyone else.

When rationalization attempts to cover up motives which one is trying to keep hidden, it necessitates the use of *additional* rationalizations, thus creating a process which, like lying, becomes progressively more difficult to keep track of.

In summary, rationalization is the tendency to explain or understand reality in such a manner that self-esteem is enhanced; occasionally, this involves repressed motives, memories, wishes or desires, but this is not always the case.

Projection

Projection is the tendency to assume that another person has motives, feelings, or desires similar to those which one has oneself. Projection, like rationalization, is a way of looking at reality so that it enhances the self.

Projection is understood in two general ways. The first includes the ascribing of attributes, desires, and wishes to others *which one knows are characteristic of oneself.* A shoplifter would say, "Everyone does it", or "Everyone will steal if they just have the chance." The shoplifter attributes personal behaviour to others. This form of projection is referred to as *assimilative projection.* The second type of projection occurs when individuals assume that others possess motives or feelings which they themselves have denied or repressed in their own life. Adolescents who repress sexual impulses because they cannot deal with them without anxiety may project these sexual desires to another, not recognizing that they are merely reflecting their own psychological state. This is called *disowning projection* because people attempt to disown their own feelings by projecting them to someone else.

Disowning projection is the more serious because it involves a more complete denial of reality and, also, forces the person into a condition of self-alienation (being alien to one's inner self). Disowning projection is more likely to be completely false than assimilative projection because individuals have little way of checking their frame of reference because their own feelings are repressed and disowned. Both forms of projection are common to the adolescent years.

One might suspect disowning projection if (a) the motives imputed to

others are derogatory and immoral, (b) these same motives are vigorously denied in one's self, (c) little evidence exists to support the belief
that the other person has those particular, motives and (d) the person
using projection gives evidence of these imputed motives.

Sawrey and Telford underline the extent to which projection is also a
normal, commonplace element in daily living.

> These research findings, as well as everyday observations, indicate
> that we perceive the world in terms of what we are. Those who are
> honest and virtuous see others as honest and virtuous. The deceitful
> see others as deceitful. We perceive our own moral lapses reflected
> in others. When we are afraid we read fear on the faces of others.
> (1967, p. 43)

Projection, as is true with all defence mechanisms carried to extremes, has the potential to distort one's view of inner and outer reality;
when used moderately, it seems to be part of the normal adjustive
pattern, warding off anxiety, defending the self from injury or insult,
and allowing the individual to survive in his or her social world without
collapsing from the pressure inherent to it.

Identification

Identification is the process where one defends oneself against feelings of inadequacy and weakness by viewing oneself as the same as (or
as part of) some figure of power, status, or dominance. Like most
defence mechanisms, identification occurs during all age levels and,
when carried to extremes, can be a form of pathology. Identification is
characteristic of the *normal* child who identifies with parents, teachers,
or authority figures in general. It is considered normal during middle
childhood when boys identify with sports heroes, during pre-
adolescence when girls identify with idols and entertainment heroes,
during post-adolescence when young adults identify with the prowess
and excellence of a literary figure or a politician, and during adulthood
when adults identify with a boss, colleague, or predecessor. Identification is unhealthy when it prevents the individual from formulating a
personal self-concept; when one becomes continuously subservient,
never exerting one's own independence or autonomy; when the only
sense of achievement comes from vicarious involvement in others rather
than self-pride in personal activity and participation. Identification
requires less use of repression than any other defence mechanism and,

except for rationalization, is probably the most widely used and least destructive of all the defence mechanisms.

Occasionally, identification is directed more toward the benefits of being a certain person or holding a certain position than toward the actual person with whom an identification has taken place. For example, an adolescent athlete may identify with a famous sports hero because of the attention he receives and his outrageously high salary rather than because he is able to carry a football over an artificial surface without being knocked over by a behemoth adversary.

There are, of course, positive consequences of identification: young children modelling after their parents; the student modelling after the brilliant teacher; the assembly line worker identifying with the company product and therefore working more efficiently and conscientiously than might otherwise be the case. Strong identification also makes less intense the "identity crises" of adolescence.

The precise reasons why some adolescents require exaggerated defensive measures to protect themselves from the stress of day-to-day living are not clearly understood. However, it is thought that the following personality factors contribute to the degree to which life situations are more overpowering for some adolescents than others and therefore make defence mechanisms necessary.

Overview

The defence mechanism is a means of psychological protection employed by adolescents to reduce stress and strain. Virtually all youth use defense mechanisms in one form or another, therefore, in terms of percentages, they can be thought of as "normal". However, the continued use of defense mechanisms cause the adolescent to distort reality, to misperceive the motives of others, and to deny authentic feelings. From this perspective they may be considered "abnormal".

The index of whether a defense mechanism is harmful is the consequence it encourages. A clinical psychologist, therefore, might assert that the *identification* of one youth is considerably less harmful than the *disowning projection* of another. The clinician might also observe that virtually all adolescents use rationalization and regression in their daily behaviour without visible negative effects.

One of the more serious side effects associated with the prolonged use of defense mechanism is that they tend to elicit *neurotic coping reac-*

tions. These reactions are an extension of the defense mechanism in that they rely upon distortion and denial; they are more serious, however, because they are accompanied by elaborate *patterns of behaviour* which are intended to reduce personal anxiety but which add immeasurably to it. Here we shall take a look at some of the more prevalent neurotic reactions to adolescent stress.

Rigidity The inflexible adolescent, unable to bend and shift with changing pressures, experiences tremendous social pressure which tends to skyrocket anxiety level.

Low stress tolerance The adolescent who possesses only limited stress tolerance finds *normal* life crises more stress-producing than do adolescents with greater tolerance of psychological pain.

Lack of "helpers" Adolescents require someone in whom they can confide in times of personal crises. When helpers are sufficiently strong, most adolescents weather life problems without resorting to neurotic symptoms. Individuals who lack helpers must encounter their problems in solitude and this diminishes their ability to master them. Adjustment crises, of all types and for all ages, are especially difficult to handle without helpers. Unfortunately, the life-style of the immature adolescent tends to distance people rather than to bring them close.

Limited self-evaluation For some adolescents self-evaluation is contingent upon successful functioning in the environment. When the environment goes awry or creates an undue number of problems, one tends to perceive oneself as unworthwhile, insignificant, or meaningless. This encourages one to give up, to fail to assert one's autonomy and individuality, or to hide behind facade and custom. Most adolescents are capable of recognizing their integrity regardless of how the environment fluctuates and changes. Consequently, they are not totally dependent upon environmental reinforcement for a sense of personal strength. The adolescent of low self-evaluation, however, "falls apart", "breaks up", "comes unglued" when the environment becomes stressful.

Suffering The extent to which the adolescent has learned that suffering and pain are part of human life which must be coped with rather than avoided affects the ability to cope with daily anxiety. Many adolescents are "psychological cowards" who fear any form of anguish or anxiety. They flee from it with a horror which frequently is more acute than the anxiety from which they hide.

Neurotic Reactions to Adolescent Stress

Adolescents do not emerge unscathed from their struggle with stress and anxiety. Occasionally, they are forced to rely upon what personality psychologists call *neurotic reactions*. These reactions include anxiety, phobic, somatic, obsessive-compulsive, and depressive reactions. ⑤

Stress reactions serve the same general function as defence mechanisms: they attempt to keep the world within manageable limits and preserve ego strength. Neurotic reactions are self-defeating because they *increase* anxiety rather than reduce it; they *alienate* the person from others; they make problems *more difficult* because they cause the adolescent to avoid real problems and deal only with surface issues.

Anxiety Reaction

Occasionally, anxiety will swell to uncontrollable proportions filling the person with fear, panic, and apprehension. One becomes unable to function with usual effectiveness; one is preoccupied with inner feelings of anguish and is unable to deal effectively with other people. Such an experience is referred to as an *anxiety reaction*. Usually these are of short duration, lasting not more than several hours, although in extreme cases they may last for several days or weeks. Adolescents usually know enough about their anxiety to explain what brought it about: "I always get this way when my mother meddles into my business." Or, "These episodes come every term around examination time." Or, "Whenever I worry too much about money these anxiety streaks hit me." Statements of this variety are commonplace among adolescents for whom anxiety reactions occur. Insight, however, rarely deals with the repressed fears or desires which trigger anxiety reactions.

Phobic Reaction

A phobia is a strong, persistent, nonrational fear of something which presents little *actual* danger to the person. Numerous phobias have been defined, three of the more common being *claustrophobia* (fear of closed places), *acrophobia* (fear of heights) and *agoraphobia* (fear of open spaces). Phobic adolescents usually are aware of the nonrational nature of their fear but rarely are able to do anything (so they claim) about it. Some psychologists claim that phobias are *substitutes* for other sources of anxiety. For example, the fear of being laughed at, or the fear of ridicule, might be replaced by a fear of groups; fear of falling might be replaced by a fear of elevators; a fear of sexual intercourse might be replaced by a fear of some phallic symbol. Phobias are most likely to occur when it is difficult to consciously fear or hate *the true source of anxiety*. A son who fears his mother, (but who also requires her approval) might be able to keep his life relatively intact by substituting his fear of her for a fear of female teachers.

Phobias sometimes originate from learning rather than displacement. A young child bitten by a dog might develop an overpowering fear of dogs or sharp-toothed animals. This example of phobia stems from specific learning; however, most phobias are not of this variety.

Phobias, whether of the conditioned or displaced variety, are difficult to extinguish because they provide a source of sympathy and attention from others. Phobias have "nuisance value" and, consequently, are good for getting attention. Many adolescents are sufficiently starved for recognition to exchange ridicule for no attention at all. Some phobias are relatively harmless and exert minimal influence on day-to-day behaviour, whereas others are crippling because they involve a fear which is integral to everyday functioning. A fear of meeting new people would create a staggering number of crises for a woman who made her living selling insurance; the same phobia held by a fur trapper would be negligible.

Somatic Reaction

Reactions which affect the body and its proper functioning are called somatic reactions. One group of somatic reactions, referred to as *asthenic reactions,* include symptoms of tiredness, lack of energy, loss of strength, and fatigue. These symptoms tend to disappear during activities the adolescent enjoys or which have little anxiety associated with them.

A more severe form of somatic reaction is *psychosomatic reaction* which is *actual* physical disorder that results from excess tension, worry, or anxiety. The classic psychosomatic disorders of our culture include peptic ulcers, various forms of asthma — (especially bronchial asthma) migraine headaches, and hypertension. None of these disorders is *exclusively* psychosomatic, but they are the most recurring disorders which result from excess tension.

All somatic reactions serve at least two basic functions: (1) they narrow the range of personal experience and allow one (in a socially acceptable manner) to be totally absorbed in oneself, and (2) they remind one of one's own existence, and centredness, thus standing in opposition to environmental realities which minimize self or cause insecurity. (A frequent third factor is sympathy and attention received during illness. This contributes to psychosomatic disorders, but is not a *sustaining* factor for the truly psychosomatic adolescent.)

Obsessive-Compulsive Reaction

An *obsession* is a recurring thought, idea, or wish which the individual cannot dispel. It might be a rather harmless obsession, such as fearing theft of one's credit cards, or more serious such as the persistent idea that one will be struck dead. A *compulsion* is the persistent impulse to carry out acts in a ritualistic manner. Compulsions, like phobias, are varied in number and content. Some of the more widely-known compulsive acts include the impulse to steal (kleptomania), the desire to continually cleanse onself — to wash or shower, and the compulsion to set fires (pyromania).

Obsessions relate to repressed fears or desires. A young man who has repressed his sexual desires because they make him feel dirty may develop the obsessive thought that he is being contaminated by impure objects in the environment. He may develop a fear of dirt (mysophobia) and consequently develop the compulsive act of washing-cleansing-bathing.

Compulsions are not always harmonious with obsessions. Sometimes they *counter* an obsessive thought by forcing opposite behaviour. The adolescent with the obsession that things are falling apart, that life is on the verge of chaos, might counter with a compulsion for orderliness or meticulousness. She would demand everything always be in its place — and, of course, for her there would be a place for everything. Generally speaking, carrying out compulsive acts provides relief from anxiety. The compulsive adolescent may experience acute anxiety when not permitted to act out compulsions.

The basic function of obsessions and compulsions is to maintain the world within manageable limits and to keep the mind absorbed in activity. Compulsive gamblers, for example, receive many residual benefits from their compulsion: all other problems disappear — nothing else matters. Only the present, as radically experienced, is relevant to gamblers. Economic problems, marital problems, sexual anxieties — none of these matter *during the moment* of a compulsive act. For the person who has the need to escape life problems, a compulsion is an *escape* vehicle.

Depressive Reaction

Depressive reactions are experienced as intense feelings of remorse, sorrow, and self-blame with a corresponding lack of activity, loss of interest, and a preference for seclusion. Periods of depression are precipitated by experiences which the healthy adolescent is able to take in stride. During depression, a total loss of interest in outside activity occurs.

Adolescents who experience depressive reactions usually are characterized by an immature yet rigid conscience, vivid ideas about guilt, and a strong propensity for self-blame when things go wrong. The misconception that one should be perfect heightens adolescent guilt feelings because it makes impossible achievement of personal expectations.

The onset of depression is hard to predict. It may last from less than an hour to several days. During depression, the individual is not able to concentrate for sustained lengths of time, is restless yet tired at the same time, and is extremely sensitive to comments which can be construed in a negative way. Because psychic energizers are readily available a psychological dependence on medication to ''snap out'' of depression states often develops. Adolescents for whom depression is common find themselves suceptible to the ''better living through chemistry'' logic which pervades our time.

While experiencing depression, the adolescent is not much affected by conversation, diversions, or maneuvers designed by others to reduce melancholy.

Overview

In this section neurotic reactions to adolescent stress were briefly outlined. It should be made clear that in actual life these reactions rarely display themselves in such clearly-defined symptoms. Each reaction overlaps with others, causing psychologists to speak of ''clusters'' of reactions rather than specific reactions. It is instructive to note that phobias, compulsions, and obsessions are closely interrelated. A fear of sexual relationships (phobia) may foster the idea that women (men) are evil (obsession) and result in the uncontrolled habit of avoiding women (men) (compulsion). Fear of sexual relationships may also foster a *reaction-formation* which prompts the individual to act out the opposite — an endless series of affairs which prove mastery over the fear-object.

It is difficult to predict those teenagers who will develop neurotic reactions. It is equally difficult to predict which youth will "outgrow" them. It is for certain, however, that many youngsters develop an increasing dependence upon their neurotic reactions and become even more deeply entrenched in psychological disturbance as their adolescent years advance. Minor neurotic reactions sometimes snowball into full-fledged psychopathology, the consequences of which are considerably more severe and enduring.

Adolescent Psychopathology

Adolescence, especially *late* adolescence is not a healthy time of life as far as mental health is concerned. *Conflict* is inevitable because the adolescent is leaving behind the security of childhood and venturing forth into the uncertainty of adulthood. *Anxiety* is inevitable because many basic needs are held in a state of dissatisfaction while others are gratified inconsistently. *Hostility* is commonplace because the adolescent is more adult than child, but is treated by society much more like a child than an adult. Sexual *frustration* is abundant because many adolescents are experiencing peak sexual arousal but have no conscience-sanctioned way to express it. *Self-doubt* is, for many individuals, at its greatest level since early childhood and from it springs self-hate and self-debasement.

The transitional nature of adolescence assures that life is not only stormy and turbulent, but in many instances, more than the adolescence can cope with. Two serious forms of psychopathology, depression and suicide, increase dramatically during late adolescence. The early adolescent is *comparatively* exempt from major psychopathology, although one often sees symptoms of illness incubating within the evolving personality.

Our tendency to view the carefree side of adolescence makes it easy to overlook the fact that it is a time of dramatic stress. This oversight distorts our perceptions, as Keniston has noted, "Admirers and romanticizers of youth tend to identify youth with virtue morality, and mental health. But to do so overlooks the special youthful possibilities for viciousness, immorality, and psychopathology." He then goes on to note:

> Every time of human life, each level of development, has its characteristic vices and weaknesses, and youth is no exception. Youth is a stage, for example, when the potentials for zealotry and fanaticism, for reckless action in the name of the highest principles, for self-absorption, and for special arrogance are all at a peak. Furthermore, the fact that youth is a time of psychological change also inevitably means that it is a stage of constant recapitulation, reenactment, and reworking of the past. This reworking can rarely occur without real regression, whereby the buried past is re-experienced as present and, one hopes, incorporated into it. (1975A, p. 22)

A time of life which witnesses dramatic increase in the incidence of suicide, homicide, depression, and schizophrenia is indeed a difficult time. Psychopathology during adolescence, quite obviously, does not characterize all youth. Its incidence, however, is sufficiently high to merit our attention. In order to better understand all aspects of adolescent life stress we shall here take a brief glimpse into some of the psychology of adolescence.

Adolescent Neurosis

Neurosis is a term which indicates that an individual is experiencing great difficulty coping with life stress. In the attempt to void overpowering anxiety, unrealistic coping devices develop which increase anxiety and make impossible the alleviation of conditions which cause psychic problems. The neurotic adolescent evaluates everyday events as threatening and dangerous and experiences severe anxiety when required to deal with ordinary events which non-neurotic youngsters take in stride. Although neurosis takes many forms during the adolescent years, its common denominators include: *the subjective experiences* of tension, anxiety, and fearfulness and *somatic symptoms* such as headaches, generalized aches and pains, heart palpitations, stomach distress, and digestive problems.

Neurosis during adolescence is difficult to diagnose because normal teenage behaviour often appears neurotic to the outsider. Anna Freud, who views adolescence as an extremely turbulent phase in the life cycle, claims that:

. . . adolescence constitutes by definition an interruption of peaceful growth which resembles in appearance a variety of other emotional upsets and structural upheavals. The adolescent manifestations come close to symptom formation of the neurotic psychotic or dissocial order and merge almost imperceptibly into borderline states, initial, frustrated or fully-fledged forms of almost all the mental illnesses. Consequently, the differential diagnosis between the adolescent upsets and true pathology becomes a difficult task. (1968, pp. 16-17)

The difference between normal and neurotic distress is that the latter lasts longer, leads to more severe crises, and prompts the use of defensive reactions such as denial and projection which make interpersonal relationships difficult and short-circuit the ability to satisfy basic needs such as love, belonging, and esteem. Normal distress periods, when they have run their course, do not leave adolescents plagued with neurotic coping devices or interpersonal habits which completely alienate them from others.

Neurotic adolescents meet stressful situations with withdrawal, retreat, and sometimes indifference; they fail to cope with problems so that they can be solved; they fail to encounter anxiety in such a way that it will eventually be overcome. The neurotic character structure is inclined toward compulsiveness, inhibition, and rigidity. In short, neurotic adolescents do not cope well with their inner self nor with their outer world; they hide from problems or confront them unrealistically; they do not believe in their own worthwhileness nor do they believe in their ability to deal with ordinary life stress. One is merely a shell of a person, filled with anxiety and trembling at the prospect of living.

The constant stress of the troubled adolescent exacts a tremendous price on all body systems. Anxiety interferes with sleep and diet habits, thereby denying the adolescent the rest and nutrition required for normal existence; anxiety fosters hyperactivity and general nervousness which result in undue fatigue. Stomach troubles become fairly commonplace as tension impedes normal digestion. In short, psychological tension is devastating to the biological body.

The effect of stress on the adolescent growth cycle is graphically demonstrated by the fact that when the adolescent is experiencing chronic stress there is an overproduction of adrenal steroids which inhibit physical growth by working against the growth hormone from the pituitary. Although it is uncertain exactly how this mechanism works, it is thought that prolonged chronic stress exerts a significant influence on adolescent growth patterns.

Adolescent Depression

Adolescence is the first time in the life cycle when psychological depression becomes fairly commonplace. Although some examples occur during childhood, they are extremely rare when compared with the incidence during adolescence. Depression is a condition of discouragement and sorrow characterized by prolonged periods of apathy, listlessness, and passive resentment; the depressive adolescent exhibits very restrictive interests, diminished activity, and extreme reluctance to get involved in social or recreational activities. Self-confidence is nonexistent; concentration is minimal; initiative is zero; feelings of hostility and resentment appear to be the major emotional states. Body complaints such as headaches, loss of appetite, tiredness, tension, restlessness, and fatigue are common.

Depression goes against every developmental need of adolescence and serves no constructive function. Depression is an illness brought about by a history of anxiety experiences within a personality which has not learned to cope with life stress. Certain environmental conditions are more likely than others to precipitate depressive reactions, especially those which pose constant threat to the ego and provide little love or reassurance. Certain adolescents are more likely than others to experience depression, especially those who have low stress tolerance, strong feelings of inadequacy, and disturbed interpersonal relationships. Depression is comparatively rare among early adolescence, more common during middle adolescence, and reaches its peak during late adolescence.

Some authorities believe that late adolescence is a period of life when the normal experiences of living predispose youth to depression or other psychological difficulties. Consider this:

> Phenomenologically, youth is a time of alternating *estrangement* and *omnipotentiality*. The estrangement of youth entails feelings of isolation, unreality, absurdity, and disconnectedness from the interpersonal, social, and phenomenological world. Such feelings *are probably more intense during youth than in any other period of life*. In part they spring from the actual disengagement of youth from society; in part they grow out of the psychological sense of incongruence between self and world. Much of the psychopathology of youth involves such feelings, experienced as the depersonalization of the self or the derealization of the world. (1975A, p. 10)

Depressed adolescents have extreme difficulty going about the business of being adolescents. They shun social gatherings and thus fail to develop competency skills with peers; they hide from potential sources of anxiety and thus fail to cultivate the ability to endure normal life stress; they give virtually no affection and thereby alienate those who could provide the love and esteem they so desperately crave. Depression during adolescence sets the stage for more serious disorders, including schizophrenia, which is perhaps the most severe of all psychogenic disorders no matter what age the victim is.

Few cases of *schizophrenia* appear before the age 15; however, a significant percentage of *all* schizophrenia admissions fall in the 15 to 29 age bracket. Neubauer, for example, reports that of all new admissions to a state mental hospital less than one percent are under age 15, but about 16 percent are between 15 and 29. This data indicates that hospitalization due to psychological disturbance, whatever the reason, dramatically increases during late adolescence and early adulthood.

Adolescents who experience considerable stress, or whose behaviour is linked with delinquency, drug abuse or serious school problems tend to have *unique perceptions of their parents*. In a study conducted by Nihira et al., (1975) an attempt was made to discover how disturbed teenagers viewed their parents. The research took place in an adolescent "crisis ward" during a two-year period and involved 86 youth between the ages of 12 and 18. The youngsters were in four distinct crisis groups — suicidal, aggressive, psychotic, and drug-induced psychotic. Each of the patients completed a questionnaire which asked how their parents acted towards them. The findings stressed two relevant themes:

1. The parents of these adolescents were seen *by the adolescents themselves* as being more punitive, restrictive and as placing higher achievement demands on them than did adolescents from a control sample.
2. There was no noticeable difference in parent perception among the four patient groups even though the kinds of disturbed behaviour they manifested varied considerably.

Interestingly, even though the adolescent patients in this study held rather negative perceptions of their parents, they attributed *circumstances in their daily lives* as being more important to the crises they were currently experiencing. These circumstances included: use of powerful drugs; lack of close friends and a feeling that their peers did not like them; losing people who were important to them; physical punishment by parents; and, being out of school or unemployed.

Among many youth a life space known as *existential neurosis* appears. This condition encourages depression although, unto itself, it is not as serious as depression. Here is how Salvatore Maddi describes it:

The way I have defined it, the existential neurosis is characterized by the belief that one's life is meaningless, by the affective tone of apathy and boredom, and by the absence of selectivity in actions. This symptom cluster is, to judge from the writing of many psychotherapists, sociologists, and social crisis . . . rampant in contemporary life. It may seem as if what I am talking about as existential neurosis is much closer to alienation from self, than it is to alienation from society. But on reflection, it should be clear that the existential neurotic would be separated from deep interaction with others as well as from his own personal vitality. Therefore, I find the existential neurotic to be alienated both from self and from society. (1969, p. 44)

Existential neurosis results in what Maddi describes as a "rather comprehensive psychological death where there is no longer even anguish or anger to remind the person that he is a person, and a very dissatisfied one at that." (Ibid.) Thus, the characteristics of existential neurosis include: loss of personhood, absence of strong feeling, inability to consider oneself worthy of significance, and inability to believe in the importance of anything.

Closely related to existential neurosis is a condition which I have labeled *psychogenic nihilism*. The cluster of symptoms which typify it include the following:

1. a cognitive view of meaninglessness which fosters cynicism, pessimism, and fatalism and which encourages adolescents to think of themselves and the people near them as meaningless;
2. an emotional state of boredom, monotony, apathy, and non-selectivity of actions which prevents the adolescent from becoming involved in relationships (or activities) which counter feelings of worthlessness;
3. low to moderate activity levels and "drift" behaviour causing actions to be unpredictable and boundaries nonspecific, which, in turn, makes it virtually impossible to predict what behaviour the adolescent will partake in;
4. absence of commitment, enthusiasm, and activeness and the presence of defence mechanisms which claim that such behaviour is stupid or self-defeating;
5. absence of belief in the worthwhileness or effectiveness of self; This should not be overlooked because individuals who do not believe in any form of higher values have nothing which can

establish their own personal validity and, consequently, come to define themselves with the same sense of neutral equivalence by which they define the rest of the world. Therefore, what we call poor self-image, low self-concept, and feelings of insignificance appropriately describe psychogenic nihilism.

6. social as well as personal alienation which make difficult the gratification of interpersonal needs such as love, belonging, and esteem;
7. an absence of intimacy relationships, I-Thou relationships, "helper" relationships, and love relationships;
8. a selfish, hedonistic approach to social relationships with minimal concern for the rights or subjective feelings of others;
9. radical absence of self-extension, self-transcendance, and self-pride and consequently, little activity which can help the adolescent overcome feelings of emptiness and noninvolvement.

Adolescent Suicide

No one knows for certain why adolescents kill themselves. Theories and viewpoints proliferate but consensus does not exist. Youth who fail in an attempt at suicide do not fit a uniform composite sketch, nor do they exhibit identical psychological mannerisms. In different societies, suicide has different meanings; therefore, it is difficult to generalize about it as a universal phenomenon. In North American society, however, a few constants present themselves for inspection. The vast majority of adolescents who attempt suicide (whether successful or not) are severely depressed, have recently experienced a series of ego-shattering experiences, or have a history of psychiatric disturbance. Except in examples of suicide occurring under the influence of drugs, adolescents who take their own life had found their existence to be meaningless, futile, and racked with unredeemable pain. As a rule, North American adolescents take suicide very seriously and attempt it only as a last gesture of compulsive self-affirmation, usually as an unconscious plea for help rather than a demand for the termination of life.

Considering the circumstances required to attempt suicide, one cannot help but wonder at the statistics which relate to it. Suicide is the fourth-ranking cause of death among 15- to 19-year-olds in our society, and the second-ranking cause of death among university students. Some experts estimate that one in every 35 deaths in the 15 to 19 age bracket results from suicide, and these estimates are conservative since many parents claim that their adolescent died of natural causes or an unavoidable accident. Reliable statistics concerning the ratio of suicide attempts to actual suicides are unavailable; however, estimates from 5:1 to 100:1, with most experts believing the true ratio to be somewhere in the vicinity of 50:1. Only one adolescent in every 50 who attempt suicide dies from the attempt.

The incidence of suicide increased dramatically during the 1950s and continued to rise during the 1960s, especially among the late-adolescent population. If a nucleus of causal factors contributes to adolescent suicide, it appears that these factors are increasing in intensity rather than decreasing or even remaining constant. In the United States, adolescent suicide rose nearly 50 percent during the 1950s, increasing from 4.0 per 100,000 to 5.9 per 100,000 (Toolan, 1966). The rate among 15-24-year-olds has increased by almost 300 percent during the past 20 years.

Most suicide victims are *not* psychotic or medically insane. Most of them suffer from feelings of hopelessness and despair and view their lives as empty and meaningless. The most consistent pre-suicidal symptom is "a deep, all-encompassing depression" and a belief that death is the only solution to life's struggles. Although it is common for adolescents to experience self-doubt, suicidal adolescents become almost paralyzed by feelings of helplessness. Youth who attempt suicide usually have lost the ability to communicate their feelings directly, and their outward symptoms of despair and sullenness tend to push people away from them, thus they become further isolated and estranged from meaningful interpersonal exchange (information taken from Klagsburn, 1976).

F. Klagsburn claims that there are several general indicators of an impending suicide attempt:

> There are other signs of suicidal depression: Some kids will give away all their possessions, as though they were preparing for a long trip. Some show radical changes in behaviour. A good student may begin to fail at school, and struggle to master work that once seemed easy. A normally cooperative, even-tempered youngster may become irritable and disruptive. An excellent athlete may give up all team activity and complain of aches and pains that have no medical basis.

> Persistent drug abuse or heavy drinking, running away from home, and even delinquent behaviour are other symptoms of the kind of despair that may lead to suicide.

Miller's investigation of adolescent suicide (1975) uncovered other factors. Miller found that one common denominator to teenage suicide was the loss of a loved person which caused unusual reactions within the adolescent. Adolescents may so strongly identify with the lost person that they want to "join" the person in death; sometimes there occurs magical thinking where adolescents believe they are being beckoned by the deceased.

Miller concurs with most investigators when he claims that the common emotion of suicide victims is depression. However, it is not always apparent to the observer because the depression may be interpreted as boredom or restlessness. Miller also concludes that many young people do not possess a "realistic" interpretation of death and somehow fail to recognize its finality.

Following a thorough investigation of psychological disturbance among *university students*, Ryle (1973, pp. 34-37) disclosed the following information. During the course of an undergraduate career, between one and two percent of all students will experience severe *psychiatric illness* of a type requiring hospitalization. The majority of this group will suffer from psychotic illness, some with schizophrenia, and some with affective psychoses such as manic-depression. A further 10 to 20 percent of the student population will encounter emotional problems serious enough to require some therapeutic treatment. Of this group, about one-third suffer from "relatively serious" neurotic and personality disorders. Approximately another 20 percent of the undergraduate student body will report transient or psychosomatic symptoms representing "reactions to the *normal* stress of their age and environment". This information, combined with the unusually high suicide rate among university students, causes us to conclude that university students (predominantly comprised of late adolescents and early adults) experience considerable psychological and biological stress in their daily lives.

Suicide among *early* adolescents is extremely rare. In an important study conducted by David Shaffer (1974) not one suicide was reported in the under 12 age group in a seven year period. Although suicide during this age period is rare (fewer than 1 in 800,000 12-14-year-olds take their own lives) a few noteable patterns emerge: (1) About twice as many boys as girls commit suicide. (2) Suicide victims of this age tend to be slightly above average in intelligence. (3) Almost half of the suicide victims had discussed, threatened, or attempted suicide prior to their successful attempt. (4) One circumstance appeared more than any other before the suicide: anti-social behaviour and the child's realization that the behaviour would be reported to the parents. (5) Two personality patterns were noted among many of the early-adolescent suicide victims. One pattern included superior intelligence, solitary and isolated social habits and distance from their parents. Another pattern included impetuous, aggressive, or violent outbursts; extreme sensitivity, and powerful resentment of criticism.

In conclusion, even though early-adolescent suicide occurs much less frequently than late-adolescent suicide, a few patterns emerge which distinguish it from suicide during other ages.

Table 1   *Mortality from five leading causes of death in the United States in 1970*

Cause	Number	Percentage	Rate/100,000
AGES 10 TO 14			
Accidents	4,218	49.9	20.3
Malignant neoplasms	1,078	12.8	5.2
Congenital anomalies	352	4.2	1.7
Influenza and pneumonia	307	3.6	1.5
Homicide	244	2.9	1.2
Other causes	2,247	26.6	10.8
Totals	8,446	100.0	40.6
AGES 15 TO 19			
Accidents	12,188	58.0	63.9
Homicide	1,536	7.3	8.1
Malignant neoplasms	1,389	6.6	7.3
Suicide	1,123	5.3	5.9
Influenza and pneumonia	406	1.9	2.1
Other causes	4,387	20.9	23.7
Totals	21,029	100.0	110.3
ALL AGES			
Major cardiovascular diseases	1,007,984	52.5	496.0
Malignant neoplasms	330,730	17.2	162.8
Cerebrovascular diseases	207,166	10.8	101.9
Accidents	114,638	6.0	56.4
Influenza and pneumonia	62,739	3.2	30.9
Other causes	197,774	10.3	97.4
Totals	1,921,031	100.0	945.3

Source: U.S. Public Health Service, National Center for Health Statistics 1974.

Mortality Among the Adolescent Population

During the adolescent period the number one killer of youth in North America is accidents. This holds true for early, middle, and late adolescents. However, significant differences exist in the second through fifth major causes of death. As Table 1 indicates, the second, third and fourth leading causes of death among *early* adolescents are major illnesses. Homocide, the fifth leading cause, accounts for less than three percent of total deaths. In the 15-19 age range, however, a different picture appears. Accidents remain the leading cause of death, but homocide is in second place, and suicide fourth. Combined they account for 70 percent of all deaths. Compared with the total population, this is dramatically out of scale. For *all ages* (see Table 1, 10.149) diseases account for about 84 percent of all deaths, with accidents and "other causes" totalling only 16 percent.

Table 2   *Sex ratio of mortality from leading causes of death, by age, United States, 1970*

Cause of death	\multicolumn{5}{c}{Number of female deaths per 100 male deaths by age groups}
	All ages	Under 1	1-4	5-14	15-24
All causes	57	77	81	63	36
Diseases of heart	50	72	87	92	63
Malignant neoplasms	69	115	81	78	60
Cerebrovascular diseases	83	69	57	76	78
Accidents	35	87	70	46	25
Influenza and pneumonia	58	77	76	103	73
Bronchitis, emphysema, and asthma	24	73	64	†	†
Cirrhosis of the liver	49	70	†	†	†
Suicide	39	†	†	†	31
Diabetes mellitus	107	†	†	†	116
Arteriosclerosis	79	†	†	†	†
Homicide	25	91	102	70	24

Source: Metropolitan Life Insurance Company, *Stat. Bull.*, August 1974.

Sex Differences in Adolescent Mortality

Adolescent boys and girls do not die from the same causes at the same rate. For example, in the 15-24 age group only 31 girls die from suicide for every 100 male suicides; only 24 girls die as a result of homocide for every 100 male deaths. Girls are more likely to die from diabetes mellitus, but excepting this disease, their death rate in every major category is lower than that of boys in this age bracket. (See Table 2 for further information.)

Summary

1. Virtually all youth experience growth tension. It is a matter of disagreement whether this tension is overpowering and results in a fundamental shift of the adolescent personality or whether it is coped with in the same general ways as life stress during other developmental stages. The "storm and stress" psychologists claim that adolescence is a traumatic life stage. Other psychologists are more moderate. Offer, for example, observes that many youth grow through the adolescent years in a rather smooth and uneventful progression.

2. There is no doubt that *many* adolescents experience considerable stress and strain. In their attempts to cope, they employ defense mechanisms and, periodically, neurotic coping devices.

3. The age of the adolescent influences the kinds of stress which must be coped with. During *early* adolescence, problems relate to adjustment to the developing body, concern with sexual feelings, apprehension about growing out of childhood and its protective structure. During middle adolescence, the stress of individuation from parents becomes more intense; self-consciousness about the attractiveness and acceptability of the maturing body bothers many youth, as does worry about sexual attractiveness and adequacy. During *late* adolescence, stressors assume a more "adult" dimension. Concern about one's masculine or feminine identity increases as does uncertainty about permanence in social and sexual relationships. In our society, anxiety about future employment and life career also take on added importance.

4. Late adolescence is the period when the greatest brunt of adolescent stress and strain registers. Virtually all forms of serious psychopathology increase over their middle or early-adolescence incidence. Suicide and homocide also increase during this time.

5. Defense mechanisms reduce the stress and strain of adolescent life

by distorting reality. They are self-deceptive because they originate in the unconscious, and because they reduce anxiety at the expense of perceptual accuracy. Although defense mechanisms are used by "normal" adolescents, they are the basis for serious behavioural problems known as neurotic coping devices.

6. The most typical of the defense mechanisms include: repression, the pushing of a thought, wish or memory into the unconscious where it is unable to cause ego anxiety; regression, using behaviours appropriate for a younger age in order to gain attention or to escape responsibility; rationalization, the tendency to explain events so that they flatter one's self-esteem; projection, the tendency to believe that other people's motives are the same as one's own; identification, the process whereby one identifies with the strengths of another in order to enhance personal feelings of strength.

7. Youth most likely to depend upon defense mechanisms in order to cope with the pressures of daily living include those who are rigid and inflexible, those who have low stress tolerance and who lack close friends, those who hold a low image of themselves and have difficulty handling the suffering which accompanies normal stress and strain.

8. When the stress and strain of daily living increases beyond the individual's ability to cope, and beyond the ability of defense mechanisms to distort reality so that it becomes manageable, it is not unusual for *neurotic reactions* to become part of the adolescent personality. Neurotic reactions involve a global behavioural influence which negatively affects virtually all facets of daily behaviour. The most typical include *anxiety reactions* where the individual experiences acute anxiety, fear and panic; *somatic reactions* where body discomfort and pain preoccupy the youth and force the forgoing of virtually all other involvements; *obsessive-compulsive* reactions where the person is continuously haunted by a recurring idea or attitude which cannot be escaped, or by the overpowering inclination to act out unusual behaviour; and finally, *depressive reactions* which cause sorrow, detachment, disinterest and reduced physical energy.

Neurotic coping reactions are more serious than mere defense mechanisms and often require help of a trained psychologist, counsellor or medical doctor. Some youth "work through" their neurotic reactions and become fairly normal adults. It is difficult to predict who will follow this pattern and who will become progressively more disoriented and disturbed.

9. *Depression* and *schizophrenia* are among the most severe forms of

adolescent psychopathology. Both conditions are more serious than any of the neurotic coping reactions and belong more to the classification of what clinical psychologists call *psychoses*. They involve a dramatic loss of personal maintenance and a seriously reduced ability to make decisions or form interpersonal bonds. Suicide is sometimes the outcome of a history of adolescent trauma. It rarely occurs to youth experiencing only transient problems.

The most severe psychopathology tends to occur during late adolescence or early adulthood. The earliest years of adolescence are characterized by an absence of severe disturbance, but this is not true for the later years.

Chapter Eight

Adolescent Sexuality

Sexual Behavior

Age is directly related to the outward manifestations of sexual activity *and* to the inward experience of sexual passion. The *early* adolescent tends to be sexually *in*active. The incidence of intercourse is low, as is petting and genital play with a partner. The *desire* for sexual play is strong for some youth this age, but not for most; sexual desire is as much based upon curiosity, experimentation and social competence as genital urges. During *middle* adolescence sexual urges become more a function of endocrinological changes; sexual appetite sharpens and leads to an increase in *all forms* of sexual activity. The incidence of pregnancy increases sharply over the child-adolescent phase, when it was virtually non-existent. In locales where abortion is legalized, its incidence also increases dramatically. In terms of *the total adolescent population,* however, sexual intercourse remains a minority experience; sexual adventuring exists in limited style, but is sufficiently rare that a sexual adventurer is known as such to his or her peers and holds unique status as a result. By *late* adolescence, sexual activity reaches its pre-adult peak. A great deal of it, however, takes place among couples who consider themselves bonded in one form or another, a significant percentage of whom aniticipate that their relationship will result in marriage. Sexual adventuring increases over its middle-adolescence rate, and intercourse *without* pregnancy becomes more likely.

However, to describe late adolescence as highly sexual is a misrepresentation. Only slightly more than half of all 19-year-old girls have *ever* had sexual intercourse; of the 15-19-year-old girls who have had intercourse about half of them have had only one sexual partner. About three-fourths of all girls between the ages of 15 and 19 have never had sexual intercourse or have had only one sexual partner in their entire life.

Most youth recognize that heterosexuality is something they must learn to deal with at their own pace and within the limits of their own personality. Although some adolescents show an urgency about finding a sexual partner, others contextualize it within the range of their total life requirements. Offer, whose research of *normal* adolescents is among the best available, notes that: "We have found that in heterosexuality our subjects were afraid of settling down too soon, of making an inexperienced decision . . . . In fact, they never seemed anxious to set their sights above what they felt they could handle." (p. 215, 1969)

Sexuality is now more complicated in some respects because the fear of pregnancy is reduced if normal contraceptive procedures are followed. Although this may make the act of sexual intercourse less an emotional strain it also requires the adolescent to base his or her decision about sexual intercourse on grounds other than the fear of pregnancy. In this regard Offer and Offer observe:

> The inexperienced adolescent must formulate a new rationale to aid him in proceeding at his own pace toward heterosexuality. Since the advent of modern contraceptive methods, the adolescent who feared that sexual relations would lead to pregnancy must develop other reasons for postponing intercourse. (1975, p. 170)

Sexual behaviour becomes more involved during late adolescence. However, the events which lead to "advanced" levels of sexual behaviour take place during *early* adolescence.

Before age 18 about one-third of the males and about 17 percent of the females report have experienced sexual intercourse once or more (Schofield, 1965, p. 33). This is rather impressive when we consider that before age 15 only six percent of the males and two percent of the females admitted to sexual intercourse. Thus, the great majority of adolescents who experience sexual intercourse *first do so during the 36-month period between ages 15 and 18*. Sexual intercourse does not simply "happen". Sexual behaviour advances through progressive stages, *culminating* with sexual intercourse.

Some *general trends* of sexual behaviour during adolescence are demonstrated in Tables 3 and 4. We note that sexual involvement with the opposite sex most often begins with kissing, later followed by breast fondling, active and passive genital stimulation and, finally, sexual intercourse. Obviously, Schofield's list does not exhaust the possibilities of sexual play; his data however, does indicate that sexual behaviour during adolescence follows a general pattern.

The fourteenth and fifteenth years are important. Although sexual intercourse occurs for only a small percentage, kissing (including deep "passion" kissing), and breast stimulation become increasingly more

Table 3

Accumulative incidence of seven sexual activities among boys showing percentage with experience at each age

Activity	Age							
	Under 12	12	13	14	15	16	17	18
Kissing	3.2	8.9	23.0	47.7	70	82	90	92
Deep kissing	—	0.6	3.0	15.0	27	46	61	70
Breast stimulation over clothes	1.1	2.0	6.0	17.0	36	55	71	80
Breast stimulation under clothes	0.5	1.1	3.5	11.5	25	43	60	69
Active genital stimulation	0.4	1.1	2.1	6.7	16	30	45	56
Passive genital stimulation	0.2	0.9	1.6	4.4	10	22	37	44
Sexual intercourse	0.2	0.5	0.9	2.3	6	14	26	34

Table 4

Accumulative incidence of seven sexual activities among girls showing percentage with experience at each age

Activity	Age							
	Under 12	12	13	14	15	16	17	18
Kissing	2.1	6.5	25.0	54.0	80	94	95	96
Deep kissing	—	—	3.6	16.6	40	62	75	83
Breast stimulation over clothes	0.2	0.6	3.2	15.0	38	58	74	80
Breast stimulation under clothes	—	—	0.8	7.2	19	36	51	62
Active genital stimulation	—	—	0.1	0.9	4	11	19	31
Passive genital stimulation	—	—	0.1	2.2	10	21	33	46
Sexual intercourse	—	—	0.1	0.4	2	5	10	17

Source: Schofield, M. *The Sexual Behaviour of Young People*. London: Longmans, Green and Co., Ltd., 1965, pp. 33 and 34. Reprinted by permission of Longman Group Limited and Little, Brown and Company, ©1965.

common. Kissing and petting lead to sexual intercourse rather infrequently before the age of 16.* Whereas only 25 percent of the girls have participated in "romantic" kissing before age 14, over 80 percent

* This does not deny sexual intercourse does take place. Nor does it deny that boys and girls who are sexually experienced at this age may be *very* experienced. It shows that most 14- and 15-year-olds who engage in kissing and "petting" do not proceed to sexual intercourse. *Most* postpone sexual intercourse until late adolescence or the early twenties.

have done so by the end of the fifteenth year. About 16 percent of the males and 10 percent of the females have experienced genital fondling by members of the opposite sex before 16. This appears rather significant when we note that before the fourteenth birthday the same behaviour occurred for only two percent of the males and less than one percent of the females. There is little doubt that, for many adolescents, ages 14 and 15 are the years when sexual behaviour becomes more advanced.

Schofield's data was gathered during the early sixties. Some researchers maintain that sexuality (including the incidence of sexual intercourse) has increased since then. Zelnick and Kantner's data, for example, indicate that 15-19-year-old girls are more sexually active. Based on a 1977 study Zelnick and Kantner claim that about 55 percent of all girls under age 19 have experienced sexual intercourse, as compared with only 27 percent in 1971. Their research shows a steady upward progression directly related to age, as far as sexual intercourse is concerned. For instance, about 18 percent of the 15-year-old girls have had intercourse; about 25 percent of the 16-year-olds; about 41 percent of the 17-year-olds; about 45 percent of the 18-year-olds; and, about 55 percent of the 19-year-olds. This general increase also takes place, according to age, with regard to the use of contraception, and the tendency to think of one's sexual mate as a future marriage partner.

Boys experience their *first* sexual intercourse with girls near their same age in about 56 percent of the cases; girls, however, have their first intercourse with an older male in about 66 percent of the cases studied. Girls who first had intercourse before they were 17 almost always had older partners; of the girls who first had intercourse at age 15, their partners were older 97 percent of the time. In accordance with this trend, boys whose first intercourse occured at 14 invariably started with older girls. Research indicates that the younger sexual intercourse begins, the greater the likelihood that the partner is older. For adolescents as a group, about a third of the boys and two-thirds of the girls are introduced to sexual intercourse by an older partner (Schofield, pp. 59 and 60).

Interestingly, 54 percent of the males and 61 percent of the females had their *second* experience with sexual intercourse *within one month* of their first experience, and 86 percent of the boys and 80 percent of the girls within six months after first intercourse. These data indicate that once the initial experience has occurred, it is likely to occur again within a comparatively short period of time.

Sexual intercourse is not always a pleasant experience. In one study it was found that 47 percent of the girls claimed their first experience with intercourse produced reactions of shame, fear, or disappointment; 29 percent of the boys agreed that these terms described their reactions to first sexual intercourse. Only 30 percent of the girls said they "liked" first intercourse; 48 percent of the boys, however, said they "liked" their first intercourse (Schofield, 1965, p. 65).

Masturbation   Self-stimulation of the genitals does not begin during adolescence, to be sure; for most people it begins during childhood and continues through adulthood. During early adolescence, boys first experience *orgasm* as a result of masturbation. Female masturbation, likewise, takes place during adolescence, but with less consistency and with less incidence of orgasm than for boys.*

Data gathered by Kinsey (1953, p. 173) reflect the different patterns of adolescent masturbation of boys and girls. By age 15, about 80 percent of the boys have masturbated to orgasm, while only 20 percent of the girls have done so. By age 20, the respective percentages have increased to 92 and 33. Data presented by Gagnon (1972, p. 240) indicate the greater *incidence* of male masturbation. Among a group of more than 580 high school students, 77 percent of the males admitted to masturbating twice a week or more, whereas only 17 percent of the females reported this incidence of masturbation. It was also noted that only 11 percent of the boys stated they never masturbated, where 60 percent of the girls reportedly abstained from masturbation.

Boys from lower socio-economic groups tend to engage in masturbation less than do middle-class boys. The reasons for this are unclear, but it is assumed that lower-class males view masturbation as an admission of inability to secure females for intercourse, whereas the middle-class boys think of it more as pleasurable release, having nothing to do with sexual prowess.

Male sexual behaviour during the past 30 years   Few studies have been conducted on the nature of male sexual behaviour, and even fewer on the differences between the young males of the 1940s versus those of the 1970s. One researcher, however, was able to utilize the same "sex practices and beliefs" questionnaire to male college students almost 30 years apart. The 1940's males were slightly over 19-years-old, whereas

---

*It should be noted that in recent years female masturbation has been thought of more positively than in the past. Research on female orgasm indicates that clitoral stimulation, rather than vaginal penetration, is the key factor in orgasm. Most sexologists today recommend a variety of methods for female sexual arousal, including masturbation. Some doctors claim that masturbation, if not abusive to tissue, is not harmful and may contribute to a more complete sexual experience.

the average age of 1970's group was over 21, therefore, age differences may have influenced the overall results. Nevertheless, here are some of the findings of the differences and similarities between the sexual habits of young college men over a 30 year period:

1. The age of the first nocturnal emission remained the same — 13.5 to 13.8 years of age.
2. Masturbation occured in 93 percent of the 1940's group, and 95 percent of the 70's group; the age of first masturbation was about the same for both groups, however, the 70's males reported a greater monthly incidence of masturbation.
3. About 45 percent of the 40's males reported having experienced premarital intercourse, whereas about 72 percent of the 70's males claimed they did. The 70's group had their first sexual intercourse at about age 15 whereas the 40's group, on the average, at age 17.
4. The 70's group, though having a higher percentage of males who have experienced intercourse, report a fewer number of sexual partners than did the male group of the 40's.

The researcher in this study claims that male sexual behaviour has not radically changed over the past 30 years if this group of college males is typical of the entire population. (Finger, 1975)

Adolescent Sexual Involvement

Sexual expression *is* important to youth. It is *not* the dominant fact in their lives. The sexual impulse *is* strong (especially in late adolescence); it is *not* the strongest life impulse at this age. The pleasure of sexual gratification *is* intense during the teen years. It is *not* the pleasure to which all other pleasures are compared. Searching for a sexual partner *is* a fact of adolescent social life. It is *not* the dominant fact.

Adolescence is the first time in the life cycle where sexual feelings are experienced in a direct, concrete way. Hormone-induced sexual arousal begins with puberty; before then human sexuality is a mixture of curiosity, fantasy, and uncertainty. It has little urgency, nor does it grip the person with desire and passion. Therefore, the experience of sexual arousal is a new sensation to which the adolescent must adjust.

Because an impulse is natural does not mean that it fits gracefully into the personality. New impulses create new desires and cause new behaviours. When these desires conflict or when behaviour contradicts the demands of the conscience, the result is tension. The sexual impulse

160

forces the young person to change attitudes, to adopt new behaviour, and to doubt viewpoints made obsolete by the changing body.

The adolescent is not likely to risk *social rejection* or *personal ridicule* to satisfy sexual impulses. One of the major functions of adolescent courtship is to find a partner with whom sexual exploration can take place with some assurance that ego injury will be kept to a minimum. The task is not merely to find a partner with whom sexual activity *per se* may take place, but to find a partner who behaves in such a way that the emotional pressures do not prove overpowering or self-defeating. *Weaving together the subjective feelings of passion with the objective impulse of sexual desire* is the dominant predicament of adolescent sexual adventure. The sexual impulse itself plays only a single role in this complex drama; equally important players are self-concept, social acceptance, and personal morality.

It is generally assumed that males possess more intense sexual impulses than females. This conclusion is based not only upon observations in human cultures, but among other primates as well. The extent to which it can be explained by endocrinological factors more effectively than by social factors is a matter of controversy. The chief hormone during male puberty is *testosterone*. Its primary effect is to promote growth and development of the reproductive system and to enhance the development of other body tissues, such as muscles. Testosterone acts both as a sex hormone *and* a growth hormone, therefore it is incorrect to think its only function is to promote sexuality.

Males who demonstrate *a lack of sexual motivation* are sometimes adminstered testosterone. However, the administration of testosterone has no proven effect in heightening the sexual responsiveness of *healthy* males; most cases of impotence are psychogenic. Some psychologists argue that if *lack* of sexual interest is psychogenic, then an increased or overly zealous interest is probably also psychogenic. "We can therefore conclude," claims Katchadourian, "that although the presence of an adequate amount of androgen does not ensure sexual adequacy, a substantial lack of the hormone will certainly hamper it" (1977, p. 99). At any rate, it is not precisely clear why males evidence stronger sexual inclinations than females during adolescence (if in fact they do). The endocrinological facts do not make a clear case one way or the other.

The intensity of the sexual impulse is not uniform from person to person. Psychology traditionally has given special attention to those youth for whom the urge for sexual expression is strong, or those for whom it exerts a dominant influence on their fantasy and actions.

161

Without doubt, sexual energy is a major factor in adolescent life and its discharge is a central fact of teen existence. Consider, for example, the observation of Gordon Allport, one of the eminent American psychologists of this century, on the topic of *late-adolescent sexuality*.

> We should face the fact that at least in the early years of college life, crises in the sexual sphere are for the most part frankly genital in their reference. The biological drive is so powerful that the youth is concerned with it almost by itself. Its integration into mature love, into marriage, into career plans, into an embracing philosophy of life, exceeds his present capacity. He is likely to think that genitality by itself is maturity. Sexual gratification is frankly the aim, often with devastating consequences. At this stage of development, the students have much to say about sex and little to say about mature love. (1969, p. 301)

On the other hand, some evidence suggests that sexual impulses are not as strong among *all* youth as Allport believes. For example, only about half of the boys and girls have participated in genital play with a member of the opposite sex by age 18. (See Schofield, 1965.) This indicates that even though the sexual impulse may be strong, it is held in check by other powerful factors. What these factors are is subject to considerable debate, but it is clear that they exert as much influence on sexual behaviour as does the sexual impulse itself.

Adolescent Attitudes Towards Sexuality

Much of the following information concerning the sexual habits and attitudes of adolescents is based upon the research of Robert Sorensen (1973). The findings are based upon a national sample in the United States representing the adolescent population. Sorensen's investigation dealt with the sexual motives, beliefs, and attitudes of youth as well as their actual sexual behaviour. The information provided herein represents only a brief overview of Sorensen's research and is intended to illuminate some of the attitudes of adolescent sexuality.

The majority of all adolescents (69 percent) feel that more is involved in sexual relations than sheer physical pleasure. The general trend is that older age groups (16 to 19) place less emphasis on the physical pleasure aspect of sexuality than do younger adolescents. This finding accords with the assumption that as the need for intimacy increases during late adolescence, sexual behaviour takes on a deeper emotional component;

therefore, it is treated more seriously.

Most youth do not engage in sexual behaviour because they deliberately choose to break rules set up by parents or society. A stronger motivation for initial sexual behaviour is *experimentation* blended with the thrill of experiencing a pleasurable sensation. The need to experiment with one's emotions and sensations is a significant factor in adolescent sexual behaviour. Interestingly, Sorensen reports that *older* adolescents are more willing to limit sexual relationships to one person, with 76 percent of the older girls and 44 percent of the older boys claiming they would prefer one partner for long-term sexuality.

Most youth who have not experienced sexual intercourse claim that they are not as yet "ready" for it and tend not to feel that they are "missing" something of great importance. Of all youth in this study, 62 percent of the boys and 51 percent of the girls felt that with the beginning of sexual relations there emerges a new sense of maturity and growing up. This budding realization of imminent adulthood influences the entire spectrum of adolescent behaviour and requires that adults take in consideration the adolescent's escalating social and biological maturity. Although many symbols signal the onset of adulthood, it appears that the one which makes the strongest difference to the adolescent is the ability to participate in meaningful sexuality.

Adolescents are more stringent in defining their own personal standards of sexual morality than in setting standards for others. This interesting reversal of the pre-adolescent tendency to judge others more severely than oneself reflects the advances in moral outlook which take place during adolescence. Youth, while they may not openly condone the sexual behaviour of their peers, usually will not condemn it either. Most people studied in the Sorensen investigation believed that *younger* adolescents are more impelled toward sexual involvement because of peer group pressure than are older adolescents, with boys being influenced more strongly than girls. This supports the observation that during the early-adolescent years sexual behaviour is governed more by social needs and expectations than by private needs such as intimacy. Also, when we consider that many early adolescents report that they do *not* experience strong passion during sexual play it becomes apparent that the full force of chemical sexuality does not emerge until middle or late adolescence. Girls provide the most frequent exceptions to this generalization because they are approximately one-and-one-half years more developmentally advanced than boys by middle adolescence.

Many boys feel that girls use sex as a form of reward or punishment;

72 percent of the girls saw such a phenomenon occurring in *both* directions, with boys as well as girls withholding sexual favours as a form of punishment and granting sexual favours as a form of reward. Boys consistently perceive girls as using this reward-punishment scheme but rarely see themselves as using it.

About half of the adolescents studied felt that sex could be used as a diversion from the pressures of life. Most youth claim that during sexual activity they experience temporary euphoria, with physical and emotional sensations overriding the pressing problems of day-to-day life. Because sex is a relatively new experience for adolescents (most of them being only two or three years beyond puberty), its sensations are magnified by the thrill of novelty, the abstraction of maturity, and the excitement of tasting forbidden fruit.

The majority of youth feel that parental prohibition does not prevent them from experiencing sex. For example, 63 percent of all adolescents polled answered affirmatively to this statement: "Living at home with my parents does not interfere with my sex life." Despite this, only 30 percent of the older boys answered affirmatively to: "My sexual behaviour is pretty much the way my parents would want it to be." This apparent contradiction reflects the situational predicaments which give rise to adolescent hypocrisy.

Sorensen's research indicates that boys plan their sexual activities more precisely than do girls and employ more persuasive tactics. Girls, while not exempt from such calculations, tend to rely more upon their spontaneous reactions and the mood of the moment. As one would expect, sexually experienced youth are better able to handle the social and physical mechanics of sexual activity. With practice comes proficiency.

Girls *tend* to stress the importance of love in sexual behaviour more than boys. Girls are more likely to be offended when they sense that a relationship is based exclusively on physical pleasure. Despite their differences concerning the importance of "love" in sexual involvement, boys and girls alike agree that sexual behaviour is a personal matter not to be judged by others. Their concepts of right and wrong tend to be highly personalized and they show little interest in evaluating rightness or wrongness in matters of sex. However, general matters relating to sex, such as the double standard, tend to be perceived as "wrong". Interestingly, 77 percent of all adolescents studied believed that the sexual behaviour of most adolescents is unacceptable to society as a whole. Thirty-eight percent claimed they would not go against the general standards of society. However, 62 percent felt their own interests have priority over those established by society; therefore, they would not be reluctant to engage in sexual behaviour generally thought improper.

Concerning *pre*marital intercourse, 80 percent of the boys and 72 percent of the girls felt that sex before marriage is acceptable if the partners are "in love". On the other hand, few adolescents are tolerant of *extra*marital affairs, and virtually all adolescents condemn the sexual activity of adults which requires deception and lying. Ironically, most adolescents admit that their own sexual activity is characterized by deception and partial truths, especially with regard to what they tell their parents.

Despite their tendency to perceive sexual behaviour as a personal matter which should not be overly censured by others, adolescents hold fairly uniform ideas concerning sexual "responsibility", clinging firmly to the belief that certain kinds of sexual adventure are undesirable. For example, almost all youth (88 percent) questioned in the Sorensen investigation agreed that "it is *immoral* for a boy to *force* a girl to have sex, no matter what the circumstances". This finding confirms that adolescents in North America have incorporated into their sexual attitudes the culture-wide belief that sexuality should involve free consent by the partners and should exclude unwanted violence. Most adolescents agreed that "sex is immoral for people who are too young to understand what they are getting out of it". Therefore, society's rule not to exploit youngsters as well as society's belief that sexuality is "wasted" on those too young to appreciate it, is widely shared by adolescents.

Only 30 percent of the adolescents agreed with the statement. "A white girl and a black boy having sex together is something that I would consider immoral, even if both of them wanted to do it." The percentage does not change appreciably when the situation is changed. Only 33 percent agreed that "A white boy and black girl having sex together is something that I would consider immoral, even if both of them wanted to do it". Thus, we observe that even though adolescents agree with cultural beliefs concerning forced sexuality and sexual behaviour involving those too young, they seem to be at odds with the general belief that sexual intercourse between blacks and whites is undesirable. Finally, only 25 percent of all youth (and only seven percent of *late*-adolescent boys) agree that sex is immoral when the partners are not married to each other. (Sorensen, 1973, p. 105)

Very few adolescents could be described as sexually carefree. Sex is a serious matter not easily separated from their sense of personhood; they are considerably less able than young adults to partake in recreational or impersonal sexual escapades; and they are more likely to be crushed when a sexual partner does not take them seriously.

Neither are they uninhibited. To be seen in the nude, even by one's sexual partner, is embarrassing to a considerable number of teenage boys and girls because they remain shy and awkward about their "new" body and because they frequently are ignorant about their partner's body. They joke about sex, but not in a confident, matter-of-fact way, rather more along the lines of nervous bantering. As a rule, sexually active youth are conventional in positioning and other mechanical aspects of sexual intercourse. They are not daring innovators or experimentalists, therefore avant-garde sexuality does not appear. They are too inexperienced to have a great deal of confidence in their sexual abilities, therefore they tend to deal with the basics. Only a small percentage are sexually promiscuous, most of whom are late adolescents.

Adolescent boys demonstrate only a nodding acquaintance with what girls call sexual technique. They tend not to understand their partner, and appear singularly preoccupied with themselves. They are not callous or indifferent, rather, they are essentially oblivious to the differences in their approach versus their partner's approach to sexual expression. They frequently are not attuned to their partner in a romantic or chivalrous manner. Their partner is primarily an extension of their own passion. In a phrase, adolescent sexuality is egocentric, intense and concrete. It has remarkably few abstract qualities because it is too new and too engrossing to be viewed in any way except the personal.

The idea of the sexually promiscuous adolescent is encouraged by the idea that the automobile allows young people to travel unsupervised in a portable bedroom. The evidence does not indicate that the sexual habits of young people are determined by the automobile. For example, in one research study, between 40 and 50 percent of the sexually active girls had either *their first* or *their most recent* sexual experience in the home of their partner. Only about nine percent had their first intercourse in a car, and less than six percent had their most recent intercourse in an automobile. Only about five-six percent had either their first or their most recent coitus in a hotel or motel. This indicates that although mobility increases the opportunity for sexual experience, the incidence of sexual coupling in motels or automobiles is low, while the home of the partner remains the most likely location for the sexual rendezvous. (Zelnick and Kantner, 1977)

Zelnick and Kantner investigated the sexual habits of girls age 15-19 and found that among those who *were sexually active* over 60 percent had not had intercourse within the month previous to their research interview, indicating that they are not sexually active by adult standards. Among the sexually experienced girls of this age over 60 percent have had only one sexual partner, whereas only 25 percent have had either two or three partners in their sexual lives.

Girls tend to have sexual intercourse with older boys but the exact reasons why are not clear. For girls 17 or younger the chance is about 50 percent that their most recent sexual partner was 19 or older. The probable explanation is that older boys are able to cope with the subtle nuances required of sexuality and are better able to persuade a reticent female to become a sexual partner than are younger boys. Also, the chance is greater that they are sexually experienced and thus consider themselves "experts". On the practical side, they are more likely than younger adolescents to have private living quarters or friends who do, therefore, the privacy impediment to sexual relations is removed.

Even though boys and girls differ in some attitudes toward sexuality, they also share common interests and outlooks. For example, in a study conducted by Rubenstein, et al., (1976) it was found that ninth grade girls and ninth grade boys chose almost identical topics related to sexuality that they "wanted to know more about". The researchers studied the responses of 65 boys and 65 girls to a list of 112 sexual terms. The subjects were asked to list those topics about which they wanted to know more. The boys and girls *agreed on 12 of the 13 top ranked topics*.

The top 13 terms for each sex, beginning with the highest interest words for each are:

Girls	Boys
birth control	venereal disease
abortion	enjoyment of sex
birth control pill	sexual intercourse
venereal disease	birth control
pregnancy	love
love	oral intercourse
fear of sex	pregnancy
guilt about sex	abortion
rape	guilt about sex

enjoyment of sex	birth control pill
sexual intercourse	fear of sex
sex offenses	sex offenses
prostitution	prostitution

The adolescents in this study were concerned with the interpersonal aspects of sexuality more than with facts of anatomy. They wanted to know how intercourse affected their partners and the conditions under which it is likely to take place. In other words, they were as concerned with the interpersonal aspects of sexuality as with the physical aspects.

Psychological Factors in Adolescent Sexuality

The following psychological factors influence adolescent sexual behaviour: the need for intimacy; the need for belonging; the desire for dominance and submission; competence and exploratory motives; the desire for passion; imitation and identification; and rebelliousness and negative identity.

1. *Intimacy* Harry Stack Sullivan was among the first psychologists to stress the need for intimacy. Although definitions of "intimacy" vary, most of them include the need for close personal relationships with another person, the need for intense closeness and involvement with something meaningful. Intimacy can also be understood in terms of what it is not. It is the opposite of isolation, of estrangement, of alienation and is characterized by personal closeness rather than distance, by intensity rather than neutrality, by excitement rather than monotony, by general organismic feelings of completion rather than ambivalence, by a feeling of fusion rather than mere nearness. Intimacy implies sharing, taking into confidence, trusting.

The need for intimacy begins to manifest itself in pre-adolescence where the desire for a personal confidant first becomes central. With the partial disintegration of the peer group as well as the tendency toward heterosexual pairing-up, the intimacy need becomes even more accentuated. The emotional conflicts of adolescence "demand" a close companion; most adolescents find it difficult to make it through their daily existence without having someone in whom they can confide and articulate their most pressing problems.

The psychological need for intimacy is manifested physically in many ways. Embracing, holding, hugging, and general "hanging around" partially facilitate the intimacy experience. Sexual involvement is one physical expression of intimacy. Closeness, intensity, involvement, and self-surrender each are manifestations of the intimacy need.

Sexual behaviour can facilitate intimacy at levels other than the sexual. This is especially true among adolescents despite the commonly accepted maxim that psychological intimacy should *precede* sexual involvement. For adolescents with minimal meaningful involvement elsewhere, sexual behaviour is a basic avenue for creating bonds of psychological intimacy. This, of course, is not universally true but is more representative than most people (especially parents) care to acknowledge.

2. *Belonging* Most psychologists concur that belonging is a basic human need. Maslow includes it in his hierarchy, Murray in his listing of psychological needs (he calls it affiliation), and all neo-Freudians acknowledge it as a basic reality. Sociologists, perhaps more than psychologists, emphasize the need for group belonging and participation. Although Maslow distinguishes between belonging and esteem needs, it is not uncommon in general theory for them to be grouped together. The need to belong implies a sense of membership in, or participation with, another person or group. It differs from intimacy in that it need not be experienced directly in order to be gratified. That is, one's feeling of belonging can be satisifed when one is separated from that to which one belongs. Intimacy can be understood as the experiential component of a belonging need which has been satisfied.

A twofold relationship exists between adolescent sexuality and the need for belonging. (1) The need for belongingness compels adolescents toward one another. In certain instances a general compatibility or openness emerges which facilitates sexual behaviour. This can be stated another way: adolescents come together without much initial sexual attraction; however, in the course of being brought together a sense of openness, relatedness, and security may emerge. When this happens the probability is increased that sexual behaviour will ensue. In this respect the need for group affiliation prompts sexual experimentation and interaction. (2) The female acquiesces to the sexual demands of her partner because her sense of belonging (relatedness) is threatened if she refuses. This is not a case of clear-cut blackmail on the part of the male, but rather a case of the girl choosing behaviour partially out of fear of losing something she is psychologically pushed toward. This is an important consideration because usually the girl determines the degree of sexual activity. Generally, the male is more willing to engage in sexual behaviour, and usually will if he can locate a consenting female.

Thus, factors which increase the female tendency to condone sexual behaviour are related to its frequency.

3. *Dominance and Submissiveness*   A number of psychologists, Erich Fromm most notably, stress the need or desire for dominance in daily living. Although it is doubtful whether dominance meets the criteria of a psychological need, a good case can be made for its role in human sexuality. Dominance is generally understood to mean control or mastery over part of the environment. It doesn't imply the person is tyrannical or dictatorial, it simply means one exercises a working command of one's general environment.

Alfred Adler was one of the first psychologists to recognize the relationship between inferiority and dominance, and his theory asserts that each individual has relatively strong feelings of inferiority. These feelings can be coped with in a variety of ways, one of the more common being "compensatory" behaviour, which is the attempt to make up for feelings of inferiority by being dominant in other realms of life. Compensatory behaviour takes many forms: excellence in the classroom, arts, athletics, or sexual behaviour.

Submissiveness is a form of relatedness by which one accepts being controlled by another person. As is the case with dominance, this does not necessarily (but may) imply a pathological condition. In fact, many relationships are made more congenial by one partner assuming an essentially submissive role; parent-child, husband-wife, and employer-employee relationships are frequently of this variety.

By being sexually submissive (acquiescent) to the male, the female may find herself having several needs tended to at once: the need for intimacy, belonging, sexual expression, as well as her desire for submissiveness. Because our society condones female submissiveness more readily than male submissiveness, it is a more central reality among adolescent girls than boys. One might observe, however, there are strong forces at work in our present society reversing this general trend of feminine submissiveness!

4. *Curiosity and Competence Motives*   Robert White defines competence as ''an organism's capacity to interact effectively with its environment''. In the adolescent subculture, heterosexual interaction of all types is a central fact of life. In this respect, sexual behaviour is part of a personal-social reality toward which competency can be reached only by exploration, trial and error, etc. For adolescents (at least most of them) sexual behaviour is novel, exciting, and stimulating. Sexual explorations have the thrill of newness which accompanies virtually all

"first-time" behaviour, sexuality more so than most because of its intense experiential nature. Competence motives expedite the onset of heterosexual experimentation because experimentation is the only means by which competency is achieved.

It is interesting to note that parents would be quite indignant if their adolescent children showed the lack of initiative and exploratory interest in school work that is expected of them in matters sexual. To think the adolescent will not actively search out something so central as heterosexual relations is unrealistic in most instances.

It should be noted that exploratory behaviour in sexual activity does not mean that the adolescent pursues it in a cold-blooded manner. Most adolescents, in fact, require that specific conditions be met before sexual activity will occur. Usually this involves friendship, a certain amount of respect, a period of psychological intimacy, as well as sexual passion at the time of sexual behaviour. These conditions hold true especially for girls.

In summary, the concept is really quite basic. One cannot learn (whether child, adolescent, or adult) without tampering, exploring, investigating that which one is learning about. Sexual behaviour is certainly no exception to this generalization. Speaking in purely statistical terms, the incidence of sexual behaviour could be expected to increase during adolescence if for no other reason that the fact that there is no other way to learn about sexuality.

5. *Passion and Intensity*   In most realms of the adolescent life-style, itensity is sought after, preferred, desired. Adolescents are not "paced" individuals. They peak a lot. They are very up and down. When doing what they enjoy, they employ a wholehearted, flamboyant style; likes and dislikes are as intense as are attitudes. Many adolescents are prone toward experimentation simply on the recommendation that it will generate an intense experience.

Passion of all types, including the sexual have special allure. At an age when individuals are striving to assert their newly-emerging selves, this is critical. Shared passion, as in sexual behaviour, provides adolescents with even more valuable experience, since they not only experience themselves intensely, but are able to share the experience with another. Sexual passion is in essence a three-fold reality: (1) the intense experiencing of oneself, (2) an intense experiencing of another self, and (3) the experience of having someone else acknowledge the self. Passion, like intimacy, often is experienced via sexual behaviour more easily than by other means. Frequently, adolescents develop a dependency upon sexual behaviour to facilitate passion which is strong enough to be self-validating.

Most forms of passion find some takers in the adolescent subculture. Pied pipers are a dime a dozen and have a life span correspondent with their cost value: idols, heroes, and spokesmen come and go with a speed and urgency that bedazzles most adult observers. The most effective consolation for distressed adults lies in realizing that most heroes are short-term, relatively harmless, and that no one is quite sure what forms of release adolescent energy might take without them.

6. *Identification and Imitation*   Adolescents, like all people, tend to imitate and copy what they see, especially if it is socially valued or personally meaningful. In many respects ours is a sex-oriented culture. The mass media, the performing arts, the written arts as well as the visual arts abound with sexual content. Nudity decorates all of visual arts, and movies realistically portray most varieties of sexual behaviour. Even if it were not for the biological and psychological forces which push the adolescent toward sexuality, it seems probable that he or she would gravitate somewhat toward it simply by exposure through the media.

In addition to encouraging sexual experimentation, watching or reading about sexual activity is in itself arousing. By age 15, individuals without sexual experience with the opposite sex are aware they are missing something — they cannot help but be aware of this. For adolescents whose sexual drive (or psychological drives) toward sexuality are not pronounced, this is not much of a problem. However, for those strongly inclined toward sexual behaviour but who abstain because of various constraints, there is often a borderline feeling of incompleteness. This is not necessarily an intense psychological frustration, it is simply one additional variable which moves the normal adolescent toward sexual behaviour. It can be viewed in much the same way as other conformist tendencies; in itself it is not too significant but, when combined with the other conditions of adolescence, it increases the probability of sexual behaviour.

7. *Rebelliousness and negative identity*   Some adolescents engage in sexual behaviour because of a contempt for their parents. ''Negative identity'' is a term coined by Erik Erikson which refers to the ability to obtain satisfaction from engaging in behaviour contrary to what is expected. It is more than mere stubbornness or negativism, because the adolescent earns a sense of identity from this negative behaviour. Certain forms of harmless mischief are of this variety: stuffing the

172

janitor's closet with newspaper because of the predictable effect it will have on the principal's nervous stomach or wearing sweat shirts which ridicule a social value are examples of basically harmless manifestations of negative identity. As is the case with virtually all psychological factors, however, it can be carried to extremes. Moralistic or punitive parents often generate this reaction. They make themselves an object of frustration, increasing the possibility that an act of vengeance toward them will give the adolescent some consolation. Negative identity usually is manifested in such a way that it hits at the centre of a person (or symbol) who in one way or another is a "stressor" to the adolescent.

Although adolescents do not engage in sexual behaviour simply because of negative reaction toward their parents, this can be at least a fragment of their motivation (especially among teenagers who have intense conflicts with their parents). Hostility toward parents is commonly reported by teenage girls pregnant out of wedlock. These girls often admit a strong hostility, even hatred, for their parents, voicing their desire to get even with them or to cause them anguish.

Adolescent Pregnancy

In our society many adolescents get married and have children. Some adolescents have children and do not get married. Of this latter group some mothers give up their child for adoption and others raise the child themselves or with the help of their parents. The incidence of children born out of wedlock varies from year to year, but estimates place the figure at about 250,000 per year in Canada and the United States combined, with about 10 percent of the total coming from Canada.

As might be expected, it makes considerable difference whether the teenage mother is in early, middle or late adolescence. The younger the mother, the greater the range of difficulties. This section will deal with several aspects of adolescent pregnancy, including: (a) the health risks related to teenage pregnancy; (b) adolescents as parents; (c) sexual habits of girls who become pregnant; (d) the subconscious desire to become pregnant.

Health Risks

The health risks for both mother and child are considerable in teenage pregnancies. This point is worthy of special attention because most adults think of adolescents as healthy and robust, therefore, do not view pregnancy with alarm. Gordon (1973) in his analysis of the physical and mental health risks for teenage mothers and their children includes the following observations. A pregnant teenager runs a four to five times higher risk of pregnancy complications than woman in her twenties. The younger the teenager the greater the chance that medical irregularities will occur. Pregnant teenagers tend to be poor at prenatal care and they tend not to make use of the facilities available to them. The greatest pregnancy risks include toxemia (blood poisoning), premature birth and infant mortality. A premature child born to a teenager is four to five times as likely to have neurological defects or mental retardation as children of women in their twenties. The incidence of premature births is considerably greater for unwed mothers than for married mothers. The danger of child delivery for unmarried girls is considerable. The rate of *maternal deaths for unmarried mothers* is about 21 per 10,000 live births; however, for married women the rate is only about 5 per 10,000 births. The children of teenage parents tend to be shorter, underweight, behind their grade level and display greater behavioural problems than the children of older mothers. Both environmental and biological factors contribute to these increased ailments among the children of teenage mothers.

The suicide attempt rate among girls who have been pregnant is higher than for the adolescent population in general. Job opportunities for a teenage mother are low and often she becomes dependent upon welfare. When pregnancy leads to marriage the chance of that marriage ending in divorce is three times greater than for the population in general. In summarizing the incredible difficulties facing the pregnant teenager, Sarrel makes the following comments:

Pregnant teenagers are high risks medically, socially, and education-ally. Without care, they have high rates of toxemia, prematurity, and prenatal infant mortality. They fail to complete their education or obtain vocational training. When they marry, they more often than not get divorced, and when they do not marry, they often become trapped in a self-destructive cycle consisting of failure to continue education, de-pendence on others for support, failure to establish a stable family life, and repeated pregnancies. Not infrequently, depressed, defeated, and dependent, the teenage mother is poorly prepared to cope with the demands of family life and in particular, the responsibilities of parent-hood (1970).

The dramatic health risk to both mother and child is one of the major

174

reasons so many school districts are pressing for sex education in the schools. If Gordon's observation is correct, that the common denominator to pregnant girls is their lack of knowledge about the reproductive process, then education about the relationship between sexuality and reproduction may prove helpful in reducing the incidence of unwanted teenage pregnancy.

Adolescents as Parents

Teenagers as a group are not good parents. Their day-to-day frustrations are poorly coped with because their personality is immature and their identity diffuse. The tensions of parenting are often taken out on the infant. The research of V. De Lissovoy concluded that teenage parents are impatient, that they have low frustration tolerance, that they see normal infant behaviour as personal and negatively directed, and that they are apt to correct this by spanking and other physical discipline. Teenage parents are less able to control their angry feelings than are older parents and their children tend to suffer because of this (Schwartz, 1974).

It appears that a greater percentage of unmarried teenage mothers are keeping their children than in past decades. This trend, which began in the middle seventies, is documented by Creighton (1977) who claims, "The age of unmarried mothers is decreasing and they are less likely to place their babies for adoption than ever before." The tendency to keep children is partially encouraged by social workers who advise pregnant teenagers to keep their illegitimate children. In the past, social workers have consistently recommended releasing the baby for adoption. Another factor contributing to the trend is greater affluence among middle-income families which allows the teenage daughter and her child to live with the parents.

Many teenage mothers do not find parenting tolerable, and as a result more children than in past years are being brought to adoption agencies when they are 12-24 months old. Unpublished research conducted by L. Baker (Edmonton, Alberta) indicates that the younger the teenage mother the more likely she will try to keep the baby, where older teenage mothers (late adolescents) are more likely to place their child up for adoption. Middle adolescent mothers have less awareness of the difficulties of mothering, they seem to desperately crave the love of an infant, and they most consistently believe "that everything will turn out alright''. They also are the age group most likely to surrender their child after a year or two of parenting.

Sexual Habits

Many adolescents do not know much about sexuality, especially as it relates to the reproductive process. Even those youth who are sexually active often do not understand the relationship between sexual intercourse and pregnancy. "It appears there is a high level of ignorance about sex among sexually active adolescents. Surprisingly, *sexually active young people are less knowledgeable than their inexperienced peers* . . . . Early sexual experience seems to promote an unwillingness to learn about sex, partly because the individual feels he or she is already knowledgeable, and partly because there is the fear of appearing naïve if one seeks information" (Gordon, 1973, p. 16).

The tendency for the sexually active to know less than the sexually inactive has also been demonstrated among university coeds. Crist (1970) adminstered a questionnaire on sexual anatomy to 600 coeds. The girls with the least sexual experience scored higher on the questionnaire than did those girls with the most of sexual experience. From this information Gordon concludes: "the notion that increased sexual knowledge will be followed by increased sexual activity is not very impressive. Youthful ignorance goes hand in hand with greater risk taking, characterized by . . . failure to take precautions against pregnancy and venereal disease." Gordon then surmises that "a high level of knowledge tends to be associated with a more cautious and responsible approach to sexual behaviour" (1973, p. 19).

There does not appear to be a direct link between sexual promiscuity and pregnancy during adolescence. For those girls who engage in sexual intercourse few differences are found between those who get pregnant and those who do not. One research team found that the only detectable difference between these two groups was that the girls who became pregnant knew considerably less about contraception. Teenage pregnancies *tend to* result from relationships which have lasted a considerable length of time, rather than from casual sexual encounters. A study conducted in Baltimore found that only 17 percent of the pregnant unwed girls had *more than* one sexual partner during the year preceding pregnancy. Other studies also indicate that pregnant teenagers tend *not* to be promiscuous. Schofield studied sexually active girls who *were not*

176

pregnant, and found that they also were, for the most part, involved with only one sexual partner. He found that 75 percent of the girls had only one sexual partner in the previous year. Thus, it can be assumed that girls who become pregnant and those who do not (but who are also sexually active) are not significantly different in their sexual habits, but perhaps are different in their knowledge of how to avoid pregnancy. It can also be inferred that adolescent girls take rather seriously our society's ideas about having only one sexual partner, and that this partner be a person with whom one is "in love". This supports the view that adolescents probably are more conventional in their sexual practices than are the adults of our society, and that they behave closer to the "spirit" of sexual rules than do adults.

Some research has been conducted to ascertain if unwed mothers who place their babies up for adoption differ in their sexual habits and their dating practices from unmarried mothers who keep their child. Nettleton and Cline (1975) obtained information from 550 unwed mothers in an attempt to discover how dating habits, sexual habits, and general relationships with men were influenced by being an unmarried mother. They found that unmarried mothers *who kept their children* reported a lower rate of dating, but that their incidence of sexual intercourse and their use of contraceptives was about the same as those mothers who had placed their children up for adoption. The survey also indicated that unmarried mothers who kept their children are equally as likely to marry as those who give up their children. Of special relevance was the finding that within 18 months of having the baby, nearly three times as many unmarried mothers who kept their child got married as those who had given up their child.

Some other findings of the Nettleton study include:

1. 86 percent of unmarried mothers reported they were dating at the time of the study.
2. More of the mothers who gave up their children were dating than those who kept their child.
3. About half of all of the unmarried mothers were having intercourse (which is about the same percentage as among 19-year-olds who have never been pregnant); however, 75 percent were using contraceptives (which is a higher percentage than among late adolescents who have never been pregnant).
4. In general, unmarried mothers are not turned away from men, dating or sex.

The Unconscious Desire to Become Pregnant

Disagreements exist among authorities as to the importance of sexuality not only during adolescence, but adulthood as well. Part of the problem derives from the fact that adolescent girls who seem to understand the ovulation cycle nevertheless engage in sexual intercourse during periods when the chance of pregnancy is high. For some girls this is a complete break from their general life-style where they do not risk so boldly. Some experts have concluded that among them there exists a *subconscious desire* to become pregnant. By becoming pregnant they are able to satisfy many personal desires and wishes. Jense is one authority who agrees with the "subconscious desire" theory. He says: "Whereas it may appear at first glance that most adolescent pregnancies are the result of accidents of contraception or misinformation, repeated studies have shown that *the great majority of teenage girls get pregnant because they want to."* He then goes on to point out that most girls knew about contraceptives but did not use them. "Generally, the motivation for pregnancy is unconscious, although some girls readily admit that they wanted to become pregnant." The most common reasons, according to Jense, for wanting to become pregnant include:

1. to prove that she is a woman and that her body works the way it should;
2. to have someone, the baby, to love;
3. to please a man who wanted to impregnate her;
4. to get back at her parents for hassling her about her sexual behaviour;
5. to get away from her rejecting home environment, her boring school, and the "awful town" she lives in;
6. to satisfy her parents' covert wish for her to get pregnant and have the baby;
7. to get a man to marry her; and
8. to relieve loneliness and depression. (1976, p. 148)

Teenagers who become pregnant find that their pregnancy *rarely* effectively satisfies any of these needs or wishes. On this point, experts agree, whether or not they believe in the "subconscious desire" to become pregnant.

Many social workers and youth workers do not agree with this theory. They claim that most pregnant girls, from the moment they discover they are pregnant, wish it were not so. Many adolescents who become pregnant do not demonstrate the need to prove that they are able to have a child, to get even with their parents, or to satisfy the desire of a boyfriend. With the increased availability of medical abortions taking place in hospital settings more teenagers than ever before are electing to terminate their pregnancy. This would indicate that their desire to become pregnant (or at least to remain pregnant) is not strong.

Sol Gordon strongly disagrees with the theory. He claims that in the majority of teenage pregnancies it is extremely doubtful that the girl wanted to become pregnant. The research which indicates that girls are motivated to become pregnant is weak, and after the fact. "However, the evidence shows that the only trait pregnant teenagers share, besides sexual experience, is a lack of knowledge about the reproductive process and birth control." Pregnancy among teenagers is best explained not by the unconscious desire to become pregnant, but rather, from the lack of information about preventing pregnancy, according to Gordon (1973, p. 37).

Some research indicates that teenagers who become pregnant have weak concepts of themselves as individuals. Zongker (1977) studied a group of teenage mothers in an attempt to compare their self-concept with that of adolescent girls who never had been pregnant. Several findings highlighted this research, including:

1. the pregnant adolescents exhibited a decidedly low self-concept in most areas;
2. the pregnant girls were extraordinarily low in self-identity, family, and social relationships;
3. pregnant girls held a low opinion of themselves but had accepted the presence of these feelings;
4. about 60 percent of the school age mothers were without fathers or stepfathers in their home as compared to 18 percent of the control group;
5. school age mothers were older but at a lower grade level than the control group;
6. pregnant adolescents were dissatisfied with their looks, bodies and physical performance.

All research does not portray as "negative" a picture of the pregnant adolescent as does the data gathered by Zongker. Some critics of the study claim that it may have been overly influenced by socio-economic factors. Nevertheless, the information is thought provoking when cast in the perspective of the psychological variables in adolescent sexuality and pregnancy.

Contraception and Adolescent Sexuality

Contraception is the attempt to avoid pregnancy without avoiding sexual intercourse. In this section we shall take a look at some of the ways sexually active adolescents attempt to avoid pregnancy.

The most exhaustive study on this topic has been conducted by Zelnick and Kantner (1977). Their findings have greatly illuminated an issue which for the most part has not been thoroughly or rigorously researched. Their data indicate that a greater percent of adolescents are presently using *some kind* of contraceptive protection than in years past. Their study dealt only with *sexually active* adolescent girls, which is approximately 50 percent of the 15-19-year-old female population. Perhaps the most noticeable trend is that fewer couples rely upon withdrawal as a technique of contraception than in times past, and that a greater percentage of females are using the pill for protection against pregnancy. In 1971 about 30 percent of sexually active couples relied upon withdrawal to avoid pregnancy. In 1976 less than 17 percent used this procedure. In contrast, in 1971 only 24 percent of sexually-active girls used the pill for protection during their most recent intercourse, in 1976 47 percent did so. Zelnick and Kantner also discovered that about 59 percent of 15-19-year-old girls who have ever had intercourse have used the pill *at one time or another*.

Despite the fact that use of the pill is on the increase among the adolescent population, most youth do not use any consistent form of contraception. For example, when asked "What contraception was used in your last intercourse?", more than half of the girls admitted to no protection. It is worthy of note that the late-adolescent girls were much more likely than the middle-adolescent girls to have used some kind of contraception.

An interesting fact uncovered by Zelnick and Kantner was that even though the percentage of girls using contraception increased considerably between 1971 and 1976, it was also true that the percentage of girls who have engaged in sexual intercourse but who *have never used contraception* also increased. In 1971 only 17 percent of the girls who had sexual intercourse had *never* used contraception; in 1976 this jumped to almost 26 percent. This could be due to the fact that girls presently know more about the ovulation cycle, therefore, can anticipate the time of the month where pregnancy is most likely.

Addy (1977), in her review of research conducted in the United States and Canada concludes that "Sexually active adolescents are poor contraceptive users and tend to risk pregnancy by having unprotected intercourse''. The *most frequently given reason* for engaging in unprotected intercourse was a belief on the part of the adolescent that conception ''would not or could not occur''. Only a small proportion mentioned the unavailability of contraceptives as a reason for nonuse. Some researchers conclude that many adolescent girls simply do not hold a causal relationship in their mind between the act of sexual intercourse and pregnancy — at least as far as they as individuals are concerned. Some girls think they are ''magically protected'' while others hold to the fantasy that ''it cannot happen to me''. D.E. Guyatt after interviewing 112 pregnant girls aged 14-19 discovered that half of these girls had *never* used any kind of contraception. The most frequently given reason for failure to protect themselves against pregnancy was ''their inability to believe that they could become pregnant'' (reported in Addy, 1977).

Addy also reports a study in which the following reasons were given by sexually-active adolescents for not using contraceptives:

I thought that it was unlikely that I (or the girl) would get pregnant.

I didn't think that I was going to have sex at that time.

Neither of us thought that it was necessary to use a contraceptive.

By having a contraceptive available, it would have appeared to my partner that I was planning to have sex.

Except for birth control pills, most other methods are just too much trouble to use.

I was too embarrassed to go to the doctor or the drug store to get something to prevent pregnancy.

I didn't use a contraceptive because I was afraid someone might find it.

Jense, in his analysis of adolescent sexuality, lists the following reasons why adolescents do not use contraceptves more consistently or effectively:

1. The adolescents do not believe they will become pregnant if intercourse is infrequent.
2. They do not believe they can get pregnant easily — that is, they doubt their fecundity.
3. They think they are having intercourse in the safe period.
4. Some contraceptives are difficult to get; the pill and the intrauterine device require a doctor's prescription and, legally, a parent's permission. Most teenagers are afraid to face their

parents with the fact that they are sexually active, knowing that their parents disapprove of premarital sex. Few teenagers feel comfortable talking with their parents about any aspect of sex.

5. Because of the general disapproval of premarital sex, and because it is often against the law, teenagers do not want to admit to their parents or themselves that they are sexually active. Unmarried teenage girls deny the realization of past, present, or future sexual activity. "Nice girls don't plan ahead" is a common belief, and taking the pill would be an admission of intent. "It won't happen to me" is the typical attitude toward the possibility of pregnancy from unprotected intercourse.

6. Contraceptives are considered by many to be unnatural. About 25 percent of teenage girls regard the pill as potentially harmful. Boys, particularly, believe that a condom decreases the pleasure of intercourse.

7. Some adolescents hope to get pregnant, although this wish is usually unconscious.

8. Adolescents are afraid that clinics and physicians will not be confidential and will tell their parents. (1976, p. 147)

Even though many adolescents are amazingly unrealistic about the probability of a pregnancy after unprotected intercourse, there is some evidence that the *most sexually active* girls are better at contraception than the *least active*. Zelnick and Kantner report that about 66 percent of the girls who had intercourse six or more times during the previous month used contraception, compared with about 47 percent who were less sexually active. This data, however, does not agree with that of Gordon, who claims: "The more sexual experience a young person has had, *the less he or she is likely to know about the facts of sex*" (1973, p. 16).

In summary, the following points seem fairly well established with regards to adolescent sexuality and the use of contraceptives:

1. Teenagers are using contraceptives more consistently and with greater regularity than did adolescents in the early seventies.

2. The use of contraceptives is greatly influenced by age: *early* adolescents are infrequent and sporadic in their contraceptive attempts; *middle* adolescents are more prepared, but still (by adult standards) unprepared; *late* adolescents are the most likely to anticipate the use of contraception, to approve of it, and to employ it effectively.

3. The pill is increasingly used by adolescents as a birth control device, whereas withdrawal is used less frequently,

4. Many adolescents seem to *believe* that they will not become pregnant even after numerous unprotected sexual episodes, while at the same time they admit pregnancy would likely happen to someone else with similar sexual habits.
5. Many adolescents view contraception as unnatural, as embarrassing or as an indicator that they are crass or "premeditated" about their sexuality. This is especially true among early and middle adolescents, and holds true for males and females alike.
6. Adolescents, as a group, are not good at avoiding pregnancy in relation to the amount of times they experience intercourse. The age group most likely to become pregnant (in relation to total numbers of times intercourse has taken place) are middle adolescents.
7. Overall, many adolescents are irrational in their outlook toward pregnancy and the role played by contraception in avoiding it.

Sexual Abstinence During Adolescence

Just as it is not precisely understood why adolescents engage in sexual intercourse, neither is it clearly understood why they *do not*. Most youth are biologically capable of normal sexual relations by middle adolescence and virtually all are ready by late adolescence. If sexual desire is "natural" for adolescents, why then do not more youth engage in sexual intercourse?

Several reasons contribute to the lack of sexual involvement including: (a) moral reasons; (b) fears and anxieties; and (c) partner-availability reasons. By briefly overviewing these factors we can obtain a more complete picture of adolescent sexuality.

Moral reasons: Many adolescents believe that sexual behaviour before marriage is morally improper, therefore, they are reluctant to engage in it. Generally speaking, three types of moral objections characterize adolescent thought. The first are *beliefs and convictions learned from adults*, especially parents. Youngsters who have been taught since childhood that sexuality is bad, unhealthy or evil often assimilate this teaching into their own outlook. The second are *beliefs acquired from a religion or philosophy*. This is perhaps a better example of a "moral reason" for opposing sexual intercourse, than the first, which is more an example of social learning. Some adolescents subscribe to the Puritan belief that sexual pleasure is unto itself bad; others adhere to the Stoic belief that all desires (including the sexual) should be held in check;

others believe in the Buddhist maxim that those people who have no desires suffer no disappointments, therefore, to not desire sex is to never be disappointed by it. The third example of moral objections to sexual involvement include *beliefs and convictions learned from personal experience*. Some youth learn that dealing with another person on a sexual basis is emotionally strenuous, that it creates more problems than it solves. They conclude that — for the moment at least — sexual involvement is not for me. Closely related is the widespread belief among adolescents that sexual behaviour between couples is acceptable only when they are "in love". Sexuality without intimacy, and emotional attachment simply is not acceptable. Another personal reason for avoiding sexual involvement is the belief that one should wait until marriage for sexual relations.

Age trends are evident in these matters. Early adolescents are likely to oppose sexual involvements merely because that is the viewpoint of their parents, church or friends. Middle adolescents are inclined to give greater weight to philosophical and moral principles, but they remain greatly influenced by home and upbringing. Late adolescents are more impressed by personal experience than either of the two younger ages, and are also more likely to think of sexuality as a personal matter that must be worked out on an individual basis.

Apparently some sex differences exist (or at least are *perceived* by late adolescents to exist) in the matter of personal morals. In responding to the question "What do you think prevents teenage *girls* from engaging in sexual intercourse more frequently", about 55 percent of a university undergraduate class answered: personal beliefs and moral convictions. However, in response to the same question regarding *male* sexual behaviour only 29 percent of the same students claimed boys were impeded in their sexual activity by personal beliefs and moral convictions.

Fears and anxieties: Adolescents, like most young adults, harbour a certain number of fears and anxieties about sexuality. Some fears are social or physical, whereas others are highly personal.

An important fear impeding sexual intercourse among youth is the fear of pregnancy. Virtually all researchers in the area of adolescent sexuality concur in this opinion. A questionnaire administered to 350 university freshmen at the University of Alberta asked students why, in their opinion, teenagers did not engage in sexual intercourse more often. Forty percent of the respondents chose "fear of pregnancy" as their first choice. Whether this will become less significant as contraceptive usage becomes more sophisticated is not known. Fear of V.D. (venereal disease) though often cited in the literature, was virtually never mentioned as a deterrent to adolescent sexuality by the University of Alberta students. Presumably this is because the vast majority of sexual intercourse during adolescence takes place between couples who have known each other for a considerable length of time, and who consider themselves "going steady", or bonded in some form or another. On the practical side is the realization by knowledgeable teenagers that most forms of V.D., if detected early, are fairly easily eradicated.

Some fears have a more social component such as the fear that engaging in sexual intercourse will foster a bad reputation. Some youth are opposed to intercourse because they know it will offend their parents, or cause them anguish if they found out. Sorenson, however, reports that couples who *strongly desire* sexual relations rarely avoid intercourse only because of parental disapproval. Many adolescents are extremely body-conscious and are reluctant to expose their body. They are uncomfortable because they are not sure if their bodies are attractive, or even if they will be laughed at. (Unlike adults, especially middle-class adults, many sexually active adolescents engage in intercourse with some or most of their clothes on). Closely related to body-shyness is the uncertain feeling held by many youth that they will not be "any good at it". This frequently is overcome by experience (and time) but for some it lasts well into early adulthood. Some youth are also simply frightened of the unknown and refuse to adventure into it.

Clinical psychologists report that among the most significant inhibitors of adolescent sex is *guilt*. *Why* sex creates guilt is not agreed upon. The most accepted viewpoint is that youngsters are taught by their elders either directly or indirectly, that sex is bad, unhealthy or unclean. This teaching becomes incorporated into the child's world view and carries into adolescence where sexuality is experimented with on a serious basis for the first time. Some teenagers "lose" this teaching rather quickly and experience virtually no guilt about their sexual episodes. Many youth, however, find that the teaching lingers on forcefully in the form of conscience pains, free-floating anxiety, guilt feelings, and a general fear of sexuality. In terms of the evidence available, including questionnaires, interviews, clinical work with youngsters, parent observations, and developmental knowledge, there is no doubt that guilt feelings represent one of the major inhibitors of adolescent sexuality. Guilt also is a major inhibitor of adult sexuality.

Partner availability: Sexual intercourse is a biological reality which takes place only after several important emotional and social realities have been taken care of. Adolescents, as a group, take sex rather seriously. Little recreational sex (in the "swinger" sense) takes place. A certain amount of sexual adventuring is found, but it is not a dominant sexual life-style among the adolescents of North America. Almost all girls, and most boys, agree with the idea that sexual intercourse should be reserved for couples who are in love, or who have some kind of commitment to one another. Most girls take offense when they think they are "being used" as a source of physical pleasure, or when their sexual expressions are made light of.

An appropriate partner is a person who a teenager knows very well, who has shared personal intimacies, who shows respect for personal vulnerabilities, and who, at the same time, is a desired sexual companion. Most adolescents find it difficult to find a partner who fits these needs; yet they tend not to engage in sexual intercourse *until* these preconditions are met.

The closely supervised life-style of youth (especially early and middle adolescents) also makes sexual intercourse awkward. Often it is difficult to find a proper location (most adolescent sexual activity takes place in the home of the boy's parents); often it is difficult to obtain privacy. These factors constrict sexual freedom.

In interviews with youth who have not experienced sexual intercourse a frequent explanation is "I just haven't met the right person yet"; or, "The right conditions haven't shown up yet". Both Sorenson (1973) and Offer (1975) report responses of this type.

Partner availability is compounded by the fact that sexuality is a complex experience made even more troublesome by the egocentrism of youth. Sexual fondling, for example, among middle adolescents sometimes resembles a mixture of wrestling, debate, and persistence. This is largely because a certain component of sexuality is more "selfish" and "self-searching" than anything else. In this matter Erikson notes: "Before such genital maturity is reached, much of sexual life is of the self-seeking, identity-hungry kind; each partner is really trying to reach himself. Or it remains a kind of genital combat in which each tries to defeat the other" (1968, p. 137). The net effect is that an "appropriate" partner becomes even more important as far as the individual adolescent is concerned.

A research study conducted by Elias and Elias (1975) casts additional light on the matter of why adolescents *do not* engage in certain kinds of sexual behaviour. In the article "The Sexual World of the Adolescent", they report that girls who did not engage in petting gave the following reasons: (1) it is wrong or immoral; (2) they were uncertain they could control their partner; (3) they never met a boy they wanted to do it with; (4) fear of parental disapproval; (5) too shy.

With regards to youth who have not experienced sexual intercourse (boys *and* girls) Elias and Elias report the following reasons (in order of importance) as contributing to avoidance of sexual intercourse.

1. the fear of pregnancy;
2. the belief that it is wrong or immoral;
3. the partner was unwilling to go along;
4. never met a boy/girl I wanted to do it with;
5. lack of opportunity;
6. fear of parental disapproval.

Even though each individual holds personal views with regards to sexual behaviour, it is apparent that a cluster of common viewpoints significantly influences those youth who choose to engage in sexual activity with a partner of the opposite sex.

Summary

1. The sexual behaviour of adolescents in North American society is radically influenced by age. As age increases so also do all forms of sexual intimacy. The middle-adolescence period is a time when sexuality begins to manifest itself as a powerful life impulse. During early adolescence, sexuality is experienced with less passion and its physical manifestations are more elementars.

Sexual involvement follows a general (but not totally predictable) progression, starting with kissing, breast fondling, genital stimulation and intercourse. About one-half of the girls have experienced intercourse by their nineteenth birthday.

The fourteenth and fifteenth years are significant because they witness the crossover to more advanced sexuality. The minor social interest in sex of the early teens is replaced with a major endocrinological push. The eighteenth and nineteenth years are also significant for many youth, because this is when sexual intercourse becomes a basic part of their sexual involvements.

2. Not all data concerning the sexual habits of youth are consistent. Schofield's data, for example, indicates that adolescents are less sexually active than does the data of Zelnick and Kantner. Data concerning

sexual activity must be viewed as general estimates rather than as precise facts.

3. Boys tend to have their first intercourse with a girl about their same age, whereas first partners for girls tend to be slightly older. First intercourse is not always a positive experience for the boy or the girl. General awkwardness, shyness and unfamiliarity contribute to the adolescent's lack of relaxed sexuality.

4. By middle or late adolescence virtually all boys masturbate to orgasm. Most girls masturbate also, but the likelihood of achieving orgasm is less than for boys.

5. The sexual impulse is not the dominant impulse of the adolescent personality. Social, psychological, and moral factors exert an equally (often more) powerful influence. Finding a viable (as contrasted with merely available) sexual partner is a major task of the adolescent period. Although situations vary from individual to individual, sexual involvements tend not to take place until a "viable" partner has been found. This holds true for both boys and girls, but more so for girls.

6. Youth do not abstain from sex merely because their parents disapprove. Boys tend to be more premeditated and strategic in their sexual adventures, whereas girls tend to be more "spontaneous" and insistent upon "proper circumstances". Girls also tend to place greater importance on "being in love", although both sexes believe that sexual involvement between couples who are in love is more proper than between partners whose relationship is casual or short term. In most regards adolescent attitudes toward sexuality are conventional and within the guidelines of the society at large.

7. Most youth do not approve of extra-marital affairs on the part of adults and especially of their parents. They also tend to view playful adult sexuality with suspicion. Few adults discuss sexual matters with their adolescent children.

8. Most adolescents are mildly inhibited by nudity, especially in the presence of someone of the opposite sex; they tend to doubt their sexual competence because they lack experience and because they have no known standard by which to compare.

9. Adolescents are not sexually active as late adolescents. Among youth who experience intercourse (about one-half of the adolescent population) it is not unusual for them to have had intercourse only once or twice during the past year. Only a small percentage of adolescents are sexually promiscuous, the majority of whom are late adolescents.

10. Several psychological factors encourage sexuality among ado-

lescents, including: (a) the desire for an intimacy partner, someone with whom to share intense relatedness; (b) the need to belong, to be affiliated; (c) the desire to dominate or to be submissive to another person; (d) curiosity about sexuality, the body, and the experience of sexual involvement; (e) the desire for passion and intensity; (f) imitating the actions of others, or identifying with their sexual accomplishments; and, (g) rebelliousness and hostility, especially toward parents. These psychological factors, unto themselves, do not *account* for sexuality. However, they add impetus to the preexisting sexual impulse and, therefore, increase the chance that sexuality will occur.

11. Adolescent pregnancy is a serious matter in contemporary society. Not only does it create considerable difficulties for the teenage mother, but for the child as well. The health risks to mother and child are considerable. The incidence of premature birth, maternal death, infant illness and defect, and mother suicide are all greater for teenage pregnancy than for older women.

Adolescents tend not to be good parents. Their ability to tolerate the stress of raising a child is not well developed, their tendency to abuse the child is greater than if they were older, and their likelihood of giving up the baby for adoption after a year of parenting is greater than that of the population in general. Early and middle adolescents are severely limited in their ability to parent because their personality is diffuse, their sense of identity is weakly established, and their capacity for long term commitment is limited.

12. Girls who become pregnant tend not to be sexually promiscuous. They tend to have been involved in a fairly long term relationship with one sexual partner. Some researchers claim that the primary difference between sexually active girls who get pregnant and those who do not is their knowledge about effective contraception.

Some psychologists believe that girls harbour subconscious desires to become pregnant in order to satisfy otherwise unmet needs in their lives.

13. Most adolescents are not good at using effective contraceptive devices. Therefore, their incidence of pregnancy per intercourse is much higher than for adults. Late adolescents are the best contraceptive users, early adolescents the worst. Many teenage pregnancies occur after the girls have experienced intercourse only two or three times.

The pill is being used by a greater percentage of adolescent girls than in past years. At the same time, there is a greater percentage of girls engaging in sexual intercourse with no protection at all.

Many girls "believe" that they will not get pregnant no matter what their sexual habits. Others believe that contraceptive devices would reduce the chance of pregnancy but they refuse to use them because it interferes with spontaneous sexuality, or makes them appear premeditated or "cheap".

14. Not all youth are sexually active. The reasons for abstaining include: (a) moral reasons; personal beliefs and convictions, some of which are taught and some of which are personally formulated; b) fears and anxieties about the uncertainties of sexuality; and, (c) lack of desirable partner.

Part Three:
Some Myths About
Adolescence

Author's Introductory Comments

In this section of the text I have brought together several controversial topics related to the study of adolescence in our culture. However, this section of the book differs dramatically from the first two sections in that it is more editorial-like and designed to prompt personal reactions from the reader. The style is not neutral or highly objective as is the trend with textbooks; rather I am giving the reader a biased viewpoint, the sense or nonsense (even semi-sense) of which each individual must conclude on a personal level.

My purpose for including a section of this type at the end of the book is to encourage investigation of our present day understanding of adolescents and the predicaments which they encounter in the course of their day-to-day existence. Some of the issues in this chapter have been elaborated more fully in my previous book, *The Adolescent Predicament,* whereas others are dealt with for the first time. I hope the reader will approach these mini-essays with an open and critical mind, and with an eye for the evidence, overt as well as camouflaged, which either supports or refutes these ideas.

J. J. Mitchell
Edmonton, Alberta
October, 1978

The Myth That We
Like Adolescents

Wherein we note that even though our culture is described as being a "youth-oriented" culture, it nevertheless is characterized by a considerable degree of resentment against youth and that many adults actually fear adolescents.

A popular myth is that adults like adolescents. Few myths are further from the truth. Our treatment of youth is similar to that of treaty Indians in that we provide for them isolated settings where they are the beneficiary of institutions; we pay lip service to their importance and uniqueness but do little to actualize either. I believe that the predominant attitude toward youth is slightly less intense than fear and slightly more profound than resentment — it is far removed from enjoyment or affection.

Youth are a mixture of nuisance, inconvenience and menace and adults do not know quite what to make of them. R. Menninger, sensing the mood, exclaims: "To put it bluntly, our adult society tends to regard the adolescent as an unfortunate inconvenience, a sort of bad moment that we half wish would go away; a distraction or maybe a disruption that gets in the way of real business of living for the rest of us; a kind of incidental way station in life that will surely pass if we wait long enough or hold our breath or look the other way." Menninger has more to say on the topic:

> It is as if the adult society regards adolescence as an unattractive extension of childhood that we must somehow put up with, until the magic of time has somehow transmuted that cute little baby of yesteryear into the adult of tomorrow. Most of us feel put upon by the very existence of the adolescent, annoyed with his parasitic nature, and the like, as if we were somehow the victim and he the aggressor. And, as with any victim, the roads of appeasement and

bribery are natural resources. So we give him a car when he asks, or a new electric guitar, or an increase in his allowance — anything, just to get him "off our backs" and out of the way. (1968, p. 324)

Fritz Redl, who is among the more refreshing of the youth watchers, is forthright in his belief that young people today are discriminated against. "Even if you happen to live, as a child, far away from where prejudices hurt, upon entering the teen-phase you become quite noticeably *part of a discredited minority group*. Sor, no matter how well the particular adults in your life may like you as a person, whenever they speak, write, and act as representatives of the adult generation they view teenagers with a jaundiced eye." He finishes with "Of course, some of my best friends are teenagers; but, never mind, as such they are a bad lot, guilty or at least not to be trusted until proved innocent" (1969, p. 88). In this stance Redl aligns closely with Edgar Friedenberg, and Paul Goodman and other social commentators of our time who believe that youth are not treated in a civil manner in our society.

Most adults do not know what to make of youth energy. Vitality unnerves them because there is uncertainty as to how it will be released. Adults want to be assured that teenage muscle will not be weighted against t em and when they do not receive assurance they are frightened.

It is easy to see why adults fear adolescents. Youth rarely have enough worthwhile work to do, therefore they congregate and mill about. Their conversation is not particularly enthralling and their behaviour is not very impressive. They talk loudly about parties and boyfriends and cars; they playfully bully one another and ridicule passers-by. Groups disband into wandering trios or foursomes which often are troublesome or disrespectful. Adults fear trouble and resent disrespect, and they hate *having to worry about either*.

Friendenberg claims that teenagers are one of several minority groups who have been accorded "hot-blooded" status, a distinction which occurs when authorities believe that if the lid is not screwed tightly it will be blown through the roof. Hot-blooded minority groups are seen as "joyous, playful, lazy, and irresponsible, with brutality lurking just below the surface and ready to break out into violence". They also are seen as "childish and excitable, impudent and improvident, sexually aggressive, and dangerous, but possessed of superb and sustained power to satisfy sexual demands" (1965, p. 68). Elders fear what they cannot control, and resent minority groups who are not "controllable".

There is more to the fear of youth than animal ardour and undisciplined energy. Foremost to many adults is the fear of disapproval. What if I put my best foot forward and am rejected by the very youth I am trying to contact? What if they think poorly of me? That I am out of date, or out of touch with new realities? In short, what if I, the adult, am rejected or thought stupid. Adults respond predictably: they reject first. They are afraid to initiate interaction and believe that anyone stupid enough to reject them deserves to be cancelled in advance. The adults cancel, the youth retaliate.

Indifference is not as painful as outright disapproval, but adults resent it almost as much — especially middle-class adults of position who are accustomed to being acknowledged by underlings. Adults who intervene in the adolescent world find that their presence is not noticed in a meaningful way. They are not rejected but neither do they carry much weight.

Adults fear that youth will reject their values and beliefs. This fear is partly founded on the facts of history because youth *do* alter the beliefs of their elders and they do accept new outlooks — though not with the consistency most adults fear. The *possibility* that the young will reject what the older generation holds sacred forces adults into the double-bind of encouraging self-reliance among young people while realizing fully that it may take feared directions.

It is not the deviant or disturbed adolescent who most agitates the adult mood. Adults are most deeply frightened of the adolescent in his (or her) *natural form*. It is this natural form which the impersonal rules of the school strive to keep under wraps.

When we closely examine school rules, we find common to them all, the *enforcement of orderliness*. Classrooms are kept quiet because teachers are convinced, or have learned from experience, that conversation leads to disruption; corridors are kept empty because administrators fear that traffic leads to congestion; gymnasia are vacant because physical activity leads to rowdiness. Rules keep youngsters in bounds, and other rules keep them orderly while within the bounds. A third set punishes them if they trespass either.

School rules are not intended to prevent genuine vandalism or physical violence. Nor are they designed primarily to prevent theft, truancy or destruction. They are designed to prevent *loitering* (because in schools one is permitted to do *nothing* only in an organized setting); to prevent *spontaneous outbreaks* of laughter or conversation which may deteriorate into sexual chatter or silly commentary on the social habits of Suzie and Willie; and, most importantly, to prevent any type of *confrontation* between youths and adults. The justification for the rules is that youngsters abuse liberties, and that when given a centimetre they take a kilometre.

The average adult is emotionally frightened of the average adolescent, and it is precisely what is most natural to youth that adults fear most. Youth make security-loving adults jittery. Rules are designed to ease the jitters by replacing youthful excess with youthful orderliness. This seems reasonable, as most adults believe that excess means immaturity at best and revolution at worst; and order means maturity or, at worst, involuntary compliance. Excess is viewed as pathological. Exhuberance, the emotional runoff of excess, is tolerated only when it is directed toward accepted goals, particularly those contrived by the school to divert energy from its natural object. Order, a legitimate character trait, and a necessary condition for institutional smoothness, is viewed as the cardinal virtue of civilization. Lapsing from it invites the resurgence of primitive man.

The prime function of rules is to devitalize youth and to strip them of the robust vitality which is at the core of their creative energy, their sexual energy, and their intellectual enthusiasm. In this devitalization youth lose much more than bargained for. They lose in raw curiosity, thus they are less gifted in science and invention. They lose enthusiasm, and staying power, and thus are less able to stick with long-range projects. They lose spontaneity at an age when it is their chief social asset. They lose sexual openness (a great relief to their elders) and they learn to live with deception and deceit as though it were a natural part of sexuality.

School administrators fear youth who have nothing to lose, but also secretly admire their freedom and their forthrightness. They resent impulsiveness because they have spent years overcoming it within themselves (to survive middle-class life) and cannot cope with its arousal. The teacher who has lost spontaneous vitality and the ebullience which is its natural companion, who opposes youth in whom it is not as yet repressed, is not fundamentally different from the sexual phobic who has lost touch with sexual feelings and who converts their desirability into a repulsion, and who is repulsed by the sexual activity of others, especially those who dare to enjoy it. They fear immature people who are too naïve to understand the importance of orderliness in maintaining institutions, but at the same time who are too in tune with their natural impulses to exchange it for what feels good. Friedenberg, I believe, has said it as well as anyone:

When a society sees impulsiveness and sexual exuberance as minority characteristics which unsuit the individual for membership until he is successfully naturalized, it is in pretty bad shape. Adolescents, loved, respected, taught to accept, enjoy, and discipline their feelings, grow up. "Teenagers" don't; they pass. Then, in middle age, they have the same trouble with their former self that many ethnics do. They hate and fear the kinds of spontaneity that remind them of what they have abandoned, and they hate themselves for having joined forces with and having come to resemble their oppressors . . . . I am convinced that it is also the source of the specific hostility — and sometimes sentimentality — that adolescents arouse in adults . . . . Their effect is to starve out, through silence and misrepresentation, the capacity to have genuine and strongly felt experience, and to replace it by the conventional symbols that serve as the common currency of daily life.   (1965, p. 70)

Our most revealing gesture of youth fear is the way we isolate them from virtually everything our society considers important. Except for the school dropouts, adolescents spend most of their daylight hours in schools. The school is isolated from the total community in almost every regard: youth are not allowed out in the community, and citizens of the community are not welcome in the school. Youth are excluded from almost all experiences which enhance a respectable job. "The adolescent is now the only totally disenfranchised minority group in the country. In America *no minority group has ever gotten any respect or consistently decent treatment* until it began to acquire political power" (1965, p. 77). At present there is no prospect of attaining this power.

We encourage "game proof"; the procedure by which a person establishes personal worth by achieving expertise in games. Whether they are highly-structured athletic games, cultural events such as drama or music, or interpersonal games such as peer eominance, matters little because their mutual feature is that they are removed from the real world and do not, unto themselves, affect anything important. Game proof is the means by which a person with no real power acquires a substitute for it through invented rituals. Minority groups who cannot be disposed of, but who have the potential to be troublesome, are ripe for game proof. That government or private industry has created almost no *socially productive* or *personally rewarding* ways for youthful energy to be constructively employed indicates our belief that youth should not play important roles. Until we understand our fear of youth we will not make sense out of how we discriminate against them; nor will we comprehend the "naturalness" of their alienation.

Ages: Fear and resentment of youth is not equal for all ages. Toward the early adolescent, comparatively little fear *or* resentment is directed. This holds true because youth of this age are neither physically nor sexually mature and the basis for substantive disagreement with the parent society has not yet been forged. Early adolescents *irritate* adults with their scraggly appearance, their lack of manners, and their vile language, but they do not pose a significant threat to be genuinely feared. They are saved by the child side of their makeup. The *middle* adolescent is more victimized by minority status, and more likely to engage in the kinds of activity which generate resentment in adults. By middle adolescence most girls have acquired their adult body and many boys are rapidly approaching it. They want adult-like treatment even though they are inexperienced in attaining it. They straddle childhood and adulthood with typical adolescent floundering.

The *late* adolescent receives the lion's share of adult and institutional discrimination. In relation to talents, ambitions and personal desires they unquestioningly are the most constrained of all adolescents. School for many of them is little more than a social wasteland. Legitimate opportunities in the work forces are nil. Even the possibility for constructive *volunteer* work is limited. This happens at an age when adolescents are adult in almost every aspect of their personality, but have access to almost no adult social roles. Their life-style estranges them from the best of their maturing personality and encourages in many a sense of defiant rebellion and among others apathetic withdrawal. In our society, it is the late adolescent whom we most fear and resent, and, with the exception of those who go to school, they are the youth for whom we provide the fewest opportunities.

The Myth of Adolescent Sexual Vitality and Promiscuity

Wherein we discover that adolescents are not nearly as sexually active as adults, that they take sexuality very seriously, and that their involvements are rather conservative when contrasted with adult sexual activities.

The belief that adolescents are sexually active, that they are able to find a willing partner at a moment's notice, and that they experience powerful sexual arousal is a myth which has found considerable audience among the adult population. As with most myths or stereotypes, it holds a particle of truth but in no way embraces the whole truth. Several factors contribute to the perpetuation of the myth, some based upon the sensual and open nature of youth gatherings, and others upon the unconscious projections of envious adults. I will not dwell upon the clinical observation that adults whose own sexuality is suppressed and smoldering see rampant sexuality camouflaged as teenagers at every turn. Its factualness is so clear as to need no elucidation, yet, being a subjective phenomenon it lies beyond the realm of empirical confirmation.

The *behaviour* of adolescents is sufficient to destroy the myth that they are adventurous, confident, sexual predators constantly on the prowl. *By virtually every criteria, adolescents are less sexually active, less easily aroused, less abstract and calculating, and less effective in their sexual ambitions than are adults.*

Very few adolescents could be described as sexually carefree. Sex is a serious matter which is not easily separated from their sense of personhood; youth are considerably less able to partake in recreational or impersonal sexual escapades than are young adults, and they are more likely to be crushed when a sexual partner does not take them seriously.

Adolescent boys demonstrate only a nodding acquaintance with what girls call sexual technique. They tend not to understand the frame of reference of their partner, and appear singularly preoccupied with themselves. They are not callous or indifferent, rather they are essentially oblivious to the subtle differences in their approach versus their partner's approach to sexual expression. They are not attuned to their partner in a romantic, detached, chivalrous manner. Instead, their partner is primarily an extension of their own passion who shares in it as well. In a phrase, adolescent sexuality is highly egocentric, intense and concrete. It has remarkably few abstract qualities because it is too new and too engrossing to be viewed in any way except the personal. From the adult point of view it is remarkably unromantic.

Nothing shatters the myth of adolescent sexual vitality more convincingly than the fact that only about one-third of *all* girls between the ages of 15 and 19 have ever had sexual intercourse. This acquires additional impact when one realizes that most of the girls who have *not* had sexual intercourse have been in a situation where it was possible ("even sensible" as one teenage girl told me) but have refused. The consuming passion for sexual intercourse that some people attribute to adolescents *as a group* simply is not there. For the majority of youth, the conditions, the circumstances and the partner are more important than the sexual activity itself.

In North American culture, girls especially are susceptible to sexual misinterpretation. Young girls who have attained their full adult figure by age 14 or 15 exude an erotic image in their T-shirts and cut-offs of which they are likely to be completely unaware. Because experienced adults see them as full-blossomed and sexually attractive, and also because adults are more attuned to unspoken sexual messages, a genuine confusion takes place. The middle-adolescent girl who knows she "turns on" older boys and men may not be completely aware of the consequences. She herself may not be aroused in a sexual sense, but flattered by the response she receives.

In a similar vein, boys and girls alike often attach little sexual significance to coyness or aggressiveness in a social context. The point often lost on adolescent watchers is that behaviour which *appears* sexual often is not because the youngster does not perceive the abstract nature of the sexual overture, or give it precedence over the social dimension of peer interaction. This consistently holds true during early and middle adolescence.

The inconsistent use of contraceptives demonstrates the adolescent's sense of urgency about sex. As of this writing (1978), few girls, and even fewer boys, employ effective contraceptive devices to avoid pregnancy. This derives partly from ignorance about the reproductive process (most teenagers do not know when conception occurs during the ovulation cycle).

Social workers in homes for unwed mothers note that many girls knew they would become pregnant if they had sexual intercourse. Despite this realization no precautionary measures were taken. The answer most frequently given by these girls for not using contraceptives is that they believed that contraceptives destroyed the passion of sex, or interrupted its spontaneity and, therefore, were unacceptable. This suggests that their "philosophy" of sexuality is based upon immediacy and passion, and contradicts the image that they are detached or frivolous in their sexuality. They are passionately earnest, and with regard to unwanted pregnancies it is their downfall.

The myth of the sexually promiscuous adolescent is ignited further by the belief that the automobile allows young people to travel unsupervised around the countryside in a portable bedroom. The evidence does not indicate that the sexual habits of young people are determined by the automobile. For example, in one research study it was found that between 40 and 50 percent of the sexually active girls had either their first or their most recent sexual experience *in the home of their partner*. Only about nine percent had their first intercourse in a car, and less than six percent had their most recent intercourse in an automobile. Only about five-six percent had either their first date or their most recent coitus in a hotel or motel. This information indicates that although mobility increases the opportunity for sexual experience, the incidence of sexual coupling in motels or automobiles is low, while the home of the partner remains the most likely location for the sexual rendezvous.

Other data indicate that adolescent girls are not as sexually adventurous as many people believe. For example, only about 18 percent of all 15-year-olds and about 25 percent of the 16-year-olds have ever had sexual intercourse. Zelnick and Kantner investigated the sexual habits of girls age 15-19 and found that among those who *were sexually active* over 60 percent had *not* had intercourse within the month previous to their research interview, indicating that they are not sexually active by adult standards. Among the sexually experienced girls of this age over 60 percent have had only one sexual partner, whereas only 25 percent have had either two or three partners in their sexual lives.

Girls tend to have sexual intercourse with older boys but the exact reasons why are not clear. For girls 17 or younger the chance is about 50 percent that their most recent sexual partner was 19 or older. The probable explanation is that older boys are better able to cope with the subtle nuances required of sexuality and are better able to persuade a reticent female to become a sexual partner than are younger boys. Also, the chance is greater that they are sexually experienced and thus consider themselves "experts" who can guarantee their product. On the practical side, they are more likely than younger adolescents to have private living quarters or friends who do, therefore, the geographical impediment to sexual relations is removed.

In summary, even though adolescents often exude an image of outward sensuality, and even though they may appear to the adult observer as sexually adventurous, the evidence indicates that for the majority of youth this is not an accurate portrayal of their sexual nature. The data indicate that most early- and middle-adolescent youth have not as yet experienced sexual intercourse.

Youth tend to take their sexual behaviour seriously and are less likely than adults to engage in "recreational" sex or to clearly differentiate a casual sexual escapade from a serious personal encounter. Very few girls use effective contraceptive measures before late adolescence, therefore, unwanted pregnancy is more frequent per sexual intercourse during middle adolescence than during late adolescence.

Adolescents do not necessarily view youth, *per se,* as a symbol of sexuality whereas adults are more likely to equate youth with sexual vitality. On the whole, adolescents are not nearly as sexually active as young adults and they view sexuality as a serious theme in their personal lives. They tend to be "monogamous" and they place considerable importance on partner fidelity. The belief that they are casual about sex, promiscuous, or sexually adventurous is, for the most part, a myth.

Myth Number Three

The Peer Group Myth

Wherein we discover that the peer group is not nearly as important to adolescents as most "experts" want us to believe; that peer group preoccupation reflects a lack of options and derives from being isolated from the real world and from spending most of their time in segregated schools.

The role of the peer group in adolescent life is considerably misunderstood. Let us examine the facts to see how they stack up in terms of what we knoa about humans in general and adolescents in particular. First, adolescents *do* like their friends and they spend considerable time in their presence; when given a free choice they frequently choose peers rather than parents, grandparents, or any other adults. Second, the peer group influences behaviour. The weak-willed are often stamped by the strong-willed or the muscular. The peer group has leaders, and a distribution of power. Sometimes it is cruel, sometimes charitable. It can excite members to plateaus of nastiness they would not attain on their own. Third, the group manipulates for its own interests and for the interests of its leaders. Most experts agree that these statements are true of adolescent peer groups. Unfortunately, experts fail to point out that these statements also are representative of *adult* and *child* peer groups. *They are essentially statements about the nature of groups rather than statements about the nature of adolescents.*

A look at day-to-day adolescent life does not clarify all matters but it certainly casts insight into the issue of peer obsession. The typical adolescent rises about seven a.m.; assuming that he/she has no morning household chores or outside jobs (which is the norm in contemporary North America) he/she leaves for school about eight a.m. From then until about four p.m. he/she is in school where the only people he/she interacts with are youth, the overwhelming percentage of whom are within two years of his/her own age. Teachers are nearby but not genuinely accessible. Virtually no other adults are permitted in the schools. Near four p.m. the youngster heads for home accompanied by peers; he/she checks in about five. Between five p.m. and ten p.m. the typical adolescent spends three-fourths of one hour eating, and three hours watching television. Bedtime is in the vicinity of eleven p.m. On a 24-hour clock, the breakdown goes like this: eight hours of sleep, eight hours of school, including travel time; one hour "hanging around" with peers; one hour (minimum) eating; three hours television; three hours miscellaneous. For time spent in social interaction nothing comes close to the amount of time spent with peers. An alien might infer that parents and adults could be omitted from adolescent life together if the decision were based on a typical day routine.

Adolescents are isolated in their daily routine from adults. They do not interact on any constructive plane. If a mysterious disease wiped out every adolescent in North America it would not seriously affect any *important* industry or institution (other than the schools) because youth contribute in no vital way to the maintenance or operation of our society. They are the recipients and the consumers of artifact industries who spend the vast percentage of every waking day in the presence of one another. It is no wonder they depend on their peers. Peers *are* their world.

There is no escape. The days when youth could run away from over-schooling or a world filled only with peers are gone. Even when the environment is so utterly inferior as to be intolerable, youth cannot slip away and start afresh. "One of the most important coping devices the youth of our pioneer days had available was, of course, *the constructive and therapeutic runaway* — leaving home or unbearable conditions and making something of yourself. In the young-adolescent years, even the best attempts of this sort are now out. Even well-intended and reason-ably mature attempts at this sort of self-cure invariably and ingloriously end at the desk of that nice lady from the Traveler's Aid at bus, railroad, or air terminals." (Redl, 1969, p. 88)

The single most significant event in the contemporary adolescent life-style came about with the introduction of compulsory education. In the late nineteenth century, public compulsory education for youth age six to 16 became widespread throughout North America. This broke the custom of English common law where the parents had control of the education of the child. In a court case where the father tried to disobey the law of compulsory education the court decreed:

> The course of study to be pursued in the public schools of our state is prescribed either by statute or by the school authorities in per-

suance thereof. These schools include not only elementary schools, but high schools as well . . . . A parent, therefore, is not at liberty to exercise a choice in that regard, but, where not exempt from some lawful reason, must send his child to the school where instruction is provided suitable to its attainments as the school authorities may determine.

Even a parent who is proven competent may not assume the responsibility of educating the child.

We have no doubt many parents are capable of instructing their own children, but to permit such parents to withdraw their children from the public schools without permission from the superintendent of schools, and to instruct them at home, would be to disrupt our common school system and destroy its value to the state. (See Bakan, 1972, p. 76)

The historical offshoot of the compulsory education laws was beyond the imaginings of even the most visionary futurists. We now have a massive educational structure which embraces almost every young person in the country. (Between 97 and 98 percent of all 14-15-year-olds attend school.) The educational benefits of this system are undeniable, but for the moment they are not the focus of concern. What is of concern is the degree to which compulsory education has *created an artificial youth world* for which no precedent exists in either North American or European history.

Home life also is more isolated than in past generations. Rarely do more than two generations share the same house; grandparents live elsewhere and their grandchildren do not know them as individuals nor do they know about (or respect) their historical roots. Suburban families are compact thus adolescents know virtually nothing first hand about young children. Among the professional classes, mother and father are so busy that home is little more than a pit stop, or rest centre, where children are best kept in the stands. The young person does not hold a substantial basis for identifying with parents and thereby becomes even more attracted to the peer world.

Adolescents have no concrete ideas about the *competence* of their mother or father. They have never seen them in action. They have not seen them do what they do best; often home is where they are at their worst — or least competent. They have not seen other adults ask their parents for advice, nor have they seen them solve difficult problems. The point I make is that not only are youth isolated into same-age peer communities, but the links which would meaningfully connect them with adulthood are weakly forged and easily broken by the strain of normal tension. In the most real sense, youngsters simply do not know their parents because they do not share vital work with them, nor the pleasure and sorrow which comes with it. The peer group receives no viable competition from adults. No wonder it wins the allegiance of young people.

Being excluded from the adult community has greater impact on the mood of the adolescent than heretofore imagined. In a practical vein it means only peers remain. Some youth are resentful because they feel abandoned. An even greater number, however, simply don't care. The apathy contributes dramatically to the alienation of the young. Indifference toward the adult society increases the magnetism of the peer community.

Youth do not inherently value peers more highly than adults. They learn to do so. Neither do they inherently dislike adults. This they acquire from lack of meaningful affiliation with them. We misread youth because we do not understand what they need; we concentrate too much on what they do wrong and not enough on what they do right. We see their actions as caused by age, but they are better understood if we concentrate on social dynamics. This is especially true with regard to peer groups.

It pays to remember that youth *do* like their peers and are genuinely influenced by them. It does *not* pay to think that the peer group is the most important fact in their lives, or that its notch on the hierarchy cannot be replaced. An obvious "for example" is romance. In our culture it is a trend for late adolescents to forsake the coterie for a steady. Boyfriends or girlfriends do not break up the clique, but they consistently build inroads into its power and prestige. Likewise with good employment. Most youth will abandon what was thought to be an inseparable peer group for a job which pays well or which permits constructive work. If the person-to-person relationship is civilized, many youngsters chose to spend time with their parents rather than with their age mates. The same holds true for sports, for drama, or any activity in which people are taken seriously, receive praise and do something they consider important. Counsellors who have a feel for youth and who avoid condescending attitudes find a steady stream of youngsters trickling in and out of their office. Adolescents do not avoid adults who deal with them in a dignified way. On the contrary, they are attracted by the experience, power and insight inherent to adulthood.

As holds true for adults and children, there are times when the adolescent prefers *only* to be with peers. This is especially true for matters essentially adolescent in nature. Young boys do not want adults hanging around when they are talking up what a great body Cynthia has, or how they almost scored with Marie. Neither do they care for them when working through interpersonal problems or low feelings. Adolescents know there is much about their play and silliness that adults do not care for, and when they are in the midst of it, or planning it, adults are not wanted. Learning important things is sometimes impeded by the presence of adults. Peers have a legitimate desire to be among themselves, with adults only as outsiders. However, their *whole life* is not this way; to think that it is shows how effectively the peer-group myth clouds our understanding.

Youth become hooked on peers when they represent the *only way* to achieve importance. In these conditions, without peers they are nothing. Existentialists call it the fear of nonbeing; its anxiety is awesome but nevertheless acted out in the adolescent arena with regularity. The sense of emptiness it carries compels one to fill the gap by being with others. The mere presence of companions offsets the anxiety of being nobody. When peers are the only way to preserve one's centre, they become the centre of one's life.

Adults misunderstand youth gatherings, believing that because youth huddle together they are bound together psychologically in a pact of inseparable allegiance. This is not so. As Friedenberg points out in *The Vanishing Adolescent,* "Groups of juveniles are not friendly; and strongly felt friendships do not form among them, though there is often constant association between members of juvenile cliques." Necessity, as much as choice, brings them together. "They are not there to be friendly; they are there to work out a crude social system and to learn the ropes from one another." In this regard appearances deceive.

Youth *do not* become hooked on peers when other ways to achieve importance exist. I have suggested two involvements which consistently weaken the peer grip: romance and work. Other factors also weaken peer group obsession: a relationship with parents which is basic and earthy, where the youngster sees parental competence or expertise also counters peer dominance. Dealing with younger and older generations (so that one's personal age-frame is not exaggerated out of proportion) also helps.

Kurt Lewin, one of the most perceptive of the social psychologists, once observed that the adolescent "does not wish any longer to belong to the children's group, and at the same time, knows that he is not readily accepted in the adult group. In this case he has a position similar to what is called in sociology the 'marginal man' ''. Unfortunately, we require youth to remain marginal when their impulses are to grow out of marginal status into adulthood. Their glamourization of themselves and their peers derives almost exclusively from their lack of meaningful ties with the adult community, from being herded into segregated schools where peers are their only companions, and from no one other than peers taking them seriously. There is nothing about adolescence, *per se,* which gives the peer group the paralytic power it holds in western culture. It results from our boycott of their personhood.

Ages: The psychological importance of the peer group changes during the course of the second decade of life. During *early* adolescence the peer group is, in essence, the young person's lifeline with the outer world: it demarcates the first major split from the family. Its social significance is hard to *over*-estimate as the tentacles of its influence probe every corner of life. The peer group is the first testing ground of adolescence where youngsters find out what others think of them and what their strengths and weaknesses are all about. Because personal identity is not fully formed the group is sought for guidance and direction. To go against the group is difficult, sometimes impossible. Of the three ages of adolescence, this unquestionably is the ascendant period of peer power. As *middle* adolescence approaches, youngsters gain a stronger grip on themselves. They know themselves better, therefore, are not as manipulable as the ''marginal'' youth of yesterday. They also know more what they dislike, and are better skilled at avoiding it. They anticipate better, therefore, are duped less frequently. Their sense of morality is further developed, making them less coercible; and their intellect more complex, making them better able to view themselves from a rational distance. We should not make them sound too aloof from the pressure of peers because they still very much want to be held in their favour, and they also need their comfort and comraderie. As a group, middle adolescents are distinguishable from early adolescents by their greater sense of autonomy, and their increased ability to oppose social pressure. Late adolescents are more their own people than during either of the other periods. Close friends, intimacy partners, and companions which are welded together by common interests are more likely at this age than the random collections of friends and activities of early adolescence.

The aptitude to think for oneself becomes so fully developed in *some* late-adolescent youth that not only does the peer group lose influence, so also does the society at large. Late adolescents assess themselves more in terms of competence and intimacy than mere social acceptance.

The Generation Gap Myth

Wherein we discover that adolescents, as a group, are not fundamentally different from adults as a group; that what we consider important generational differences are often little more than differences in outlook for achieving the same goal; and that genuine generational differences in our culture do not take place until late adolescence.

Adults, we often are told, are considerably distanced from youth by ideology and outlook. This so-called "generation gap" creates differences which make it impossible to reconcile the nature of youth with the nature of adulthood. Conservatives blame the gap on the insipidness of youth; liberals, always more wordy, attribute it to a resentful unconscious or to institutional deficiencies which prevent youngsters from getting on the right track. The next consequence of the generation gap is that youth are not able "to communicate clearly" with adults, and that adults are unable "to socialize" their youngsters in the manner they see fit. If the lines of communication were more open the gap would close and the generations would live in greater harmony — we are told.

When we say "generation gap", what do we mean? if we mean that adult-adolescent disagreements are of *a uniquely profound nature,* then I think it is misleading. If we mean that differences between the generations are *based upon lack of communication,* then I think it is misleading. If we mean that it is a "gap" which *exists because of deficiencies within either adults or adolescents,* then I think it is misleading. Theoreticians who so explain "generation gap" fail because it is precisely the opposite of these concepts which constitutes "generation gap".

Not so many generations ago, but more than most of us want to believe, one of our most enduring thinkers commented: "Our adolescents now seem to love luxury. They have bad manners and contempt for authority. They show disrespect for adults and spend their time hanging around places gossiping with one another . . . . They are ready to contradict their parents, monopolize the conversation in company, eat gluttonously, and tyrannize their teachers." When Socrates uttered these words he probably received nodding approval from his listeners, just as he would today.

I don't believe in generation gap because I do not like the metaphor. Gap implies a cleft or a crevasse which separates but which has no substance; mere space serving as an obstacle. It does little credit to the *fundamental nature of the differences,* and is like labelling the differences between the Germans and French a "nationality gap". Generations are not separated by a "gap" but by differences in impulses and actions. Some genuine differences in ideology exist but they are not nearly as dramatic as most people think — especially the nervous ones.

To assume that generation gaps are based upon lack of communication is to misread the argument. Communication is clear between the generations: conflict exists because the older generation chooses one option and the younger another. The messages of each to the other are fairly clear, they simply are unacceptable. Hence a power struggle. Most power struggles between adults and adolescents in our society have to do with *specific preferences rather than general beliefs.* Parents struggle with their children on dress habits, check-in times, friend selections, and sexual habits. These struggles represent the differences between what the parent wants and what the youngster wants to do. They are differences brought about by differences in impulse and responsibility. Establishing clear communication lines does not reduce basic differences although it *may* bring about a better understanding of each other's viewpoint. These conflicts are in no way *fundamentally* different from the power struggle between the toddler and the parent, except that the participants are a decade or so older. Generation gap is not based upon lack of communication; it is grounded in the clarity of it.

To claim that adult-adolescent conflicts are of a uniquely profound nature is myopic. In many respects the conflicts which take place between adult and adolescent are calm when compared with conflict among adolescents themselves. The rift between late adolescents and early adolescents, for example, is greater than that between most late adolescents and the adults they interact with — which is saying quite a bit. Early adolescents are almost never considered equals with late teens and their opinions carry virtually no weight. They live worlds apart. On occasion peers are treated savagely. Erikson observes that young people are "remarkably clannish, intolerant, and cruel in their exclusion of others who are "different", in skin colour or cultural background, in tastes and gifts, and often in entirely petty aspects of dress and gesture arbitrarily selected as the signs of an in-grouper or an out-grouper'' (1968, p. 132).

Some ''generation gap'' problems are relatively minor, particularly the conflict which exists between *early* adolescents and adults. Offer's research shows that these conflicts disrupt the household and cause ill feelings, however, to think of them as a *profound* struggle is to overstate the case. ''Rebellion in our normal subjects is characterized by chronic infighting (lasting one to two years) with parents and school teachers in the pre-high school years. This infighting is over issues that seem small or undramatic. The rebellion does not involve serious or repeated delinquencies, nor does it involve the plunging and rising of great emotional states. *Bickering is the word most characteristic of these disturbances* (1969, p. 186).

The belief that generation gap is caused by deficiencies within either the adolescent or the adult is, for the most part, incorrect. Differences exist precisely because each generation knows its own mind, remains true to its beliefs, and strives to do what it thinks best. That adults do this without clear understanding of youth is regrettable, and less defensible than the youngsters' equal lack of empathy. But to infer that it derives from a fundamental *deficiency of character* is to miss the point.

On occasion, however, conflict between the generations is based upon a deficiency in *aptitude*. Some adolescents who ''reject'' society do not hold any fundamental objections against their society: their distance stems from the fact that they do not possess the necessary skills to succeed in the outside world and therefore either rebel or lose interest. Keniston notes: ''In assessing the sources of alienation, we must try to strike still another balance: *between those who cannot meet the demands of their society,* and those *who choose not to do so.''* Many youth simply cannot meet the expectations placed upon them. ''Countless men and women simply lack the requisite human qualities for anything approaching success in American society: they go jobless, they cannot 'achieve', they do not succeed, they are not wanted, and they become embittered, sour, and rejecting of our society as a whole.'' (1960, p. 386) On the surface these embittered youth strike us as being fundamentally at odds with society and the older generation as well, but their grievance is personal rather than societal, and it may or may not affect their allegiance to the dominant society. Paradoxically, some of society's most consistent ''losers'' are the staunchest defenders of the status quo.

Power is the ability to effect or to prevent change. Those who cannot effect or prevent change have no power. When a person (or a group) wants to effect change, and is opposed by another person (or group) a *power struggle* ensues. Generation gap is *a power struggle of conflicting desires and impulses between the older and the younger, the vast majority of which modify so persistently with age that it is only a matter of time before the younger generation sides with the older generation against the new wave.* Socrates' grandfather probably held a view of youth similar to that which Socrates himself expounded, although if he had said it to Socrates as a youth, he would have had an argument, maybe a rebellion, on his hands.

Consider the following. Parents (or school authorities for that matter) do not condone excessive "displays of affection". They do not approve of petting, and most certainly not sexual intercourse. They do not approve of "arousing" clothing or conversation laced with sexual innuendo. Nor do they much like playful wrestling or any other excuse for unnecessary contact between the sexes. Presumably adults think as they do for good reasons. They believe that sex is important and should be taken seriously. That sexual promiscuity is undesirable because it leads to undesirable consequences. They believe that intimacy should preceed sexuality. They believe that young people should act "like young adults". These are the general beliefs upon which they base their expectations. With virtually all of these general beliefs *the adolescents are in complete agreement.* None seem foreign to them. In their private lives they are remarkably true to them. The objection comes with the specifics. Who says public displays of affection are cheap? Who says my wardrobe is "arousing", better yet, what if it is? Isn't arousing and being aroused part of natural sexuality? What is wrong with playful wrestling? Nothing serious comes of it. It's fun, but certainly not wrong unto itself.

The important differences between the older and the younger are remarkably slight. The *minor* differences are what grate. Unfortunately, they are not differences which really make a difference to the issues at hand, but they make considerable difference in the way the generations treat one another, and in the ways they artificially lose respect for one another.

The mood of the late seventies and the early eighties differs dramatically from that of the middle sixties. Outright resentment has been replaced by the struggle to turn society to one's personal advantage without being swamped by it. The fight no longer is to overthrow the system but to siphon its strengths into oneself. Nor is the sense of hostile alienation as powerful as it was during the sixties. The following statement by Theordore Roszak in *Making a Counter Culture,* was an apt description of youth *at that time,* but it no longer rings true:

> For the fact is that cultural innovation in America is becoming more and more the captive of youth who are profoundly alienated from the adult society. For better or worse, most of what is happening that is new, provocative, and engaging in the arts, in politics, in education, in social relations (love, courtship, family), in journalism, in fashions, and entertainment, is very largely the creation either of the discontented young or of those who address themselves primarily to the young. (p. 1)

The relationship of youth to the dominant society is a touchy subject. Youth are the successors to the throne; its strength and viability depends upon them. When they show signs of corruption or deviance, elders become worrisome. In North America today, the generations, by modern world standards, and by almost universal historical standards, are quite compatible. Our misunderstanding is that we have not accentuated enough the *viable* or *tolerable* differences between the generations, nor have we appreciated the improvements we have made *because of* generational differences. After all, it was the youth who set in motion the shutting down of the war in Vietnam. And it was the adults who opened the free drug clinics for adolescents who were destroying themselves on chemicals. Differences in outlook have produced viable improvements. Adult experience counters the naïveté of youth, and the boldness of the young challenges the caution of their elders. Without generational conflict adolescents become old before their time and adults are robbed of rejuvenating confrontation with upstart challengers. In Canada and the United States *genuine* belief differences between the generations are minimal and, on the whole, the tension they create is not destructive. (If an exception exists, it holds for late adolescents and their consistent mistreatment by the *institutional power* structure.)

Nor is the alienation of inner-city youth the result of a generation gap. Their separateness derives from active oppression, not a gap. Abuse is accorded them because of economic status or race rather than age. It is a significant problem which leads to dramatic youth pathology but it is not fundamentally an *age* problem because it does not improve with time, and it equally existed before adolescence. Psychologists have never well understood juvenile delinquency among low income youth because they try to understand it independent of the *oppression* which is its true cause.

Differences between the generations are of two general types: young people who reject the *life-style and ideology* of their elders and who actively strive to create genuine alternatives disagree on one level, and young people who fight over specific issues which effect their immediate family or small segments of their day-to-day routine disagree on another level. In North America almost all generational differences are of the second type. On the grand scale, society is little threatened; on the personal scale, individuals are threatened and experience pain. The damage usually takes place *in the confrontation:* youngsters run away, quit school or in any number of ways jeopardize their future. The consequence of the disagreement frequently is greater than its substance. It's a shootout over an insult.

Ages: As with most adolescent realities, differences between the generations are influenced by the phase of adolescence being lived. The differences are not hard and fast, but sufficiently consistent to be noted. During *early* adolescence, some shaky periods take place which result in anything from minor arguments to irreconcilable rifts. Conflicts tend to centre around specific behaviour rather than general ideology and invariably originate because a youngster refuses to do what is expected, or else insists upon doing something taboo. In short, conflicts are what adults call "discipline" or "behaviour" problems, and what the young call "bossiness" or "not being able to do my own thing". Serious consequences at the personal level may flow from these altercations. If the differences are patched up, however, no *categorical reason* exists for adult and adolescent to disagree. During *middle* adolescence, subtle changes take place which increase the likelihood of generational differences. The thought process becomes more sophisticated and is better able to isolate philosophical differences; youth are able to dislike an adult for what he represents not merely how he disciplines. They see adults in a more comprehensive way. Their god-like qualities disappear. In addition, *the basis for specific conflicts increase* because the middle adolescent demands greater freedom and expects more mature treatment. If denied he rebels. Spending money is easier and this increases freedom, taking the young person that much further away from adult control. However, the adolescent remains heavily invested in peers, in school and sometimes with a romantic partner. The adult world is peripheral; if it does not cause pain it often goes unnoticed. Thus, in the radical sense of a revolutionary looking to overthrow the authorities, there exists little fundamental "generation gap".

With late adolescence, the problem worsens. This is an "age of

214

ideology" and with it comes the realization that they view important matters in a *fundamentally different* way than does the parent society. It is a time of tension between person and society, when youth *actively resist* socialization they disagree with. Late adolescents can shun wealth to which they have grown accustomed, or give up pleasures if they are philosophically objectionable. To start a revolution, a hippie generation, a drug colony, a student government association, or a ban the bomb movement, this is your age. Forget the *early* adolescents: they are pre-ideological and believe in dogma more than principle, and give up when the going gets tough. *Middle* adolescents are ideological but inclined to accept that which currently is in power. *Late* adolescents, *as a group,* are also followers of the status quo, but among them one is most likely to find young men and women who have genuine and definable grievances with their society who are willing to fight for them and to be poor for them. Of the adolescent ages, late adolescence is the only period where genuine ideological "generation gap" exists. The Red Guard, the Storm Troopers, the American Revolutionaries, and the French Resistance drew heavily from this age group and so also will future revolutionary movements.

Myth Number Five

The Turmoil Myth

Wherein we discover that all youth do not experience adolescence as an age of extreme anguish or turmoil; that much of our thinking about adolescence has been clouded by extremist writing and the indiscriminate use of outrageous metaphors.

In the minds of many otherwise clear thinking adults, adolescents are a dangerously unstable group of people. Their life is thought of as a constant struggle with overpowering tension and ceaseless turmoil. As a generalization about youth this simply is not true. How it has come to be thought of as true is unclear, but it derives in part from the way many social scientists describe the adolescent experience.

According to some psychologists the adolescent is like a runaway locomotive on a collision course with whatever (or whoever) happens to be on the tracks. Anthony (1969) has documented some of the more vivid metaphors used to describe youth. One author says: "One cannot analyze an adolescent in the middle phase, *it is like running next to an express train*". Another writer likens adolescence to *"an active volcanic process* with continuous eruptions taking place, preventing the crust from solidifying". In the clinical litterature the use of terms such as "turbulence", "chaos", and "turmoil" are frequent. Blos, for example, has stated that early adolescence is a period of profound emotional reorganization "with attendant and well-recognized *states of chaos"*. Scary images indeed! After reviewing these assessments of youth, Anthony insightfully notes "Once the psychotherapist gets it into his head that he has to deal with a bomb that might explode or a volcano that might erupt or an express train that will outpace him . . ." his view of youth is likely affected for the worse. (1969, p. 57)

Mark Twain, on his return from a European lecture series, was met by a reporter who informed him that it had been reported that he was dead. Twain replied, "Those reports were exaggerated". Reports of adolescent life are equally exaggerated. There is no question that some turmoil

216

accompanies adolescence; for *many* youth it is the most turbulent time of their lives. On the other side of the coin, our understanding is inaccurate if we infer that *all* youth experience storm and stress, that grief and turmoil are *necessary ingredients* of the adolescent years, or that *for all young people* adolescence is the most emotionally taxing period of their lives.

Close inspection of youth who are not disturbed in a psychological sense nor significantly deviant in a social sense (which represents the majority) indicates that the images conjured by the storm and stress authors do not stack up very well. Offer makes an important observation when he states: "Investigators who have spent most of their professional lives studying disturbed adolescents stress the importance of a period of turmoil through which all teenagers must pass in order to grow into mature adults. On the other hand, investigators who, like us, *have studied normal adolescent populations tend to minimize the extent of the turmoil*" (1969, p. 180).

Much of the problem is related to the fact that adults do not hold consistent views as to what adolescent turmoil means. Is the nervous fretting, the edgy stomach of one's first date adolescent turmoil? Is the resentment youth harbour toward their parents turmoil? What of the suppressed anger they hold toward school? If these tensions occurred during childhood or adulthood would we think of them as "turmoil"? Or would we be more inclined to think of them as life difficulties each individual learns to cope with?

Turmoil is significant in relation to three measures: (1) the extent to which it interferes with attaining goals; (2) the extent to which it creates *overpowering* anxiety; and, (3) the extent it carries *into the future* and creates havoc therein. Life experiences which influence the adolescent in these ways can rightfully be understood as turmoil-ish. Our tendency to elevate minor life skirmishes such as peer struggles or romantic feuds into major life catastrophes makes the youth experience more filled with turmoil than it often is. Conversely, we overlook genuinely serious maladies, such as the lack of worthwhile work, or the stifling boredom of school, and reduce them to minor ailments when they are not.

We must distinguish when turmoil is fleeting and transitory from when it is harmful to personal growth. This distinction is clouded by the adolescent's ability to egocentrically magnify self-experience into a grand display of existential urgency, and by an equal ability to adjust to harsh circumstances with amazing dexterity. It is further obscured by the adult tendency to *under-estimate* the needs of youth, to assume that they are able to deny their budding adultness without regressing into childish drivel, and that they enjoy their isolated and impotent roles in family and society.

That adolescence is not categorically a time of unbearable stress becomes more seemly when one places into perspective the varying ingredients of adolescent turmoil, and when one is not overly impressed with metaphors such as erupting volcanoes and runaway express trains.

Offer suggests that adolescent turmoil represents a "significant disruption in the psychic organization of the adolescent that leads to psychological disequilibrium and tumult, resulting in fluctuant and unpredictable behavior." Experiences must be more than merely inconvenient, stressful or bothersome to be thought of as turmoil. Offer draws the following conclusion:

> *We have not found turmoil to be prevalent in our normal adolescent population.* Behavioural and emotional indices gained through interviews of the adolescents and parents, teacher ratings, and analyses of psychological testing all deny the existence of turmoil on a grand scale in our adolescent subjects. The concept of adolescent turmoil should be seen as only one route for passing through adolescence, one that the majority of our subjects did not utilize. Rebellion was seen in the early adolescence of our subjects; in all but a few cases the rebellious behaviour was not a part of a total picture of turmoil but was coped with before it grew to chaotic proportions for the individuals involved. (1969, p. 179)

Youngsters learn to stand on their own feet, to admit to strengths *and* limitations, and to make important decisions about the future. For the most part, adolescents face up to these tasks successfully. Normal adolescents lack the turmoil of disturbed adolescents "precisely because their ego is strong enough to withstand the pressures. In their task they are greatly helped by their parents" (1969, p. 184).

Youth who *do* experience considerable turmoil may be experiencing a normal rather than an neurotic crisis. Erikson points out that "adolescence is not an affliction but a normative crisis, i.e., *a normal phase of increased conflict* characterized by a seeming fluctuation in ego strength and yet also by a high growth potential". On the other hand, *neurotic crises* are self-perpetuating, they waste growth energy, and they deepen psycho-social isolation. The normal crises hold some advantage, they

> . . . are relatively more reversible, or, better, transversible, and are characterized by an abundance of available energy which to be sure, revives dormant anxiety and arouses new conflict, but also

supports new and expanded ego functions in the searching and playful engagement of new opportunities and associations. What under prejudiced scrutiny may appear to be the onset of a neurosis is often but an aggravated crisis which might prove to be self-liquidating and, in fact, *contributive to the process of identity formation*. (Quoted in Offer, 1975 p. 162)

Ages: Adolescents in different phases experience different kinds of turmoil. During the *child*-adolescent period the greatest difficulties evolve around peer conflicts, survival within the school, and lack of self-confidence. Turmoil at home is founded upon bickering between parent and child and the tendency for parents to not pay attention to their youngsters; however, disagreements tend to be based upon specifics of conduct such as when to report home, whom to associate with, achievement in school, and other day-to-day realities, rather than upon major disagreements requiring a philosophy of life. Turmoil during *middle* adolescence tends to be like the *sturm und drang* believers claim. Emotional upheavals are more noticeable, romantic feuds more intense, and disagreements with parents more substantial. During these years turmoil leads to more serious consequences both personally and socially. In the *late*-adolescent period, turmoil is experienced as tension with society at large and the future in general. It is adult in composition and closely resembles the inner torment characteristic of normal adulthood. Conflicts concerning career plans and separation from parents are common at this age.

From the foregoing we may infer that during the adolescent years many youth experience considerable turmoil and distress. On the other hand, many youth experience only mild turmoil bouts. Some youth appear to be as exempt from turmoil during adolescence as they were during childhood. The belief that *all* youth experience chronic turmoil during the teen years is a myth which has been encouraged by an excessive preoccupation with troubled adolescent sub-populations such as juvenile delinquents, or the emotionally disturbed, and insufficient analysis of the normal adolescent.

The Hypocrisy Myth

Wherein we discover that youth are much more prone toward hypocrisy, in-fighting and power politics than is commonly thought; that their abhorance of hypocrisy relates to its presence in others much more than in themselves.

Some adolescent watchers emphasize that the teen years are a period of idealism. Because of this they conclude that youth are strongly opposed to any form of deceit or deception, and that they place profound emphasis on the truth. They also conclude that "to be true to oneself" is the paramount axiom of the adolescent years. In a phrase, many adolescent commentators argue that youth are not hypocritical.

For the most part, this is a myth. Youth *are* idealistic, however, they also are pragmatic and in many instances they will do whatever is required in order to achieve personal advancement.

The hypocrisy myth achieves impetus because youth are keenly aware of the hypocrisy *of others* and are not afraid to speak their mind against it. However, merely pointing out the hypocrisy of others does not insure its absence in oneself. In the following pages I shall outline some of the developmental factors which contribute to hypocritical behaviour among adolescents, and also describe some of the social and interpersonal situations which increase its probability during this time of life.

Of all the pre-adult growth stages, adolescence is the one most filled with hypocrisy and hypocritical behaviour. Teenagers are hypocritical because their desire for social acceptance, their need to explore forbidden pleasures, and their preoccupation with the present incline them toward social pragmatism and self-centred expediency — the nuclear ingredients of all hypocrisy.

Four general categories of behaviour frequently observed during the adolescent years can justifiably be described as hypocritical in nature. These include: (1) the tendency to pretend to be what one is not; (2) the tendency to pretend not to be what one is; (3) the tendency to talk negatively about peers in their absence but positively about them in their presence; and (4) the tendency to behave and speak in whatever manner is most expedient or advantageous to one's self. The adolescent is inclined toward all these forms of hypocrisy for numerous reasons, some of which are developmental in nature and will be outgrown.

Not everyone can be hypocritical because hypocrisy requires certain skills and talents which are not abundantly available during the pre-adolescent years. For example, to be hypocritical one must recognize the distinction between public appearance and private experience and understand that it is possible to manipulate the conclusions other people draw. Hypocrisy requires the ability to remember accurately and plan systematically a complex series of actions, always clearly distinguishing within one's own mind that such behaviour is a mixture of parade, charade, and fact which must appear genuine to the observer. Hypocritical behaviour, in many respects, is beyond the limited developmental capacities of the child, especially the preschool child, who does not clearly understand that thought is private and cannot be read infallibly by outsiders; nor does the child understand that motives are personal and cannot be omnisciently detected. The adolescent, on the other hand, is aware that thought is private, that motives are ambiguous, and that deceit often goes undetected. Teenagers are better at hypocrisy than their younger brothers and sisters because they possess the tools for its proper execution and can better transact the complex procedures required.

Adolescents, of course, are more impressed with the hypocrisy of adults than with their own. Adolescents usually can be relied upon to document the daily hypocrisies of their elders, but the intelligence which allows such insight is not impartial enough to bring under investigation the hypocrisy generated by itself. Stated succinctly, adolescents are aware of the hypocrisy of others to a much greater degree than of their own hypocrisy. (The flamboyant social criticism, typically found wherever adolescents congregate, is a by-product of this peculiarity.) In fairness to adolescents, we must report that their understanding of adult hypocrisy is often sophisitcated and, on occasion, exceeds that which adults themselves possess. The issue, however, is not how accurately adult hypocrisy is understood, but how inaccurately adolescents perceive their own hypocrisy.

Numerous factors contribute to the tendency to engage in the types of hypocrisy earlier stated. Adolescents, for example, are constantly confronted with situations where they are expected to pretend to be what they are not. They are expected to be content with school when they rarely are; they are expected to be openly honest but, when they are, chastisement is often the reward; they are expected to conform to parental viewpoints and beliefs which they do not agree with. Viewed objectively, adolescents are constantly expected to be other than what they are and, therefore, the stage is set for one type of hypocrisy: pretending to be what one is not.

Pretending *not* to be what one is also is observed in the adolescent arena. Adolescents are expected *not* to be angry or resentful but, in fact, they often are; they are expected *not* to engage in behaviour which will hurt their parents when they often must in order to be honest with themselves; they are expected *not* to feel hatred, jealousy, or possessiveness even though these feelings surge through their being, ripping the fibre of inner emotion. In essence, adolescents are expected by peers, adults, parents, and teachers *not to be, not to feel, not to desire* those very things which constitute a genuine share of their total existence. They are expected to deny inner feeling and, eventually, they learn to behave accordingly — usually without cognizance that to do so is, in part, hypocritical.

These first two types of hypocrisy are, in great measure, a logical consequence of living in a social world filled with contrary rules and expectations.

More serious forms of hypocrisy also come into play during these critical years including slander and self-centred expedience.

Adolescents are, in many respects, status seekers and pyramid climbers. Especially during *early* adolescence, they are strongly influenced by peer pressure, power politics, and the need to belong: thus, they become prospects for the web of social maliciousness we sometimes associate with junior executives. When the need for group acceptance becomes overwhelming, as it indeed does for many adolescents, the ability of the group to manipulate the person is proportionately increased; on the other hand, when the group strongly desires to admit particular persons, the greater is their ability to manipulate the group. Adolescents who find themselves on the weak side of the exchange, constantly seeking admission and attempting to prove that they deserve acceptance, are easily enticed into a vast array of behaviour to which they otherwise would never consent. Of the extremes to which an adolescent will go in order to win group acceptance, hypocrisy is one of the more moderate.

A common adolescent ploy is to debase or ridicule peers competing for group acceptance, thereby elevating one's relative importance at the expense of a fellow adolescent. If the peer group values honesty, it is an easy matter to point out the dishonest nature of a competitor; if the group values toughness, it is elementary to point out the frailties and weaknesses of another peer seeking group acceptance. In short, the adolescent is not immune to lying, slandering, or defaming other people if this will lead to a more secure footing on the slippery social ladder.

The adolescent who is not burdened with moral imperatives is able to breeze through the 'requirements' of cut-throat social life more easily than a companion who reflects upon the moral rightness of one's conduct. Inevitably, the adolescent must come to grips with the non-authenticity of hypocrisy, whether it is socially effective or not. Thus, a natural consequence of adolescent social interchange is a crisis in moral viewpoint, usually occurring during the late-adolescent years after the turmoil of early adolescence has taken its toll.

The final form of adolescent hypocrisy is the tendency to do *whatever is required* to achieve maximum results in the present without considering what will accrue in the future as a result of such actions. In other words, the hypocrisy of expediency. The adolescent who says only what the school principal *wants* to hear, who behaves only in the way the gang leader *expects,* who feigns sincerity in order to win the confidence of a sweetheart engages in the hypocrisy of acting out a role in order to receive maximum returns for that role. Role playing is not itself hypocritical. However, when one attempts to persuade another person that the role being played *is an accurate portrayal of one's real self when it is not,* that person becomes hypocritical. On this count, the adolescent is guilty time and again. Adolescents learn to feign sincereity and to manipulate others by appearing innocent when they are not or by appearing expert when they are but novices. Hypocrisy of this type can be likened to that of the imposter, the conman, or the charlatan, and even though such prototypes are somewhat stylish nowadays, hypocrisy and deceit are central to their style.

Samuel Johnson was partly correct when he stated that 'no man is a hypocrite in his pleasure'. His intention was to point out that people will, if nothing else, be forthright in pursuing those things which bring them pleasure. One is tempted to surmise that Johnson's insight is geared more to adults than adolescents because the latter are steadfastly hypocritical about their pleasure, convincing themselves that they like things which they do not and assuring others that they do not like things which they do. As mentioned before, this is partially attributable to the fact that adolescents are required to live by rules which do not take into consideration either their need structure or their advancing developmental status.

Our society and other technological societies do not truly require the adolescent to comply with the fundamental principles of honesty and consistency except in matters involving private property and bureaucratic efficiency. For the most part, our society does not care whether adolescents are honest or dishonest as long as they do not create inconvenience or wander beyond narrowly-prescribed expectations. Because of this, many adolescents merge into adulthood only marginally convinced that honesty is better than deceit or that justice is better than expediency.

Adolescents tend to outgrow their unique brands of hypocrisy, replacing them in time with typical adult variations. Adolescents are comparatively exempt from the universal adult hypocrisy which decrees that others should 'do as I say, not do as I do'. Adolescents believe in doing their own thing, and tend not to be overly prescriptive about what others (especially peers) should do.

Adolescent hypocrisy is worthy of close analysis. It tells us a good deal about their pressurized life and allows glimpses of the ways in which personality preserves itself in a social network which does not take it seriously. Adults are obligated to take a long look into the matrix which perpetuates adolescent hypocrisy; not to do so is a hypocritical gesture by a group pretending to promote their children's welfare but, in fact, often conspiring against it.

Only when adults allow adolescent honesty to be significantly more important than dishonesty will hypocrisy diminish. As of now, our society fails to encourage honesty, instead it rewards semi-honesty and marginal deceit. Adolescent hypocrisy is one of the consequences.

The Incompetence Myth

Wherein we discover that youth are much more competent than is generally thought; that their apparent lack of abilities stems from the ways in which they are excluded from important work and by the unwillingness of the schools to allow them to engage in meaningfully productive work; and that until the past generation adolescence has always been a time of social productivity.

A misconception exists within the contemporary public mind which would have been impossible three or four generations ago. It assumes that adolescents are basically incompetent at performing important life skills. The myth also claims that youth are incapable of effective or complicated work, and that they would experience intense difficulty surviving in the outside world if given a chance. This myth is openly supported by the schools which almost universally claim that young people should not be permitted out in the community even when it demonstrably improves the quality of their education. The myth is supported by business and labour, both of whom refuse to hire adolescents except for menial jobs.

Several generations ago the myth would never have gotten off the ground because it is a falsehood only the affluent can afford. As I sit at my typewriter, I overlook a massive Canadian prairie which 75 years ago was virtually devoid of people. It now stands as one of the richest agricultural and mineral centres in the world. The soil was broken, the towns were planned, the hospitals constructed, and the highways built by a spirited assemblage of pioneers, many of whom were middle and late adolescents who had only marginal schooling. People of this age were not incompetent then and they are not incompetent now.

Competence is the ability to deal effectively with important realities. In a technical sense it refers to being legally qualified and capable. To lack competence is serious business.

Adolescents *appear* to have no important kinds of competence. The settings where we observe them: the shopping malls, the walkways to and from school, the public hangouts, are, not much suited to doing what they do best. The emphasis of their school learning is academic thus, they do not require tangible skills which make them *appear* competent.

One distinguishing trait of both lower *and* higher-class youth is that they have nothing to do when they are not in school. (Middle-class youth are more likely to hold part-time jobs). Therefore, they hang around; and even though this requires basic-life skills, it is rarely thought of as such by the authorities. The image of adolescents as incompetent is reinforced by the way they behave. In many respects they resemble adults who recently have been laid off their jobs. They restlessly mill around, jousting with and mocking one another, and seemingly have nothing to do, which is precisely correct because they don't have anything to do. People who have nothing to do always look incompetent, especially if they are young, poor, or belong to a disfavoured minority group.

The appearances are not totally deceiving. Many young people are, by general standards, incompetent in their work skills. Many of them have never held a job for pay, and others have never participated in essential work around their home — especially urban youngsters. Most of them lack interpersonal skills with adults because they have had so little experience that they lack know-how. Having done little of importance they lack the confidence to believe that they *are* important. This inclines them to quit or give up far too easily. The "depression adults", as youth of today sometimes refer to people in their sixties, are not wrong when they complain that adolescents of today do not know how to work. Nor are they wrong when they point out that youngsters of today lack creative ingenuity in the work world. The differences between the youth of today and yesterday, however, are not of character, aptitude, or intelligence. The differences are in the experiences of growing up. Today's youth possess a greater breadth of knowledge because of instant world-wide news coverage, and, obtain more sophisticated classroom instruction than did the older generation, *however* they have considerably less exposure than did the youth of yesteryear to life experiences which *engender important forms of competence*.

Some observers assume that youth truly *are* incompetent. The "evidence", however, is more a function of the environment and its meagre offerings than lack of aptitude. Their shortage of skills in repair and maintenance derive from the same environmental conditions as their lack of interpersonal skills in dealing with adults: they are isolated from meaningful work experiences where they could learn specific skills; they spend most of their time in schools with peers and benefit only marginally from the expertise which adults could pass along to them; and, with time, they have grown accustomed to not doing much worthwhile and accept incompetence as the nature of things. Their *potential* to learn, however, is enormous. Intellectually they have the raw power of adults, and physically they are almost as durable. Perhaps even more importantly, their *psychological need structure predisposes them to achieve competence;* failure to recognize this aspect of their personality is one of the more serious shortcomings of curriculum designers, educators and government officials.

Some Examples of Constructive Use of Youth Talent

I would like to digress from the theoretical for a moment to share a few examples of youth projects in order to provide some indicators that adolescents are more capable than we given them credit for being, and that even against imposing odds they are able to achieve constructive goals which benefit their society. It is worth keeping in mind that all of these projects except one were conducted outside the schools, without much professional assistance or guidance.*

In Sacramento, California a group of young people banded together to create a community work project they call "Share and Repair". This project combines the elemental concepts of neighbourly sharing and self-help with the pragmatic expedience of cheap labour. The project began when a welfare mother with eleven children was served an eviction notice to vacate her condemned house. A neighbour lady thought this intolerable and organized a group of local teenagers to work on the house. Within the week it had been brought up to building code specifications. "Share and Repair" is still going. The main goal of the group is to fix and mend houses in need of repair. The owners must help, but the bulk of work is done by the teenagers. Primarily they mend roofs, fix windows, repair broken screens and doors, build cabinets, renovate sagging porches and remedy faulty plumbing. They "do" one house per month. Most of the workers are high school students, but some are from junior high. The quality of work is top rate. The city building code

*Examples cited in this section are taken from *Youth Magazine,* July, 1976, Mailing address is - 1505 Race St., Philadelphia, Penn. 19102.

stands as the criteria of acceptability. The beneficiaries are low-income people who cannot afford to pay to have the work done, and who do not have the tools or the competence to do the work themselves.

In Philadephia a high school senior by the name of Joe Forish organized twenty young people and opened a V.D. hot line for the metropolitan area called "Operation Venus". Eventually it grew into one of the largest and most effective call-in information services in the world. The hot line provides a toll-free confidential telephone service to which anyone can call from anywhere in the continental United States and receive virtually any information about venereal disease. The callers are given the address of a clinic or a physician who lives in their vicinity. Operation Venus was started in response to the increasing need for information about V.D. in the adolescent community. Operators trained in the biological, medical, social and psychological aspects of V.D. are on duty seven days per week. If they were older, or held academic degrees, they would probably be thought of as experts in adolescent psychology. During its first six years of operation, more than 800 young people were trained to work on the Operation Venus hot line. Since its effectiveness has been well established, and the organization has been proven to be of superior quality, many organizations which as a rule do not hire or subsidize youth have lent financial assistance. They include the Center for Disease Control, Atlanta, Georgia; Commonwealth of Pennsylvania Department of Health; and the Community Service Corps of Philadelphia.

In New York City young people organized by the Rev. Canon Walter Dennis work with the elderly and the very young during the summer months. Day camps for children 6-14 are organized in parts of the city where facilities are virtually nil; a wide variety of activities are offered including athletics, field trips and creative arts. Parents benefit also as they are liberated from looking after their kids all day. Thousands of elderly in New York also receive benefits of this youth program. They receive information on where they can take their grievances, and which agencies can most effectively help them. They also receive assistance from youngsters in making their living arrangements more comfortable. In essence, this group of teenagers, is doing what Federal and City governmental agencies do; only cheaper, more humanely, and in several respects, better.

The Alvarado Art Workshop in San Francisco began when a group of parents realized their children were learning very little about art in school. They convinced their kids this was true, and within a few months students from Alvarado and Edison schools had begun the Alvarado Art Workshop. One goal is to beautify their schools. To accomplish this they have built stained-glass windows, constructed block-printed curtains for their cafeteria, carpeted a library with rug scraps, painted murals and pieced mosaics. One educator said: "The project is everywhere — in the hallway, in the entrance to the school, outside the school doors, in the auditorium dressing rooms, in the cafeteria . . . . The project *is* everywhere, and people respond with a friendliness and cooperation *that brings back the spirit of hope for the school to students, teachers, parents and administrators alike.* The quality of work is notable." The Art Workshop provides a splendid mix of community resources, adult initiative, and adolescent competence. The entire community benefits.

In New York State a group of high school students began a nature museum known as the Cornwall-on-Hudson's Museum of the Hudson Highlands. It presently is in year-round operation and at one time occupied ten rooms of the Town Hall. The town has since erected a special building for the museum. The museum specializes in exhibits of live animals, fish, reptiles and birds. It features wildlife native to the region, and provides tours, study guides and in-school programs for local schools. In terms of the adolescents themselves, it provides the opportunity to learn about the day-to-day operation and maintenance of a museum. It is a remarkable example of youthful competence channeled into a constructive project with adult guidance and support.

An even more productive concept is employed by Manual High School in Denver, Colorado. Here the students learn traditional curriculum through the activities required to build a house. However, rather than remain a mere abstraction, the house *actually is built.* Local union representatives oversee critical aspects of construction such as electrical wiring and plumbing. The house itself, however, is built by youth primarily under the supervision of their regular classroom teachers. Traditional high school options such as wood shop, math, vocational-education options, and civic law are taught in conjunction with the house-building project. The houses are sold to low income families who otherwise would never be able to purchase a home, therefore, the high school does not compete against home building corporations.

Several points are worthy of mention. First, in their design and execution these projects are first rate work efforts which equalled or bettered previous community conditions. Secondly, the creative energy essential to successfully complete these projects came from young people, but they required, in the beginning, the assistance of an adult or an adult organization. Third, in every instance, the competence of the adolescents was far beyond the expectations of the authorities whether it involved repairing a broken-down house or working through the problems of elderly citizens lost in the bureaucratic shuffle of city government. The projects symbolize a fact the older generations have known for decades (because they lived it first hand) and that is simply that youth are inventive, industrious and altruistic when given the chance, or when necessity dictates.

The workers were eager and enthusiastic and, as a rule, put in longer hours than they originally bargained for. They did not receive pay, yet worked more rigorously than most salaried adolescent workers. The nature of their work elicits the best from young people (and adults for that matter): it provided a public service the effects of which were visible; the youth were identified with their work by the community and they held a personal interest in the success of the projects; the youth were really in charge as contrasted with being merely token participants. Adolescents work well under these conditions and demonstrate competence beyond what adults expect.

Youth are not good workers, they lack creative ingenuity, and they are incompetent *only when the older generations actively conspire against their natural talents.* When given the opportunity to prove what they can do; and when provided with quality assistance — especially in the beginning of a project; and, when the efforts of their work yield genuine results they do not lack competence at all. We have invented the myth that youth are incompetent in order to avoid the blatant fact that our system, as it presently exists, offers insufficient opportunity to develop life skills. By perpetuating the myth that youth are incompetent we assure that they become progressively more so until one day it became a self-fulfilling prophecy.

Ages: During adolescence two kinds of competence are most noticeable: the first is being capable and efficient within the universe of peers and the constellation of experiences related to it; the second being skills and abilities which permit humane survival in the "outside" (what adults call the "real") world. It is necessary to distinguish between these two types of competence to properly understand the adolescent experience. For the *early* adolescent a vast majority of life competence is related to school, the peer group and the family. Early adolescents are learning about themselves and society and are not ready to assume roles society deems important. By middle adolescence, the pendulum

230

swings closer toward meeting adult responsibilities. Here youth obtain their first job — although some do not until late adolescence or early adulthood. It also is the age at which they can be expected to reliably carry out jobs which require adult concentration and dependability. Skills increase considerably from the previous age but remain less advanced than in late adolescence. Youth who are not gifted in the classroom, either because of intellectual limitations or behavioural incompatabilities, knowing they are "allowed" to withdraw from school at 15 or 16, begin to think seriously about life in the outside world. By *late* adolescence, youth have achieved the *potential* for considerable competence valued by society. Their interpersonal skills are better than during early or middle adolescence although for many they remain weak from lack of interchange with adults. Their knowledge about themselves is more realistic. They tend to know, for example, if they are better at tinkering or fixing than at working with people. The majority, however, have had little life experience to reliably check out their images and beliefs about themselves.

In terms of the competence society is looking for in young people, *late* adolescents are unquestionably the most gifted of all adolescents. When locked out of important interaction with the larger society they also are the most short-changed. Isolating the *middle* and *early* adolescent in the North American tradition does not yield any tremendous advantages (except that it keeps them out of society's machinery) but it does not create the disadvantages for them that it does for the *late* adolescent who is more ready to step out of school into the outside world.

Summary

Many important aspects of adolescent psychology are shrouded by myths which interfere with a clear understanding of youth phenomena and contribute to the falsification of the adolescent experience. In North America not only do myths about youth fill our thinking, so also do myths about the elderly and other minority groups. In this chapter I have tried to expose some of the fictions regarding adolescence.

One myth we presently hold is that our culture, as a whole, likes young people and continually strives to do what is best for them. This is at best a partial truth because it overlooks the considerable resentment adults harbour toward youth, it underplays the degree to which we segregate adolescents from the important facts of the dominant society, and it fails to acknowledge our attempts to devitalize young people.

Our ability to understand adolescents and their problems is cast in a more solid context when we admit to the fact that many adults fear and resent youth, and that they impede the growing up process. Without this realization a good deal of adolescent behaviour seems bizarre and far fetched; as a result they are perceived as a "hot-blooded" minority group whose behaviour is steamy and unpredictable.

The school system has many dimensions of youth resentment built into it, and I request the reader to reflect upon their own school experiences to search out examples of it. The most indicting, however, is the refusal of school officials to take students seriously, and to require them to live within a token social world where they do almost nothing of importance. Paul Goodman, who has written brilliantly about youth predicaments, entitled his classic book *Growing Up Absurd*. The title has notable merit and deserves reflection because, in many respects, we create absurd realities which interfere with noble growing up.

The second myth claims that youth are highly sexual creatures who constantly seek new ways to satisfy their sexual urges. This myth is easier to deal with than youth resentment (even though it is a direct by-product of it) because weighty empirical evidence speaks against it. Research on adolescent sexual habits consistently point out similar trends, most of which counter the belief that youth are highly-active sexually. During *early* adolesence, very little sexual behaviour occurs; during *middle* adolescence, youth become more sexually active, and during *late* adolescence, even more so. However, even among unmarried 18 and 19-year-olds sexual intercourse is not as typical as one might suspect.

The opposite myth, that youth do *not* experience sexual passion and that they do not engage in sexual intercourse, is likewise foolish. However, it also has fewer takers! Youth, like adults, take sex seriously. During their periods of initial sexual experimentation youth tread cautiously rather than flamboyantly.

The third myth reflects one of the more enduring fictions we hold about adolescents. It claims that teenagers are dominated by peer groups, that their psychological alliances are almost exclusively affixed to other teens, and that their innermost impulses incline them toward intense involvement with the peer group and away from adults. This outlook is encouraged by psychologists who observe the day-to-day behaviour of youth without questioning the root causes of the behaviour they observe. Youth are *peer oriented* because it is from comrades and acquaintances that they find out about themselves, and it is from peers that they acquire social power. However, and this is where many psychologists and educators misperceive the dynamics of youth, youth in our culture are peer *dominated* because they live almost exclusively in a segregated world where peers are the only people available to them.

The myth that youth *really* want to spend all their time with peers permits adults to defend adolescent isolation from mainstream society. However, a good case can be made that adolescents desire adult companionship, and that they enjoy the company of younger children when given a position of responsibility in relation to them. Likewise, many youth are not enthralled by their age-mates but gravitate toward them because no other option exists.

The fourth myth is the myth of the generation gap. It is nourished by the misperception that youth prefer peers to adults, but it has an independent existence of its own. This myth, like that of sexual promiscuity, is easily dispelled because of the convincing evidence which speaks against it. Offer's research on "normal" adolescents is among the best. His findings indicate that youth are not terribly different from adults in their important outlooks, and that they tend to respect differences which exist between themselves and their elders.

The myth of the generation gap is lessened when we realize that youth are in the midst of formulating their own ideas and outlooks, and frequently they know much better what they *dis*like than what they like. When their dislikes contradict the likes of their parents some people wrongly infer that a *crucial* rift has taken place.

Differences between the generations *are* important, and in many ways they contribute to a wholesome mutual exchange. It is unusual, however, for adolescents to hold radically different viewpoints than their parents with regard to important social values and beliefs. The age where significant differences are *least* noticeable is early adolescence, whereas they are *most* noticeable during late adolescence.

Another important myth is the belief that the adolescent years are *inherently* a time of turmoil and anguish. An offshoot of this myth claims that all youth inevitably experience intense frustration *merely because* they are teenagers. This is not the case. Many youth breeze through the adolescent experience with only minor difficulties — certainly no more than they experienced as children or pre-adolescents. Other youth encounter urgent life stress, but they cope with it in an effective way. A third group of youth, (and it is *their* experience which has monopolized our understanding of youth) find adolescence an extremely stressful life stage, their problems overwhelm them and create powerful turmoil in their personal lives. This third group, however, is not the majority. Neither is it adolescence, *per se,* which causes their problems — it is a combination of personal, social, and environmental difficulties which cripple the adolescent personality.

Another myth assumes that youth are *not* hypocritical and that they are genuinely offended by people who are. This is not so. Adolescents are probably more hypocritical than virtually all children are, and they are considerably more hypocritical than many adults. The conditions of the adolescent life-style encourage hypocrisy. The struggle for peer recognition and acceptance is not easy for many youngsters; for others the discrepancy between what their parents expect of them and what they prefer is reconciled best via hypocrisy. In many instances adolescents are expected to be what they are not, and in others they are expected not to be they are. All of these circumstances increase the chances of hypocritical behaviour.

The final myth discussed in this chapter deals with youth competence. The myth claims that adolescents are not competent at important life skills and, even more relevant, that they lack the ability to acquire the competencies necessary for survival in the adult world. This outlook is a comparative newcomer in North America, and contradicts the viewpoint of three or four generations ago which assumed that by middle adolescence, boys and girls should assume important familial and *social* responsibilities.

The schools encourage youth incompetence more than most adults realize and considerably more than school officials admit. The unwillingness to permit students to venture out into the community, and the refusal to concentrate the vast talents of adolescents into socially constructive projects are both indicators that the schools prefer to keep students under wraps. At the turn of the century 15, 16, and 17-year-olds were building houses. Now they cannot even enter the building sites where construction projects of this type are taking place.

Despite the myth of youth incompetence, numerous community projects throughout North America confirm that youth are competent, and close analysis of their psychological makeup indicates that they are strongly impelled by the desire to acquire competence.

Bibliography

Addy, C. "American and Canadian Studies of Adolescent Sexual Attitudes and Behaviour", at Symposium on Adolescent Sexuality. Regina, Sask., May, 1977.

Adelson, J. "The Political Imagination of the Young Adolescent", in *12-16: Early Adolescence* edited by J. Kagan and R. Coles. New York: W.W. Norton and Co. Inc., 1972.

Allport, G. "Crises in Normal Personality Development", from *The Young Adult,* edited by G.D. Winter. Glenview, Ill.: Scott, Foresman and Co., 1969.

Anthony, J. "The Reactions of Adults to Adolescents and Their Behavior", in Caplan, G., and Leboxici, S., *Adolescence: Psychosocial Perspectives.* New York: Basic Books, 1969.

Ausubel, D. *Theory and Problems of Adolescent Development.* New York: Grune and Stratton, 1954.

Bakan, D. "Adolescence in America: From Ideal to Social Fact", in *12-16: Early Adolescence* edited by J. Kagan and R. Coles. New York: W.W. Norton and Co., Inc., 1972, pp. 73-89.

Balswick, J. and Macrides, C. "Parental stimulus for adolescent rebellion". *Adolescence,* Vol. 10, No. 38, Summer 1975.

Bandura, A. "The Stormy Decade: Fact or Fiction?" in *Adolescent Behavior and Society: A Book of Readings.* New York: Random House, 1975, pp. 25-33.

Bixenstine, V., DeCorte, M., and Bixenstine, B. "Conformity to peer-sponsored misconduct at four grade levels". *Developmental Psychology,* May 1976, Vol. 12, No. 3, pp. 226-236.

Blos, P. "The Child Analyst Looks at the Young Adolescent", *12-16: Early Adolescence* edited by J. Ragan and R. Coles New York: W.W. Norton and Co. Inc., 1972.

Broadfoot, B. *The Pioneer Years 1895-1914: Memories of Settlers Who Opened the West.* Toronto: Doubleday Canada, Ltd., 1976.

Cantril, H. "A Fresh Look at the Human Design", *Journal of Individual Psychology.* 20, 1964, 129-136.

Charles F. Kettering Foundation. *The Reform of Secondary Education: A Report of the National Commission on the Reform of Secondary Education.* New York: McGraw-Hill Book Co., 1973.

Clifford, E. "Body Satisfaction in Adolescence", in *Adolescent Behavior and Society: A Book of Readings.* New York: Random House, 1975, pp. 80-85.

Cohen, Y.A. *The Transition from Childhood to Adolescence*. Chicago: Aldise Publishing Co., 1964.

Coleman, J.S. "The Transition from Youth to Adult", in *Adolescent Behavior and Society: A Book of Readings*. New York: Random House, 1975, pp. 627-633.

Collins, K. "Adolescent Dating Intimacy: Norms and Peer Expectations", *Journal of Youth and Adolescence*. 3, 1974, 317-328.

Conger, J.J. *Adolescence and Youth: Psychological Development in a Changing World*. New York: Harper and Row, 1973.

Cottle, T.J. "The Connections of Adolescence", in *12-16: Early Adolescence* edited by J. Kagan and R. Coles. New York: W.W. Norton and Co., 1972, pp. 294-336.

Covington, M., and Beery, R. *Self-Worth and School Learning*. New York: Holt, Rinehart and Winston, 1976.

Cox, R.D. *Youth into Maturity: A Study of Men and Women in the First Ten Years After College*. New York: Mental Heath Materials' Center, 1970, pp. 145-146.

Creighton, J. "Unwed Mothers Age Down", *Edmonton Journal*, June 24, 1977, p. 23.

DeVaron, T. "Growing Up", in *12-16: Early Adolescence* edited by J. Kagan and R. Coles. New York: W.W. Norton and Co., 1972, pp. 337-348,

Douvan, E., and Adelson, J. *The Adolescent Experience*. New York: John Wiley and Sons, Inc., 1966.

Dreyer, P. "Sex, Sex Roles and Marriage Among Youth in the 1970s", from *Youth: The 74th Yearbook of the National Society for the Study of Education*. Chicago: University of Chicago Press, 1975, pp. 194-223.

Elias, J. and Elias, V. "The Sexual World of the Adolescent". *The Counseling Psychologist*, Vol. 5, No. 1, 1975.

Elkind, D. *Children and Adolescents: Interpretive Essays on Jean Piaget* (2nd ed.). New York: Oxford University Press, 1974.

Elkind, D. *A Sympathetic Understanding of the Child: Six to Sixteen*. Boston: Allyn & Bacon, Inc., 1971.

Entwisle, D. and Greenberger, E. "Adolescents' Views of Women's Work Role". *American Journal of Orthopsychiatry*, Vol. 42 (4), July 1972.

Erikson, E. *Identity, Youth and Crisis*. New York: W.W. Norton and Co., 1978.

Family Planning Advisory Committee. *Report of the Family Planning*

Advisory Committee to the Committee of Ministers on Family Planning. Saskatchewan, Canada: Government Pub., April, 1975.

Finger, F. "Changes in sex practices and beliefs of male college students over 30 years". *The Journal of Sex Research,* Vol. 11, No. 4, November 1975, pp. 304-317.

Flacks, R. *Youth and Social Change.* Chicago: Markham Publishing Co., 1971.

Fort, J. "Youth and the Drug Crisis", in *Youth in Contemporary Society.* Beverly Hills, California: Sage Publications, Inc., 1973, pp. 191-210.

Freud, Anna. "The Ego and the Mechanisms of Defense", *The International Psychoanalytical Library,* No. 30, 1937, pp. 149-150.

Freud, Anna. "Adolescence", from *Adolescence* edited by Alva E. Winder and Dow L. Angus. New York: American Book Co., 1968.

Friedenberg, E. *Coming of Age in America: Growth and Acquiescence.* New York: Random House, 1965, pp. 1-27.

Friedenberg, E. *The Dignity of Youth and Other Atavisms.* Boston: Beacon Press, 1965.

Gagnon, J. "The Creation of the Sexual in Early Adolescence", in *12-16: Early Adolescence* edited by J. Kagan and R. Coles. New York: W.W. Norton and Co., 1972, pp. 231-257.

Gagnon, J., and Simon, W. "Youth, Sex, and the Future," in *Youth in Contemporary Society.* Beverly Hills, California: Sage Publications, Inc., 1973, 211-250.

Gallatin, J. *Adolescence and Individuality: A Conceptual Approach to Adolescent Psychology.* New York: Harper and Row, 1975.

Gessel, A., Ilg. F.L., and Ames, L.B. *Youth: The Years From Ten to Sixteen.* New York: Harper and Row Brothers, 1956.

Goodman, P. *Growing up Absurd: Problems of Youth in the Organized Society.* New York: Vintage Books, 1960.

Gordon, C. "Social Characteristics of Early Adolescence", in *12-16: Early Adolescence* edited by J. Kagan and R. Coles. New York: W.W. Norton and Co., 1972.

Gordon, S. *The Sexual Adolescent: Communicating with Teenagers about Sex.* North Scituate, Massachusetts: Duxbury Press, 1973.

Hall, C., and Lindzey, G. *Theories of Personality.* New York: John Wiley and Sons, Inc., 1957, p. 133.

Havighurst, R. "Objectives for Youth Development", in *Youth: The 74th Yearbook of the National Society for the Study of Education.* Chicago: University of Chicago Press, 1975, pp. 87-92.

Havighurst, R., and Gottlieb, D. "Youth and the Meaning of Work", in *Youth: The 74th Yearbook of the National Society for the Study of Education*. Chicago: University of Chicago Press, 1975, pp. 145-160.

Jemilo, R. "Youth Action", in *Children, Psychology, and the Schools: Research and Trends*. Glenview, Ill.: Scott, Foresman and Co., 1969, pp. 224-234.

Jense, G.P. "Adolescent Sexuality", in *The Sexual Experience* edited by B. Sadock, H. Kaplan, and A. Freedman. Baltimore: Williams and Wilkins Co., 1976, pp. 142-155.

Josselyn, I.M. *Adolescence*. New York: Harper and Row, 1971.

Justice, B. and Duncan, D. "Running Away: An epidemic problem of adolescence". *Adolescence*, Vol. XI, No. 43, Fall 1976.

Kagan. J. "A Conception of Early Adolescence", in *12-16: Early Adolescence* edited by J. Kagan and R. Coles. New York: W.W. Norton and Co., 1972, pp. 90-105.

Katchadourian, H. *The Biology of Adolescence*. San Francisco: W.H. Freeman and Co., 1977.

Keniston, K. "Prologue: Youth as a Stage of Life", in *Youth: The 74th Yearbook of the National Society for the Study of Education*. Chicago: University of Chicago Press, 1975, pp. 3-26.

Keniston, K. "Youth: A 'New' Stage of Life", in *Adolescent Behavior and Society: A Book of Readings*. New York: Random House, 1975, pp. 43-52.

Kiell, N. *The Universal Experience of Adolescence*. New York: International Universities' Press, Inc., 1964.

Kimmel, D. *Adulthood and Aging: An Interdisciplinary Developmental View*. Toronto: John Wiley and Sons, Inc., 1974.

Kinsey, A.C., Pomeroy, W.B., and Martin, C.E. *Sexual Behavior in the Human Female*. Philadelphia: W.B. Saunders Co., 1953.

Klagsbrun, F. *Too Young to Die: Youth and Suicide*. Boston: Houghton-Mifflin, 1976.

Laufer, M. *Adolescent Disturbance and Breakdown*. London, Ont.: Penguin Books in assoc. with Mind, 1975.

Lerner, R., Karabenick, S. and Stuart, J. "Relations Among Physical Attractiveness, Body Attitudes, and Self Concept in Male and Female College Student", *The Journal of Psychology*, 1973, 85, p. 119-129.

Lerner, R., and Karabenick, S. "Physical Attractiveness, Body Attitudes, and Self Concept in Late Adolescence", *Journal of Youth and Adolescence*, 3, 1974, pp. 307-316.

238

Lerner, R., and Knapp, J. "Actual and Perceived Intrafamilial Attitudes of Late Adolescents and Their Parents", *Journal of Youth and Adolescence,* 4, 1975, pp. 17-36.

Maddi, S. *Personality Theories: A Comparative Analysis.* Homewood, Ill.: Dorsey Press, 1969.

Manaster, G. *Adolescent Development and the Life Tasks.* Boston: Allyn and Bacon, Inc., 1977.

Martin, E.C. "Reflections on the Early Adolescent in School", in *12-16: Early Adolescence* edited by J. Kagan and R. Coles. New York: W.W. Norton and Co., 1972, pp. 180-198.

Maslow, A.H. *Toward a Psychology of Being.* Princeton, N.J.: Van Nostrand Co., 1962.

May, R. *Love and Will.* New York: W.W. Norton and Co., 1969.

May, R. *Power and Innocence.* New York: W.W. Norton and Co., 1972.

Menninger, R. "What troubles our troubled youth", from *Mental Hygiene,* Vol. 52, July 1968.

Miller, J. "Suicide and adolescence". *Adolescence,* Vol. X, No. 37, Spring 1975, pp. 11-24.

Mitchell, J.J. "Adolescent Hypocrisy", *Journal of Moral Education,* Volume 5, Number 1, 1975.

Mitchell, J.J. "Adolescent Intimacy", *Adolescence,* Summer 1976.

Mitchell, J.J. *Adolescence: Some Critical Issues.* Holt, Rinehart and Winston of Canada Ltd., Toronto, 1971.

Mitchell, J.J. *Human Life: The Early Adolescent Years.* Holt, Rinehart and Winston of Canada, Ltd., Toronto, 1974.

Mitchell, J.J. "Moral Dilemmas of Early Adolescence", *The School Counselor,* September 1974.

Mitchell, J.J. "Moral Growth During Adolescence", *Adolescence,* Summer 1975.

Mitchell, J.J. *The Adolescent Predicament.* Holt, Rinehart and Winston of Canada, Ltd., Toronto, 1974.

Musgrove, F. *Youth and the Social Order.* London: Routledge and Keegan Paul, 1964.

Mussen, P., Sullivan, L.B., and Eisenberg-Berg, N. "Changes in political-economic attitudes during adolescence". *The Journal of Genetic Psychology,* 1977, 130, pp. 69-76.

Muuss, R.E. "Adolescent Development and the Secular Trend", in *Adolescent Behavior and Society: A Book of Readings.* New York: Random House, 1975, pp. 56-67.

Nettleton, C. and Cline, D. "Dating patterns, sexual relationships and use of contraceptives of 700 unwed mothers during a two-year period following delivery". *Adolescence,* Vol. X, No. 37, Spring 1975, pp. 45-57.

Nihira, K., Yusin, A., and Sinay, R. "Perception of parental behaviour by adolescents in crisis". *Psychological Reports,* 1975, 37, pp. 787-793.

Offer, D., and Offer, J.B. *From Teenage to Young Manhood: A Psychological Study.* New York: Basic Books, Inc., 1975.

Offer, D. *The Psychological World of the Teen-Ager: A Study of Normal Adolescent Boys.* New York: Basic Books, Inc., 1969, p. 178.

Oliveus, D. "Aggression and peer acceptance in adolescent boys: Two short-term longitudinal studies of ratings". *Child Development,* 1977, Vol. 48, pp. 1301-1313.

Paton, S., Kessler, R., and Kandel, D. "Depressive mood and adolescent illicit drug use: A longitudinal analysis". *The Journal of Genetic Psychology,* 1977, Vol. 131, pp. 267-289.

Pearson, G. *Adolescence and the Conflict of Generations.* New York: W.W. Norton and Co., 1958.

President's Science Advisory Committee. *Youth: Transition to Adulthood.* (Report of the Panel of Youth of the President's Science Advisory Committee) Washington, D.C.: U.S. Government Printing Office, June, 1973.

Redl, F. "Adolescents — Just How Do They React?" in *Adolescence: Psychosocial Perspectives* edited by G. Caplan and S. Lebovici. New York: Basic Books, 1969.

Rubenstein, J., Watson, F., Drolette, M., Rubenstein, H. "Young adolescents' sexual interests". *Adolescence,* Winter 1976, Vol. XI, No. 44, pp. 487-496.

Ryle, A. *Student Casualties.* Baltimore: Penguin Books, Inc., 1973.

Sarrel, P. "Caring for the Pregnant Teenager", *The Family Planner,* 3, No. 4, 1970.

Sawrey, J. and Telford, C. *Psychology of Adjustment* (2nd edition) Boston: Allyn and Bacon, Inc., 1967.

Schofield, M. *The Sexual Behavior of Young People.* London: Longmans, Green and Co., Ltd., 1965.

Schwartz, B. "Having my Baby", *The Baltimore Sun,* Oct. 6, 1974.

Shaffer, D. "Suicide in Childhood and Early Adolescence". *Journal of Child Psychology and Psychiatry,* Vol. 15, No. 1, 1974, 275-291.

Shenker, R., and Schildkrout, M. "Physical and Emotional Health of

Youth'', in *Youth: The 74th Yearbook of the National Society for the Study of Education*. Chicago: University of Chicago Press, 1975, pp. 61-86.

Sorensen, R.C. *Adolescent Sexuality in Contemporary America*. New York: World Publishing Co., 1973.

Symonds, P.M. *From Adolescent to Adult*. New York: Columbia University Press, 1961.

Tanner, J.M. ''Sequence, Tempo and Individual Variation in Growth and Development in Boys and Girls Aged Twelve to Sixteen'', in *12-16: Early Adolescence*. New York: W.W. Norton and Co., 1972, pp. 1-24.

Thornburg, H.D. *Development in Adolescence*. Monterey, Calif.: Brook-Cole, Pub., 1975.

Toolan, J.M. ''Suicide in Children'', Technical Assitance Project, *Depression and Suicide*. Fairlee, Vermont: June 6-8, 1966, pp. 9-16.

Weiner, I.B. *Psychological Disturbance in Adolescence*. New York: John Wiley and Sons, Inc., 1970.

Whisnant, L. and Zegans, L. ''A study of attitudes toward menarche in white middle class American adolescent girls''. *American Journal of Psychiatry* 132:8, August 1975, pp. 809-814.

White, R.W. *Lives in Progress* (2nd Ed.) New York: Holt, Rinehart and Winston, 1966.

Winder, A.E., and Angus, D.L. *Adolescence: Contemporary Studies*. New York: American Book Co., 1968.

Wolk, S., and Brandon, J. ''Runaway adolescents' perceptions of parents and self.'' *Adolescence*, Summer 1977, Vol. XII, No. 46, pp. 175-187.

Zelnik, M., and Kantner, J.F. ''Sexual and Contraceptive Experience of Young Unmarried Women in the United States, 1976 and 1971'', *Family Planning Perspectives*, Vol. 9, No. 2, March/April, 1977.

Zongker, C. ''The self-concept of pregnant adolescent girls''. *Adolescence*, 1977, Vol. XII, No. 48, pp. 477-488.

Index

Toolan, J.M., 147
turmoil:
    and age, 219
    as universal, 217
    in youth, 216

U

unhealthy needs, 118-120

W

Whisnant, L., 16
White, R.W., 69
Wolk, S., 92

Y

youth resentment, 192-195

Z

Zelnick, M., 180, 182
Zongker, C., 179